CRIMINAL LAW FOR PARALEGALS

DANIEL J. MARKEY, JR.
MEMBER, FEDERAL BAR
MEMBER, STATE BAR OF LOUISIANA

MARY QUEEN DONNELLY
DIRECTOR OF GUIDANCE
MARIST SCHOOL
ATLANTA, GEORGIA

SOUTH-WESTERN PUBLISHING CO.

1 2 3 4 5 6 7 8 9 0 D 02 01 00 99 98 97 96 95 94 93

Printed in the United States of America

Acquisitions Editor:	Betty Schechter
Production Manager:	Carol Sturzenberger
Managing Editor:	Bob Lewis
Coordinating Editor:	Barry Corrado
Production Editor:	June Davidson
Designer:	James DeSollar
Production Artist:	Sophia Renieris
Photo Editor:	Kim Larson
Marketing Manager:	Colleen Thomas

PHOTO CREDITS

p. 29   Susan Van Etten/PhotoEdit
p. 53   John Neubauer
p. 111   Billy E. Barnes/Stock Boston
p. 155   James L. Shaffer/PhotoEdit

Library of Congress Cataloging-in-Publication Data

Markey, Daniel J., 1941–
    Criminal law for paralegals / Daniel J. Markey, Jr., Mary Queen Donnelly.
        p.   cm.
    Includes index.
    ISBN 0-538-70861-1
    1. Criminal law—United States.   2. Criminal procedure—United States.   3. Legal assistants—United States—Handbooks, manuals, etc. I. Donnelly, Mary Queen, 1940–   . II. Title.
KF9219.3.M27   1994
345.73'05—dc20
[347.3055]   93-17337
                                                                        CIP

PREFACE

The field of criminal law is an interesting and intriguing area of specialization. An important goal of this text is to present the subject in a manner that allows its flavor to saturate the instructional content of the book. To that end, the text has been written in a uniquely readable prose. Unlike most textbooks, the material in this work flows naturally so that even persons only casually interested in the subject may read the book from front to back and gain important insights into the workings of the justice system.

The book's first objective, however, is to deliver a thorough treatment of the subject, realizing that this text may be the only exposure to criminal law experienced by many students. For those who go on to work in prosecution or defense, the foundations established in this treatise will be invaluable.

In Chapter 1, the foundations of the criminal justice system—the Constitution and the amendments that have molded our justice process—are examined. We define crime, uncover the requirements for a valid criminal law, and look at some of the ways in which crimes are classified.

Chapter 2 deals with the major elements of a criminal offense—*mens rea* and *actus reus*—the intent and the deed, and we consider some of the factors that affect those elements, such as insanity. By the end of the chapter, we are ready to deal with some specifics of the system, such as the initiation of the charging process and general concepts regarding the burden of proof in criminal cases. Our text covers these matters and other duties of the prosecution in Chapter 3. Chapter 3 concludes with a look at the duties of the paralegal who assists the prosecutor.

In Chapters 4 and 5, we look at some of the duties of defense counsel and the paralegals who assist them. Some specific duties of the paralegal are set out in Chapter 4. Chapter 5 deals with pretrial motions and the duties usually performed by a paralegal engaged in that phase of case preparation for the prosecution or the defense.

The subject considered in Chapter 6 involves the preparation necessary to take a case to trial. We look at the role of a paralegal in helping to develop a theory of the case, in gathering and processing evidence exhibits and witnesses, and in preparing opening statements and closing arguments.

Chapter 7 places the student in a courtroom setting. We look at all the elements of a trial, from picking the jury to receiving the verdict. The responsibilities of the paralegal at each step in the process are examined and explained. In Chapter 8, the appeal process is examined, as are the duties of the paralegal who assists in the appellate phase of the case.

Chapter 9 deals with the juvenile justice system and compares it to the criminal justice system, which handles adult offenders. The chapter explains the procedural and terminology differences between the two systems.

The final three chapters deal with special topics of interest and importance to the paralegal who will work in criminal law. Chapter 10 considers the practice of plea bargaining. We begin the chapter with the observation that bargaining has become a necessity because of the overwhelming caseloads of most prosecutors and the courts. We go on to examine the bargain and look at ways in which a paralegal may fit into the process.

Chapter 11 deals with search, seizure, and evidence. It visits the classic decisions of the Supreme Court in the area, such as *Mapp, Miranda, Wade,* and *Furman.* This one chapter includes more than forty case citations, explaining the holdings and discussing the importance of each decision.

We finish the text at Chapter 12, with an examination of ethics situations that are important to paralegals working in criminal law. Its emphasis is on confidentiality and conflicts of interest.

THE AUTHORS

Daniel J. Markey, Jr., received a B.A. from Spring Hill College in Mobile, Alabama. He obtained his J.D. from Loyola University in New Orleans. As a student at Loyola, he worked as a research clerk in the office of the U.S. attorney in New Orleans.

Mr. Markey has served as a prosecutor in the criminal division of the U.S. attorney's office for the Eastern District of Louisiana. He has also served as an assistant district attorney in Orleans Parish, Louisiana. As director of the Metropolitan Organized Crime Strike Force, he was commissioned to represent the state of Louisiana in criminal prosecutions in five parishes (counties), comprising Metro–New Orleans. As a defense counsel, Mr. Markey has defended persons against state and federal charges for more than fifteen years. He presently serves as an appointed counsel on the indigent defender panel of attorneys for the federal courts in the Eastern District of Louisiana. His classroom experience includes two years as instructor in the criminal justice program at Our Lady of the Holy Cross College in New Orleans.

Mary Queen Donnelly received her B.A. from St. Mary's Dominican College, New Orleans; her M.A. from the University of New Orleans in New Orleans; and her state certification as a school counselor and as a Licensed Professional Counselor from the state of Louisiana. She has forty-eight hours of postgraduate credit. She is presently Director of Guidance and a member of the administrative staff of the Marist School in Atlanta, Georgia.

Ms. Donnelly has had over twenty-five years of teaching experience. She has taught on the secondary level and the postsecondary level, most particularly in a continuing education program at St. Mary's Dominican College. She organized a yearly career education program, inviting speakers from professional and paraprofessional careers within the community. In addition to her other counseling responsibilities, as Coordinator of College Counseling, she has assisted seniors in high school with selection and admission into colleges throughout the country.

Ms. Donnelly is an active member of several educational organizations, including the American Counseling Association, the National College Board, the National Association of College Admission Counselors, and the Association for Supervision and Curriculum Development. She is the author of *Skills for Consumer Success*, Third Edition, as well as articles appearing in professional educational publications.

ACKNOWLEDGMENTS

It is expected that authors thank spouses, family, and friends for understanding and accepting the withdrawal of their writing loved ones. It may be expected, but it is also warranted. Their patient acceptance of the interruptions in their lives cannot go unnoticed and unappreciated. To Betty, Bob, and all the others, we acknowledge your contributions and we thank you for them.

We also acknowledge and sincerely thank Elizabeth Richardson, our consulting editor, and Judy O'Neill, our project editor. They have been supportive and constructive during our labors. Our heartfelt gratitude goes also to those special people at South-Western Publishing Co. who gave us this opportunity. We hope your confidence is rewarded; it is certainly appreciated.

Daniel J. Markey, Jr.
Mary Queen Donnelly

Danielle Kaye

SUMMARY OF CONTENTS

CONTENTS

11   SEARCH, SEIZURE, AND EVIDENCE   193

12   PARALEGAL REGULATION AND ETHICS   215

authorized Practice Is a Crime, 219; **CONFLICTS OF INTEREST, 220;** The Classic Conflict, 220; Dual Representation in a Criminal Case, 220; Conflict between Interests of Codefendants, 220; Conflict at Sentencing, 221; Former Employment, 221; Freelance Paralegals, 221; Informal Opinion of the American Bar Association, 222; Screening for Possible Conflicts, 223; **CONFIDENTIALITY, 223;** General Rule of Confidentiality, 223; Exceptions to the General Rule of Confidentiality, 223; Paralegal's Obligation, 224; Court-Ordered Disclosure, 225; **GUIDANCE FROM NATIONAL PARALEGAL ORGANIZATIONS, 225; A FINAL NOTE, 226; ENDNOTES, 226**

1 FOUNDATIONS

INTRODUCTION

This course is about the criminal justice system. Its purpose is to create an awareness of the workings of one of the most fascinating areas of the law. Most paralegals will not find employment in the field of criminal defense or prosecution. However, not only is the paralegal who knows nothing of the workings of the criminal justice system less valuable as a professional, he or she is less complete as a person as well.

It is hoped that some of you will find an attraction for the subject of criminal law. For those of you who do, this presentation will prepare you well for the tasks expected of you as a member of the prosecution or defense team.

Our treatment of the subject differs from the traditional approach to the study of criminal law. We are not so much concerned with the specifics of various crimes as we are with the workings of the system. As we shall see, it is the *system* that sets the United States apart from other nations.

One of the chief goals of this course is to acquaint you with the fact that criminal law is not the "stepchild" of the law. If you decide to pursue a career in this area, you will be dealing with the most sacred freedoms of humankind and the most significant legal document of our land, the Constitution. It is a discipline worthy of your best effort.

THE CRIMINAL JUSTICE SYSTEM

The essential law of our nation is embedded in our Constitution. When our forbears were forming themselves into a nation, they were so concerned about the fundamental principles of the justice system that would soon control their lives that they refused to ratify the Constitution until those principles were incorporated into that document.

Criminal justice is about the balance between individual freedoms and society's right to protect its members and itself from harm. Thomas Jefferson called our personal freedoms "unalienable rights," but even unalienable rights are not totally unrestricted. We know that the right to swing one's hand stops where another person's nose begins. As a society, we recognize the fact that the individual's rights to life, liberty, and happiness are guaranteed only if everyone respects those rights in others.

When our lives and liberties are intentionally violated by another person, we call such action crime. When our lives and liberties are violated by the state, we call such action tyranny. Our society has designed a method for dealing with crime and tyranny: we call it our criminal justice system.

Police and prosecutors who defend against the criminal element, together with defense attorneys and paralegals who protect against the tyrannical, unbridled authority of the state, are society's true protectors. They are front-line defenders of freedom and our unalienable rights. They work in our criminal justice system.

DUE PROCESS OF LAW

In the United States the fundamental precept of criminal justice is the concept of **due process of law**. The phrase is first mentioned in the Fifth Amendment to the U.S. Constitution:

> No person shall be held to answer for a capital, or otherwise infamous crime, unless on a presentment or indictment of a Grand Jury, except in cases arising in the land or naval forces, or in the Militia, when in actual service in time of War or public danger; nor shall any person be subject for the same offense to be twice put in jeopardy of life or limb; nor shall be compelled in any criminal case to be a witness against himself, *nor be deprived of life, liberty or property, without due process of law*; nor shall private property be taken for public use, without just compensation. (Emphasis added)

Those who demand a hard and fast definition may have a problem understanding the notion of due process. It is a living concept. It takes different forms in different cases. It always affords an individual a fair chance to know, to understand, and to defend against adverse actions by the government.

In the context of the criminal justice system, due process of law is a constitutionally protected right that guarantees that all persons shall have the opportunity to defend themselves when charged with a crime. Judge Learned Hand declared that due process of law embodies the English sense of fair play.[1] He could offer no more by way of definition.

The idea is one of balance. Due process balances the right of the individual to act freely against the duty of society to protect the freedom of all persons. It keeps the scale from tipping too far in either direction.

BILL OF RIGHTS

The guarantee of due process is found in one of the first ten amendments to the Constitution. All of the first ten amendments were put into place before the main body of the Constitution was adopted in order to satisfy the people that the new government being created would not be tyrannical nor oppressive. To the colonists who had known oppression and had felt the heavy hand of the despot, government abuse was a true concern. Today we seem less concerned with restraining the authority of the state than were our forefathers. It speaks well of the system we have devised that such fears have diminished over our short two-hundred-year history.

We call the first ten amendments the **Bill of Rights**. Though that name refers to all ten amendments, only the first eight contain specific guaranteed advantages.

Nearly two dozen guaranteed freedoms are enumerated in the first eight amendments. Twelve of these rights pertain directly to persons accused of crime. The Fourth, Fifth, Sixth, and Eighth Amendments have particular significance for students of criminal law.

The Fourth Amendment

The Fourth Amendment deals with the right of all persons to be secure from unreasonable searches. The reasonableness and propriety of a search is a frequent issue in criminal cases.

As a paralegal working in the field of criminal law, there will come a time when you will be called upon to review the circumstances surrounding a search. If you are working for the prosecution, you may even be called upon to prepare or review the affidavit of an agent or officer supporting a request for a search warrant. If you are working for a criminal defense firm, you may examine the factors relating to the seizure of evidence from your client. In either instance, your efforts will be directed at determining if the search was properly conducted within the requirements of the Fourth Amendment.

The Fifth Amendment

We have already seen that the Fifth Amendment provides a guarantee of due process. It contains other safeguards as well. Included in the Fifth Amendment is the provision that all formal accusations (indictments) involving charges of serious crimes shall emanate from a grand jury. It also contains a protection against **double jeopardy**, that is, being tried twice for the same crime by the same authority. Further, it guarantees that the state cannot force a person to give self-incriminating testimony.

The right against self-incrimination is a broad one. It is generally thought of as pertaining only to criminal law situations. However, the right to remain silent rather than give self-incriminating testimony extends to all legal proceedings—even civil proceedings.

The Sixth Amendment

The Sixth Amendment contains eight guarantees, all crowded into one sentence of less than eighty words:

- The right to a speedy trial
- The right to a public trial
- The right to a trial by one's peers
- The right to notice of the nature of the charge
- The right to notice of the cause of the charge
- The right to confront witnesses
- The right to compel appearance of witnesses
- The right to counsel

The Eighth Amendment

The Eighth Amendment contains two guarantees relevant to our study of criminal law: the right to bail and protection against cruel and unusual punishment.

The right to bail has been interpreted to mean that bail shall not be excessive. However, the right to bail is not absolute. According to the court's interpretation, the Eighth Amendment does not guarantee bail in every situation, to every defendant, for every offense. Those students who find employment in the area of criminal defense will spend a great deal of time working to get clients released from custody on bail, pending trial.

The other Eighth Amendment safeguard, the prohibition against cruel and unusual punishment, is most frequently thought of in terms of attacks against the death penalty. At least for the present time, the courts have laid that argument to rest in capital cases. However, the guarantee does have other applications, such as reform of living conditions for prisoners.

The Fourteenth Amendment

When they were written, the safeguards contained in the Bill of Rights applied only to the federal government and its actions toward the individual. The Fourteenth Amendment to the Constitution, adopted in 1868, extends many of the guarantees in the Bill of Rights to actions by state governments. The language of the amendment has become familiar to both lawyers and laypeople:

> [N]or shall any state deprive any person of life, liberty or property, without due process of law; nor deny to any person within its jurisdiction equal protection of the laws.

JUDICIAL INTERPRETATION

How the Fourteenth Amendment affects each of the guarantees in the Bill of Rights is a matter of **judicial interpretation**. The U.S. Supreme Court retains the ultimate right to determine constitutional questions. The Court has frequently exercised that authority in matters of criminal law.

Historically, there has been much debate and diversity of opinion among justices of the highest court concerning which of the guaranteed rights are embodied in the notion of due process and, therefore, must be protected by the states. For a time the official view was that the Fourteenth Amendment only obligated the states to afford "fundamental fairness" to the accused. Under that theory, the denial of any of the constitutionally guaranteed rights in a state prosecution was viewed as merely an indication that due process had been denied.

From time to time, members of the Supreme Court have expressed opinions more liberal than the fundamental fairness theory. Justice William Douglas, for example, believed that the Fourteenth Amendment made *all* of the guarantees in the Bill of Rights applicable to state prosecutions. He believed that in some instances the Fourteenth Amendment assured an accused of rights even beyond those set out in the first ten amendments. The present state of the law is that all of the guarantees referred to above, with the exception of the grand jury requirement of the Fifth Amendment and the bail requirements of the Eighth Amendment, are binding against the states.

A point of overriding importance that must be understood concerns the authority of the courts to *interpret* the Constitution and other laws. The assurance of fairness required by the Bill of Rights and the Fourteenth Amendment is subject to judicial interpretation, all the way up to the Supreme Court. That Court is the ultimate arbiter and retains the authority, in all cases, to determine whether due process has been and is being provided.

RIGHT TO APPEAL

Every person convicted of a crime has a right to appeal that conviction to a higher court. Interestingly, the right of appeal is *not* constitutionally protected. Before the turn of the century, the U.S. Supreme Court ruled that states are not required to provide an appeal process. Regardless of that decision, every state and the federal system now provide a right to appeal.

No Absolute Right to Appeal to the U.S. Supreme Court

There is another point to be made on the subject of appeal. Even though every state and the federal court system have established an appeal process for persons convicted of criminal violations, generally speaking, there is no absolute right to appeal a criminal conviction to the U.S. Supreme Court. If we were to generalize a rule for all federal and state jurisdictions, it would be that a convicted defendant is entitled to an appeal only to the next higher court.

Writ of *Certiorari*

A defendant desiring a review by the Supreme Court must *ask* that Court to accept and review the case. This is done by applying for a **writ of *certiorari***. The significance of this fact is that the process of reviewing criminal cases is almost entirely voluntary on the part of the country's highest court. The Supreme Court justices can pick and choose which cases they want to hear. If they feel that the case presents issues worthy of their consideration, they will grant the writ. If they do not find worthy issues or if they do not want to rule on the issues presented, they will deny the writ. Most applications for a writ of *certiorari* are denied.

Thus, the Supreme Court has almost absolute control over the evolution of criminal law and the criminal justice system because it not only decides issues but also decides which issues it will consider.

DEFINING OUR SUBJECT—WHAT IS CRIME?

Now that we are familiar with the roots of the system, our study of criminal law will be made easier if we have a clear understanding of the one thing our justice system has been developed to combat—crime.

The Traditional Definition

Everyone is acquainted with the notion of crime, and each of us has our own thoughts as to what the term entails. Yet, as with many other commonplace ideas, it is difficult to achieve agreement regarding a specific definition for the concept.

There is general agreement that crime signifies a form of aberrant behavior. However, it is also recognized that not all abnormal behavior is criminal. Most people who spend any time considering the subject recognize that deviant personal conduct is not criminal unless it results in a social wrong.

Blackstone[2] said that crime is an act committed or omitted in contravention of a public law either forbidding it or commanding it. As we shall see, Blackstone's explanation is not totally satisfactory because of its misplaced emphasis.

The weakness of Blackstone's definition is that it focuses on the *act* of the offender, not on the resulting harm caused by the act. Identical actions may have (and often do have) different consequences. An illogical result will sometimes be achieved if we define crime solely in terms of the act without regard for the social harm caused by that act. Our point can be illustrated by the following example involving two similar acts.

In the first situation, Smith fires a gun at Jones. The bullet strikes Jones in the shoulder, and Jones bleeds to death before medical help arrives. In the second incident, Roe fires a gun at Doe. Doe's injury is almost identical to that of Jones, but Doe survives the attack.

Assuming that there is no justification for the conduct of either Smith or Roe, both have committed a crime. But Smith, whose victim died, could be punished for homicide, whereas Roe, whose victim recovered, would face a less serious charge.

Applying Blackstone's definition, both Smith and Roe *acted* identically and should be guilty of the same crime. Yet the consequences of each act can be vastly different. This anomaly is caused by the definition's misplaced emphasis, which accentuates the act instead of its consequences.

A Better Definition

For our purposes, it makes more sense to define **crime** in terms of the *wrong resulting from the action* rather than in terms of the act itself. Thus, a more acceptable definition, one that better fits current thinking, is given in Figure 1-1.

FIGURE 1-1 DEFINITION OF CRIME

Crime is a social evil, identified, proscribed, and punishable by law.

Applying our definition to the example of the two attackers, the crime committed by Smith is greater than the crime committed by Roe because it caused a greater social evil—the victim's death. Roe's offense is less serious, if only fortuitously so, because the social evil it caused was not as grave—the victim was only injured.

Crime versus Immorality

Thinking of crime in terms of the resulting social harm may be difficult at first because of the tendency to confuse criminality with immorality. Although typical crimes involve acts that are commonly viewed as immoral, there is nothing to confine criminal proscriptions to immoral conduct. Conversely, no legal premise makes all immoral conduct criminal.

In our example, Smith and Roe probably intended the same effect; they certainly performed the same act. If anyone were able to gauge their moral guilt, it probably would be identical. Yet the legal consequences for each attacker will be different. This is true because the law is not concerned with the morality of the conduct of Smith or Roe, only with the *results* of that conduct.

IMPORTANCE OF DEFINITION TO THE PARALEGAL

A common assignment for a paralegal working in the field of criminal law involves the review of an indictment or a bill of information to determine if it properly charges an offense.

Step one for anyone faced with such an assignment is to determine which substantive law the accused is charged to have violated. Once that has been ascertained, a primary consideration ought to be whether or not the underlying statute meets the requirements for a valid criminal law. It is doubtful that you will discover a flaw in older laws. However, the new wave of criminal statutes offers good reason to conscientiously carry out this assignment.

Many of the current generation of criminal statutes being passed by state and federal legislatures are complex and convoluted. A good example of new wave legislation, the Racketeer Influenced and Corrupt Organizations Act (RICO), is found in Title 18 of the *United States Code* (18 U.S.C. § 1961, *et seq.*) Such laws are constantly being stretched to their limits of applicability by prosecutors and challenged in the courts by defense attorneys. In your efforts to determine the validity of the substantive criminal law, you will have to determine if the statute meets the definitional standards discussed below.

Requirements for a Valid Law

Our definition of crime, you will recall, proposes two salient features: social evil and penalty. Therefore, a valid criminal law must

- Clearly identify a social evil.
- Provide a penalty for causing the evil.

Clear and Unambiguous. When we speak of the identification of a social evil, we are speaking of the principle that all persons must be given notice of the specific deed that the law forbids. The principle of **notice**, the principle that the deed that the law forbids must be specifically identified, is sacramental to our system of criminal justice. The U.S. Supreme Court has referred to the principle as "the first essential of due process of law."

In the case of *Lanzetta v. New Jersey*, 306 U.S. 451 (1939), the Court noted that one must be able to determine from the law just what conduct is forbidden so that he or she may avoid commission of the offense. It further observed that vagueness leads to unfair and arbitrary law enforcement because authorities may enforce an unclear law against some and not apply it to others.

In the United States, there is universal acceptance for the notion that criminal laws, carrying penalties for their breach, must be explicit and clear. In every state, courts have made pronouncements on the unacceptability of vagueness in criminal statutes. Figure 1-2 presents an example from a Wyoming case.

FIGURE 1-2   VAGUENESS IN CRIMINAL STATUTES IS UNACCEPTABLE

The matter of definiteness required in criminal statutes was fully discussed by us in *Day v. Armstrong*, Wyo., 362 P.2d 137, 147–148. The principles adhered to in that decision are directly applicable here and sufficient to resolve the question we are asked to decide.

For example, recognition was given in the Day case to these principles:

1. The requirement of a reasonable degree of certainty in legislation, especially in the criminal law, is a well established element of the guarantee of due process.

2. No one may be required at peril of life, liberty or property to speculate as to the meaning of penal statutes.

FIGURE 1-2   VAGUENESS IN CRIMINAL STATUTES IS UNACCEPTABLE *(continued)*

3. All are entitled to be informed as to what the state commands or forbids.

4. A statute which either forbids or requires the doing of an act in terms so vague that men of common intelligence must necessarily guess at its meaning and differ as to its application violates the first essential of due process of law.

5. The constitutional guarantee of equal rights under the law [citation omitted] will not tolerate a criminal law so lacking in definition that each defendant is left to the vagaries of individual judges and juries.

Justice McIntyre, Supreme Court of Wyoming,
State v. Gallegos, 384 P.2d 967 (1963)

No Penalty, No Crime. The second essential of our definition is penalty. In reality, penalty is the distinguishing facet of criminal law. It is what makes a criminal law different from all others (civil laws). In *United States v. Evans*, 333 U.S. 483 (1914), the Supreme Court recognized and enunciated the principle that forbidden conduct, without a penalty, *is no crime.*

Your job of determining a law's validity is not complete until you are satisfied that the law in question clearly and unambiguously describes the offense *and* provides a penalty for those who commit the offense.

Rarely in your research will you find an instance where the drafters of a criminal law have completely neglected to provide a penalty for the crime's commission. Though such instances are rare, they do occur. They are most likely to happen in situations where a statute has been revised and the punishment segment is eliminated through inadvertence. In those cases, the statute is invalid.

You will more frequently encounter a situation wherein the penalty for an offense will be made applicable by reference. For example, a statute may define a crime, such as "illegal entry into an inhabited dwelling," and declare that it shall be punishable as "simple burglary." In such an instance, a researcher must refer to the burglary statute in order to determine the applicable penalty for the crime of "illegal entry." Historically, courts have held that a cross-reference between statutes is sufficient to satisfy the penalty requirement.

Even in those instances where a penalty is provided, a good technique is to carefully examine the circumstances of the case to make sure that the punishment is relevant and can be applied. If the stated penalty is uncertain or unenforceable, the statute may have no valid application to the accused.

Before it was amended, a statute in the state of Washington provided only a penalty of imprisonment for an offense it defined as larceny. Consequently, the Supreme Court of Washington, in *State v. Truax*, 130 Wash. 69,

226 P. 259 (1924), a 1924 case cited in the Washington Reports and the Pacific Reporter, determined that a corporation, even though it had committed larcenous conduct, was guilty of *no crime* because it could not be incarcerated.

Common Law Crimes

It is relatively easy to apply our two-part test to a written statute. Because we have referred to statutes in our discussions up to this point, we may have created the impression that all criminal laws are written, but this is not the case. In the United States some jurisdictions still recognize **uncodified**, that is, unwritten common law crimes, such as murder, rape, and burglary. Unwritten criminal laws present several problems.

In dealing with common law crimes, the first problem we encounter concerns our fundamental principle of notice. The difficulty occurs primarily in situations in which the offense charged was not known to early common law. By early common law we mean law recognized prior to the year 1607. That date is used as a cut-off date in many states because it marks the founding of Jamestown, the first English settlement in America. From that point forward, the theory goes, America became disassociated from the common law of England.

Reception Statute. In some states, a year other than 1607 is specified as the cut-off date. The cut-off date, whatever it happens to be, is usually specified in a reception statute. **Reception statute** is the name given to a state law that adopts or *receives* the common law of crimes into that state's body of criminal law.

Historically, in those states that recognize common law crimes, courts have enforced uncodified crimes that were recognized prior to the date of the reception statute. Certain unwritten criminal laws can be enforced because of the legal presumption (probably well grounded) that everyone knows and understands "traditional" common law crimes. Thus, because everyone is presumed to know and understand them, there is no notice problem preventing their enforcement.

There is greater difficulty enforcing the common law against new crimes, crimes that have come into being after the reception date. Faced with such a situation, some state courts have opted to judicially expand the common law to accommodate prosecution of the new offense. The argument in favor of such accommodation is that the court is not creating a new crime, it is merely applying established common law principles to a new situation. Courts in other jurisdictions have refused to allow prosecutions for a crime if it was not recognized before the reception date, *unless it is embodied in a written statute.*

Another major problem with enforcing common law crimes concerns the question of penalty. Some states have eliminated the problem by enacting statutes that set specific penalties for felonies and misdemeanors. Determining whether a crime is a felony or a misdemeanor presents another problem that we shall discuss later in this chapter.

No Common Law Crimes in Federal Law. The U.S. Supreme Court has solved the problem of enforcing common law crimes within the federal justice system by declaring that the U.S. government cannot base a criminal prosecution on an unwritten law. Thus, since the decision of the Supreme Court in the 1812 case of *United States v. Hudson and Goodwin*, 11 U.S. 32 (1812), there has been no federal enforcement of common law crimes.

The trend today is toward codification of all criminal laws. Nearly half of the states have expressly abolished common law crimes, replacing them with encoded (written) statutes. Even in those states where common law crimes survive, you will find that they are supplemented and augmented by a substantial body of written penal statutes.

Case Law. In those instances when we are required to consider a charge based on an unwritten law, our definitional principles still apply. The test for validity is largely unaffected by the source of the law, be it a written statute or an unwritten historic concept.

The challenge presented in working with common law crimes is not as enormous as it might at first appear. The attorney or paralegal operating in a jurisdiction that enforces uncodified criminal laws must be adept at researching prior cases, for that is where the definition of common law crimes and their applicable penalties are to be found.

For the most part, unwritten criminal law pertains only to universally recognizable offenses, such as murder, rape, or burglary, as previously mentioned. In those instances, there is little cause for uncertainty as to the definition of the offense or its penalty.

Even in the case of a written law, the paralegal's job requires examination of prior decisions interpretive of the statute. Your research procedures should not be affected if you are called upon to work on a case involving a common law crime.

CLASSIFICATION OF CRIMES

In the previous section, while discussing the penalties for common law crimes, we alluded to the distinction between felonies and misdemeanors. Categorizing crimes as felonies and misdemeanors is but one of several classifications pertaining to substantive criminal laws. When first considered, grouping crimes into classes may seem very theoretical and ineffectual, but as we shall see, there is good reason to be knowledgeable on the subject.

Felony and Misdemeanor

By far, the most significant distinction is the one already mentioned between felonies and lesser crimes. **Felony** denotes a transgression of the law that causes grievous social harm. Sometimes it is described simply as a serious crime. **Misdemeanor** generally refers to any criminal offense not classified as a felony.

In this country, statutes usually distinguish between felony and misdemeanor by the nature of the penalty that may be imposed. However, there is little uniformity among the states in setting the exact penalty by which a felony is set apart from a misdemeanor.

Some states, such as Texas, make a distinction between the two by reference to the type of penal institution where the offender may be incarcerated. (Refer to Figure 1-3.) In some instances, it is the length of the sentence that determines the grade of the crime, not the place of confinement. (See Figure 1-4). In other instances it is the type of penalty, not the place or the length of sentence, that is used to distinguish between types of offenses. (See Figure 1-5).

FIGURE 1-3   DISTINCTION BETWEEN FELONY AND MISDEMEANOR BASED ON THE PLACE OF CONFINEMENT

> An offense which may—not must—be punishable by death or by confinement in the penitentiary is a felony; every other offense is a misdemeanor.
>
> *TEX. PENAL CODE § 47*

FIGURE 1-4   DISTINCTION BETWEEN FELONY AND MISDEMEANOR BASED ON LENGTH OF SENTENCE

> Notwithstanding any Act of Congress to the contrary,
>
> (1) Any offense punishable by death or imprisonment for a term exceeding one year is a felony.
>
> (2) Any other offense is a misdemeanor.
>
> (3) Any misdemeanor, the penalty for which, as set forth in the provision defining the offense, does not exceed imprisonment for period of six months or a fine of not more than $5000 for an individual and $100000 for a person other than an individual or both, is a petty offense.
>
> *18 U.S.C. § 1*

FIGURE 1-5   DISTINCTION BETWEEN FELONY AND MISDEMEANOR BASED ON TYPE OF PENALTY

> (4) "Felony" is any offense for which an offender may be sentenced to death or imprisonment at hard labor.
>
> (6) "Misdemeanor" is any crime other than a felony.
>
> *Louisiana Revised Statutes, Title 14, Section 2 (4)&(6)*

One state, New Jersey, does not even employ the term *felony*, opting instead to distinguish between *high misdemeanors* and misdemeanors.

There are several reasons why it is important for you to be able to recognize the difference between a felony and a misdemeanor. For example, the validity of an arrest may depend on the grade of crime involved. Generally speaking, an arrest may be lawfully made, without a warrant, if the arresting officer has reasonable grounds to believe that a felony has been committed—even if it is not committed in his presence.

In the case of a misdemeanor, a valid arrest without a warrant may be made only if the offense occurs in view of the arresting officer. As we progress through this course, we will see what effect the validity of arrest can have on the case against an accused.

In some jurisdictions, conviction of a felony can deprive a person from voting, holding public office, or being licensed to practice medicine, law, or other professions. Ordinarily, a misdemeanor conviction will not have such an effect. A felony conviction may serve as a ground for divorce in some states and/or deprive a person of holding certain jobs or public office.

One very important reason to know the difference between felony and misdemeanor is that in many states an accidental death occurring during the commission of a *felony* may be treated as murder. The same would not be true in the case of an accidental death occurring during the commission of a *misdemeanor.*

The classification of a crime as a felony or a misdemeanor is also significant from the point of view of procedure. In the case of federal prosecutions, felony prosecutions may only be initiated by a grand jury. The grand jury does so by returning a true **bill of indictment**. (A true bill of indictment is usually referred to simply as an indictment.) On the other hand, misdemeanor prosecutions do not require the action of a grand jury. A misdemeanor charge may be lodged by the U.S. attorney acting without consulting a grand jury. To initiate formal charges for misdemeanor violations, the government prosecutor may simply file a **bill of information** with the clerk of the district court. Both an indictment and a bill of information are formal pronouncements of criminal charges against a defendant. The classification of the crime as a felony or a misdemeanor determines which one is to be used.

Malum in Se and *Malum Prohibitum*

Although the distinction between felony and misdemeanor may represent the most significant classification of crime, it is not the only one. In your work as a paralegal, you will encounter the phrases *malum in se* and *malum prohibitum.*

Malum in se refers to an offense that is wrong in itself, such as theft or battery. **Malum prohibitum** is an offense that is wrong because it is prohibited by statute, such as public intoxication or carrying a concealed weapon.

At this point you may be inclined to ask what difference does it make if a crime is *malum in se* or *malum prohibitum?* It would not be the first time the question was asked. The answer has two parts.

First, the degree of criminal intent required to sustain a conviction may be affected by whether the offense charged is *malum in se* or *malum prohibitum*. Some courts faced with a question of intent have held that crimes that are *malum in se* require a criminal intent but that crimes that are *malum prohibitum* do not have such a requirement.

Second, but no less significant, every attorney and paralegal is aware of the distinction between *malum in se* and *malum prohibitum*. Now you can join the club.

ENDNOTES

1   Judge Learned Hand was an acclaimed American jurist who served fifty years as a judge on the U.S. Court of Appeals for the Second Circuit. The quoted reference to due process was made during his famous Holmes Lectures at Harvard University in 1958.

2   Sir William Blackstone was an eighteenth-century English jurist. His renowned *Commentaries*, a four-volume treatise on English law, and his two-volume *Law Tracts*, earned him great respect in the United States in the 1800s.

2 ELEMENTS OF A CRIME

MENS REA AND *ACTUS REUS*

We concluded the previous chapter by explaining that *malum in se* crimes generally require proof of intent. Crime is composed of two parts: the intent and the act. These two elements are usually referred to as *mens rea* and *actus reus*. **Mens rea** may be literally translated as "guilty mind." **Actus Reus**, as you may have surmised, can be translated as "guilty deed."

When lawyers and judges speak of *mens rea*, they are usually referring to the state of mind necessary to commit a crime requiring criminal intent. When discussing this subject, it has become fashionable to quote the Latin maxim *Actus non fecit reum, nisi mens sit rea*. A liberal translation would be "An act cannot be guilty without the mind being guilty." If we refer back to our definition of crime, the *actus reus* may be thought of in terms of the result or social evil stipulated by our definition.

The social evil that results when a crime has been committed may be the same for two or more types of criminal activity, but the gravity of the crimes may differ. What determines the gravity of an offense is the *mens rea*. This point may be made more understandable by the following illustration.

A drives his auto over **B** resulting in **B's** death. If **A** intended to strike **B**, to kill him or to inflict grave harm, **A** would have committed murder. However, if **A** was intoxicated, negligent, or driving at a high rate of speed, making it impossible to avoid striking **B**, he may be guilty of manslaughter or negligent homicide, but not murder.

In our example, the *actus reus* is the same in each instance. What changes is the mind-set of **A**. The *actus reus* is the killing of **B**, but the *mens rea* alters the character of the offenses.

VARIATIONS OF INTENT

Any discussion of intent must include consideration of the various ways in which the law and the courts handle this issue. We will see that the ingredient of intent is of monumental significance in determining the criminality or innocence of a person's deeds.

General Criminal Intent

General criminal intent is often used synonymously with *mens rea*. General criminal intent is made up of two elements. First, there must be an intent to do the act, which forms the *actus reus*. Second, the actor must not possess any mental impediments to the formation of the intent, such as insanity, intoxication, or mistake of fact.

General criminal intent is sufficient to satisfy the *mens rea* requirement for most classic crimes. However, the *mens rea* element for other crimes is greater than that implied by general criminal intent. In other words, to be guilty of some crimes, a person must possess *more* than a general criminal intent.

Specific Intent

Specific intent is a higher form of *mens rea* than general criminal intent; however, the majority of criminal offenses do not require specific intent. In order to establish the mental element of a crime for crimes requiring only a general criminal intent, the prosecutor must prove only that the accused performed the act and that he or she did so willingly, without being forced.

Crimes such as murder require more than proof of willingness. The prosecutor must establish that the accused did the act willingly and with the intent to cause a specific result.

As mentioned above, the crime of murder has a *mens rea* requirement of specific intent. The specific intent required for murder is *the intent to kill or cause grave bodily harm.* At the trial of an accused charged with murder, the prosecution must prove that the defendant committed the act and did so with the specific intent to cause death or grave bodily harm. Thus, the indispensable elements of the crime of murder are

1. The *actus reus*—taking a human life
2. The *mens rea*—the specific intent to kill or cause grave bodily harm

It is now easier to understand the example cited earlier. When **A** killed **B** by striking him with an automobile, the crime is not murder unless **A** specifically intended to kill or gravely injure **B**. If the incident occurred through inadvertence or neglect, the crime would not be murder.

Transferred Intent

Transferred intent is yet another variation on our theme. It is a fictional concept. It means that the accidental consequence of a calculated act has the same legal effect as the intended result.

The idea is not as complicated as it sounds—it is as simple as ABC. **A** attempts to strike **B** but misses and hits **C**. **A** did not possess the intent to hit **C**; however, the action can still be criminal. The actual intent was to commit a battery on **B**. That criminal intent will be applied to the attack on **C** by the theory of transferred intent.

Constructive Intent

Constructive intent is another term complicating the notion of *mens rea*. By inventing the concept of constructive intent, courts pay homage to the idea that intent is an element of a crime. They then excuse its absence by stating that intent can be inferred from negligence or lack of care.

Perhaps the best way to explain the concept of constructive intent is with another example. Consider the situation in which the minor child of **X** sells lemonade in dirty cups at a sidewalk stand, thus causing food poisoning in unwary customers. By application of the theory of constructive intent, **X** could be found guilty of violating a law forbidding the sale of contaminated food. The law would simply construct intent from **X's** negligence in failing to supervise the activities of the minor.

Crimes involving constructive intent are usually minor in nature. Apparently the rationale for allowing a conviction under such circumstances is that the public good accomplished by the prosecution outweighs the relatively minor harm done to the person convicted, even though that person had no intent to commit a crime.

Criminal Negligence

The principle of **criminal negligence** is similar to that of constructive intent. Perhaps the main difference between the two ideas is found in the fact that criminal negligence statutes overtly declare that intent, as an element of the offense, is replaced by recklessness.

Recklessness is not to be confused with simple negligence. Some statutes refer to the degree of dereliction required for recklessness as *gross negligence, culpable negligence,* or *criminal negligence.* Whichever term is employed, it must be understood that only flagrant negligence will suffice as a substitute for the element of intent.

A driver who recklessly speeds through a crowded intersection striking and killing a pedestrian may be charged and convicted of negligent homicide. In such a case, there is no need for proof that the driver intended to strike the victim or that he or she even observed the victim before the fatal impact. The recklessness of the driver's conduct replaces the *mens rea* normally required in cases involving homicide. (See Figure 2-1.)

FACTORS NEGATING INTENT

Since one of the constituent parts of a crime is mental, it makes sense that circumstances preventing or impairing an actor's ability to formulate intent

FIGURE 2-1   FLAGRANT NEGLIGENCE AS A SUBSTITUTE FOR INTENT

A person acts negligently with respect to a material element of an offense when he should be aware of a substantial and unjustifiable risk that the material element exists or will result from his conduct. The risk must be of such a nature and degree that the actor's failure to perceive it, considering the nature and purpose of his conduct and the circumstances known to him, involves a gross deviation from the standard of conduct that a reasonable person would observe in the actor's situation.

MODEL PENAL CODE, § 2.02(2)(D)

Copyright 1985 by the American Law Institute.
Reprinted with the permission of the American Law Institute.

may significantly affect the responsibility he or she must bear for his or her actions. In this section we will look at several conditions of the mind that have been recognized as impairments to the formulation of criminal intent.

Insanity

It is universally accepted that a person suffering from mental disease or a disorder that substantially impairs his or her cognitive powers should not be held to the same degree of legal responsibility as a rational person. We usually refer to persons with a serious mental disorders as insane. However, the word *insane* has many meanings in the law.

Even if we limit our consideration to the field of criminal law, there are several tests and criteria by which insanity is determined. A complicating factor is that there are multiple stages to every criminal proceeding. Unfortunately, the standard for mental capacity varies as a case progresses through its various phases.

The first point at which the defendant's mental state is relevant is at the time when an alleged offense is committed. If, at the time of commission of the act, the accused is insane within the meaning of the law, lack of mental capacity entitles the accused to an **acquittal**—a verdict or finding of not guilty after a trial.

The next juncture at which the defendant's mental capacity may be considered is at the time of trial. At that stage, if the accused is so unstable that he or she cannot understand the nature of the charges nor assist counsel in providing a defense, he or she is not required to stand trial. Insanity at this stage in a criminal proceeding will not result in an acquittal, but the trial will be delayed until the defendant regains his or her faculties. During the resulting hiatus, the accused is usually institutionalized.

Finally, mental problems experienced by a defendant *after* conviction may also result in legal relief from sentence execution. In a capital case, for example, if the accused is sentenced to death and then becomes insane, execution of sentence will be delayed until sanity is restored.

At each point at which an accused's sanity is at issue, a different standard must be met in order to trigger legal relief. Our purpose here is to examine the standard(s) used to determine a person's mental capacity to form the requisite intent at the time of the *actus reus*, that is, at the time of commission. It is only at that point that insanity can negate the required *mens rea*.

The M'Naghten Rule. The **M'Naghten rule** is applied in most jurisdictions to determine the criminal responsibility of an accused for actions committed while he or she may have been experiencing mental derangement. The rule takes its name from a nineteenth-century English case. The accused, Daniel M'Naghten, killed a member of the prime minister's staff, believing him to be the prime minister. M'Naghten's commission of the act was never in dispute, but there was a serious question as to his mental state at the time of the killing.

Prior to trial, the judges declared that M'Naghten would not be entitled to the defense of insanity unless, at the time of commission, he was "labouring under such a defect of reason, from disease of the mind, as not to know the nature and quality of the act he was doing, or if he did know he did not know what he was doing was wrong."

The rule is frequently stated in these terms: A person cannot be found guilty of a crime if he or she was not able to distinguish between right and wrong at the time of the offense. That language may be less than precise, but all attorneys and judges recognize its premise.

The chief difficulty in applying the M'Naghten rule lies in defining the word *wrong*. Does it mean legally wrong or morally wrong? A person may know that the *law* forbids certain behavior but may engage in that behavior anyway because he or she does not recognize the deed as morally wrong. For example, a man could be suffering from the delusion that God has instructed him to set fire to theaters showing X-rated movies. The deluded individual might undertake his "divine mission" even though he knows that there is a law against arson.

The question of the actor's criminal responsibility is not easily resolved by application of the M'Naghten rule. In our example, the defendant knew that his actions were wrong and forbidden by law, but he thought that he was doing right in carrying out God's orders. There is disparity in the resolution of such problems among the states where the M'Naghten rule is used.

Further, some persons take the position that M'Naghten disregards current psychiatric thinking. However, proponents of the rule maintain that it is just as likely to preserve justice as vague psychiatric concepts. Whatever its advantages and drawbacks, M'Naghten is the rule utilized in most state jurisdictions and in the federal courts. (See Figure 2-2.)

The Durham Test. Those who complain that M'Naghten disregards advances in modern psychiatry, usually prefer the **Durham test**. The source of

FIGURE 2-2 FEDERAL INSANITY STATUTE

It is an affirmative defense to a prosecution under any federal statute that, at the time of the commission of the acts constituting the offense, the defendant, as a result of a severe mental disease or defect, was unable to appreciate the nature and quality or the wrongfulness of his acts. Mental disease or defect does not otherwise constitute a defense.

18 U.S.C. § 20

the Durham test is a New Hampshire case that was decided in the late 1800s. The supreme court of that state recognized the difficulties presented by M'Naghten's "right versus wrong" test and decided that an accused could not be found guilty of a crime if his action "was the offspring or product of mental disease."

The court gave no definition for "offspring" or "product" but suggested that it should be a question for the jury to decide. According to Durham, an accused relying on insanity as a defense must present evidence to establish, beyond a reasonable doubt, that his or her actions were the product of mental abnormality. This has proved to be no simple task, given the difficulty in diagnosing some mental disorders and the greater difficulty in getting psychiatric experts to agree on the diagnosis.

Despite its inherent drawbacks, most psychiatrists prefer Durham over M'Naghten as a test for legal insanity at the time of commission of an offense. In the opinion of its proponents, the Durham test offers greater latitude in explaining the specific disorder of the accused without regard to the artificial "right versus wrong" standard of M'Naghten. The Durham standard is the law in only a handful of states, being far less prevalent than M'Naghten.

Irresistible Impulse. Irresistible impulse is yet another test for insanity at the time of the commission of an offense. Properly characterized, irresistible impulse is an expansion of the M'Naghten rule, not a separate standard. It allows for the acquittal of a defendant who recognizes the fact that his or her actions were wrong but who could not control his or her conduct because of an irresistible impulse. Irresistible impulse is employed only in states that recognize the M'Naghten standard, but not in all of those states.

The chief difficulty with the irresistible impulse theory lies in quantifying the impulse. How strong must the impulse be in order to be irresistible? Most psychiatrists have little difficulty in deciding whether or not the accused acted impulsively. However, they experience a great deal of trouble in declaring categorically that the impulse was irresistible.

Everyone acts in response to an impulse. In most cases, the actor recognizes the impulse for what it is and makes a conscious decision to follow the urge or to resist it. How, then, can it be determined whether an illegal deed is the result of the conscious intent to act or the product of an irresistible, overwhelming impulse? One test suggested for irresistibility is that the urge must be so overpowering that it cannot be resisted even if a policeman is at the side of the actor.

Model Penal Code **Standard.** A better answer to the insanity question seems to be offered by the ***Model Penal Code***. (See Figure 2-3.) The standard proposed in the code is something of a combination of M'Naghten, irresistible impulse, and Durham. It has been adopted in part by some states and rejected entirely by others, such as New York. The federal insanity statute, referred to earlier, was enacted after publication of the *Model Penal Code* standard; however, many states seem to be headed in the direction suggested by the penal code.

FIGURE 2-3   INSANITY STANDARD, AS DEFINED BY THE *MODEL PENAL CODE*

Mental Disease or Defect Excluding Responsibility

(1) A person is not responsible for criminal conduct if at the time of such conduct as a result of mental disease or defect he lacks substantial capacity either to appreciate the criminality (wrongfulness) of his conduct or to conform his conduct to the requirements of law. (2) As used in this Article, the terms 'mental disease or defect' do not include an abnormality manifested only by repeated criminal or otherwise anti-social conduct.

MODEL PENAL CODE § 4.01

Evidence of Mental Disease or Defect Admissible When Relevant to Element of Offense

(1) Evidence that a defendant suffered from a mental disease or defect is admissible whenever it is relevant to prove that the defendant did or did not have a state of mind which is an element of the offense.

MODEL PENAL CODE § 4.02

 POINTER: The *Model Penal Code* is a project of The American Law Institute (ALI). The ALI is an organization dominated by professors and instructors of law. Its penal code is designed as a guide for legislatures and lawmakers who are seeking to reform and improve their state's substantive and procedural criminal laws.

Immaturity (Infancy)

Another factor that can negate intent is the age of the actor.

Under the Common Law. The common law recognized criminal incapacity by reason of immaturity. **Immaturity** is a defect of intent owing to the youthfulness of the offender. Historically, a child under the age of seven years was presumed to be incapable of formulating the requisite criminal intent and, therefore, was not held responsible under the criminal law.

For a child under the age of seven years, the presumption of no intent was irrebuttable. Between the ages of seven years and fourteen years, a child enjoyed a *rebuttable* presumption of incapacity. As the child progressed in age from seven to fourteen, the presumption diminished until it passed away entirely at age fourteen. Beyond the age of fourteen years, the common law bestowed full legal capacity and responsibility upon an offender.

Under the Juvenile Justice System. Today in the United States the problem of immaturity and its effect upon criminal capacity has shifted to the juvenile justice system. All states recognize the immaturity problem, and all have established a system for handling juvenile offenders outside the criminal justice structure. The age at which a youngster is answerable as an adult for criminal transgressions is set by statute and varies from state to state. A common cut-off age is eighteen years, but the age of full criminal responsibility can range as low as fourteen. It is interesting to note that, in most states, a juvenile, not otherwise answerable for criminal offenses because of tender years, can be held responsible for offenses that carry capital or life sentences.

Instead of being found guilty of a substantive crime, a youth who is subjected to a juvenile proceeding and found to have committed the underlying act is adjudicated a juvenile delinquent. There are jurisdictions, such as California, that allow the defense of infancy to be raised even in a juvenile proceeding. We shall explore the juvenile justice system in greater detail in a later chapter.

Intoxication

Intoxication caused by alcohol or other substances can affect an actor's capacity to formulate criminal intent. In considering the effects of intoxication on the element of intent, we must distinguish between voluntary intoxication and involuntary intoxication.

Voluntary Intoxication. **Voluntary intoxication** is a defect of intent that usually does not form a valid affirmative defense. The rule is that voluntary intoxication does not negate a general criminal intent; however, when a crime requires a greater *mens rea* than general criminal intent, such as specific intent, intoxication, even voluntary intoxication, can negate the mental element.

Involuntary Intoxication. **Involuntary intoxication**, by contrast, is a defect of intent that can form a valid affirmative defense. Involuntary intoxication occurs when a person is forced to drink alcohol, or to take other intoxicants, or does so unwittingly or without knowledge of the effects it will produce. Thus, a person experiencing intoxicating side effects from prescribed medication might be declared involuntarily intoxicated.

Courts regard involuntary intoxication in the same manner as a mental disorder. The mere fact of involuntary intoxication does not itself bar prosecution, but it can result in acquittal if it prevents the accused from distinguishing right from wrong, if it creates an irresistible impulse, or if it prevents appreciation of the criminality of various actions.

An interesting question involving intoxication concerns the case of the pathologic drinker or drug user whose intoxication is symptomatic of a disease. If the offender is so dependent on the intoxicating substance as to have no control over its use, a question arises as to the voluntary nature of the person's condition. Some courts have demonstrated a willingness to handle such defendants as though they were involuntarily intoxicated. However, on at least one occasion, in the 1968 case of *Powell v. Texas*, 392 U.S. 514 (1968), the Supreme Court refused to recognize a constitutional issue in the case of chronic alcoholism. In response to that decision, some states enacted laws making alcoholism a defense against the crime of public drunkenness.

Other Defects of Intent

Insanity, immaturity, and intoxication are not the only factors affecting the formation of requisite criminal intent; however, they represent the defects that you are most likely to encounter. Others, such as duress, necessity, or mistake, are rarely seen because authorities are reluctant to prosecute individuals who act because they were forced by others or pressured by circumstances not of their making.

INCHOATE OFFENSES

Up to now, we have devoted most of our attention to the basic criminal element of intent. The subject of this section relates more to the *actus reus*.

At the beginning of the chapter, we learned that crime properly should be viewed in terms of the resulting social evil. In one of our examples, Smith wanted to shoot Jones. The gun was fired, the target was struck, and Jones died.

The example demonstrated a completed crime because intent (Smith intended to shoot his enemy) and a resulting social evil (Jones died) were present. But would there have been a crime if Smith's weapon had misfired and Jones had fled physically unharmed? The answer to that question forms the subject of this discussion of inchoate offenses. When we consider the unaccomplished goals of an offender, we are considering inchoate offenses. An **inchoate offense**, frequently a crime in itself, is a criminal transgression in which the perpetrator does not accomplish the criminal act.

Attempt

Attempt is a relatively new concept in criminal law. It is a crime in which the criminal undertaking fails to accomplish its goal. Its origin is usually attributed to a late eighteenth century English case, *Rex v. Schofield*, CALD. 397 (1784), though there is some indication within that written decision that the principle had been established earlier. In any event, until the Schofield decision, the general belief was that an unsuccessful attempt at a crime (at least a noncapital crime) was not punishable. In delivering the *Schofield* decision, Lord Mansfield declared that an attempt, even an attempted misdemeanor, could be a crime. (At that time all noncapital crimes were misdemeanors.)

Shortly thereafter, in *Rex v. Higgins*, 2 EAST 5 (1801), the same court had another opportunity to speak out on attempt. In *Higgins*, the following now famous rule was pronounced:

> All offenses of a public nature, that is, all such acts or *attempts* as tend to the prejudice of the community, are indictable. (Emphasis added)

The rule of *Schofield*, reiterated in *Higgins*, is the source of common law "attempt" crimes in this country. Most states have now codified their attempt laws, thus making it a separate statutory offense to attempt a crime. Although there is no uniformity among the states regarding how attempts are penalized, almost invariably they carry a less onerous penalty than the completed crime.

Mere Preparation. Even though every jurisdiction has criminalized attempt, there is no common method to determine when an attempt has taken place. It is, however, universally accepted that mere preparation to commit an offense does not establish the crime of attempt. An additional ingredient that goes beyond preparation must be present. In itself, **mere preparation** is a defense to the crime of attempt and does not violate the law.

In most states, courts have adopted some sort of standard to ascertain the presence of that additional factor, beyond preparation, required for the crime of attempt. Unfortunately, some state courts have enunciated no criterion for deciding when an accused's activity passes beyond the level of mere preparation.

Res Ipsa Loquitur. Some jurisdictions use the *res ipsa loquitur* analysis to determine whether preparation has reached the stage where it constitutes attempt. **Res ipsa loquitur** literally means "the thing speaks for itself." It is used as a test to determine if preparation to commit a crime is sufficient to constitute attempt. In applying the *res ipsa* standard, the activity of the accused is examined. If that activity, in and of itself, is clearly and unquestionably directed toward accomplishment of a substantive criminal act, then the accused is adjudicated to have moved from mere preparation to actual attempt. Such an analysis does not seem to answer the question What constitutes an attempt?

Substantial Act. In other jurisdictions, courts have allowed conviction of attempt merely upon proof that the defendant performed a **substantial act** directed toward accomplishing a criminal goal. The *Model Penal Code* favors this approach.

Dangerously Close. Some states employ a standard that calls for evaluation of the defendant's conduct to determine if he or she was dangerously close to accomplishing a criminal objective. In those jurisdictions, when preparation has moved the actor dangerously close to his or her objective, the line is said to have been crossed and the accused may be found guilty of attempt.

Level of Preparedness. Still other courts make a determination based on whether it seems probable that a reasonable person would turn away, that is, voluntarily desist, from his or her criminal objective, considering the level of preparedness. If the defendant's state of preparation makes it more likely than not that a reasonable person who had gone to such lengths to get ready to commit a crime would actually carry to completion the criminal objective, then the accused may be found guilty of attempt.

We can see from this review, that the courts and legislatures have had a difficult time answering the question What constitutes an attempt? None of the responses seems satisfying or even enlightening. As a paralegal working on a project involving a charge of attempt, you will rely greatly on your research skills to examine the case law in your jurisdiction. If there is an answer to our question, that is where it will be found.

One final point must be understood. Even though an attempt to commit a crime is a crime separate from the completed act, if the actor carries the act through to its completion, only one crime has been committed. At that point, the attempt is no longer prosecutable.

Conspiracy

In discussing attempt, we learned that the law may punish a person who has tried to commit a crime even though that person fails to achieve his or her objective. We will now look at another means of penalizing an offender who has been stopped short of his or her criminal goal.

When two or more persons combine to commit a crime, they expose themselves to penal sanctions by the mere fact of that confederation. Of course, we are speaking of conspiracy. As is true of the crime of attempt, **conspiracy**, an unlawful combination of two or more persons for the purpose of commission of a crime, requires the intent to commit a substantive criminal act. Also, as is true of the crime of attempt, conspiracy provides a penalty even if the substantive criminal goal is never attained. However, unlike an attempt, which is abrogated by completion of the substantive crime, the crime of conspiracy lives on, and its members may be prosecuted for the conspiracy even if they complete the underlying crime that was their objective. Stated more directly, conspirators may be convicted of both the conspiracy to commit an offense and the substantive crime that was the goal of the conspiracy.

The crime of conspiracy reaches farther into the mind of defendants than does the crime of attempt. As we have noted, conviction for attempt requires not only preparation but also an additional element beyond preparation. Conviction for conspiracy may not even require preparation—it can be based on the mere agreement between two parties. It should be noted, however, that some jurisdictions, including federal jurisdictions, do require that at least one of the parties to a criminal agreement must have taken a step in furtherance of the agreement's goal in order to establish the crime of conspiracy. Figure 2-4 is an excerpt concerning conspiracy from a federal statutory compilation, the *United States Code.*

Overt Act. A step in the furtherance of a conspiracy is usually referred to as an overt act. An overt act need not be criminal, indeed it is usually benign. It need not be indispensable or even significant to the ultimate goal of the conspiracy. It need only be committed in furtherance of the conspiracy.

Let's look at an example of an overt act. **X** and **Z** decide to steal an automobile. **X** obtains a buyer's guide to check used car values, not wanting to steal a cheap car. The purchase of the buyer's guide is sufficient to satisfy the overt act requirement of conspiracy. Obtaining a buyer's guide is not illegal, it is not indispensable to the theft of the automobile, nor is it even significant to the ultimate outcome of the scheme, but it will suffice for an overt act.

FIGURE 2-4   FEDERAL CONSPIRACY STATUTE

If two or more persons conspire to commit any offense against the United States, or to defraud the United States, or any agency thereof in any manner or for any purpose, and one or more of such persons do any act to effect the object of the conspiracy, each shall be fined not more than $10,000 or imprisoned not more than five years or both.

If, however, the offense, the commission of which is the object of the conspiracy, is a misdemeanor only, the punishment for such conspiracy shall not exceed the maximum punishment provided for such misdemeanor.

18 U.S.C. § 371

Conspiracy represents the farthest departure from our premise that all crime requires two elements, intent and deed. An overt act, even when it is required, may be inconsequential to any illegal purpose. In some respects, an overt act is merely evidence of intent. It adds nothing by way of social evil, it merely highlights the criminal intent of the parties, or at least one of them.

It would appear that conspiracy punishes a person for mere intent. However, a closer analysis reveals that the crime of conspiracy, even in jurisdictions requiring no overt act, still comprises our two classic elements, *mens rea* and *actus reus*.

Mens Rea and Actus Reus. The *mens rea* for conspiracy is apparent: it is the intent of each party to commit a criminal act. The *actus reus* is somewhat less obvious, but it is nonetheless present. It is the *combination* of the parties into a joint venture that has for its object the commission of an offense. It is not the overt act.

Misprision

Misprision (see Figure 2-5) is a third type of offense that has an obscure *actus reus*. Indeed, the crime of **misprision**, the act of concealing a crime committed by another person or the failure to report a crime, is itself obscure and is enforced infrequently, though it is recognized in many jurisdictions. We consider it at this juncture because it is illustrative of two points.

First, it is another crime that is sometimes characterized as purely mental, that is, solely a crime of intent. Second, it serves as a good example of the principle that the *actus reus* may be passive, in which case might it be more properly referred to as non–*actus reus?*

The definition of misprision cited in the preceding paragraph may convey the essence of an offense, but it adds confusion to our concept of the required elements of a crime, intent and act, because it does not specify a deed. Since we normally think of the *actus reus* in terms of a deed or action, we may be inclined to declare that misprision requires no *actus reus.*

Another definition of misprision defines the term as withholding of information concerning a crime. By couching the definition in terms of "withholding" or "concealing," the *actus reus* becomes more apparent because "concealing" is an active concept.

FIGURE 2-5   MISPRISION, AS DEFINED BY FEDERAL STATUTE

Whoever, having knowledge of the actual commission of a felony cognizable by a court of the United States, *conceals* and does not as soon as possible make known the same to some judge or other person in civil or military authority under the United States, shall be fined not more than $500 or imprisoned not more than three years, or both.

18 U.S.C. § 4

Our appreciation of criminal law is broad enough to include both crimes of *omission* as well as crimes of *commission.* It does no violence to our notion of crime that an offense is passive. Our definition of crime refers to social evil. In the case of misprision and other passive crimes, the social evil is brought about by a failure to act.

The federal statute cited in Figure 2-5 sidesteps the issue by defining misprision as an active offense (i.e., concealment). Whether it is thought of as concealment, which is active, or as failure to report, which is passive, misprision conforms to our definitional standard of a crime. There is no requirement that the *actus reus* be active. For those who cannot accept the premise that an *actus* can be passive, we have already suggested the term non–*actus reus.* Either way, it satisfies the second elemental requirement of a crime.

Principal, Accomplice, and Accessory

There are other concepts, such as principal, accomplice, and accessory, that provide for the punishment of those who may have had no part in the deeds that constitute the *actus reus.* A businessman who hires someone to kill a competitor may be found guilty of murder even though he remains miles away from the actual killing. This is true because he is a **principal** to the crime; that is, he is considered a chief participant in the crime although he employed another to act for him subject to his control and instruction.

At early common law, a distinction was drawn between a *first principal*, who was the chief performer of the crime, and a *second principal*, who aided and abetted in its performance. **Accomplice** is a relatively modern term for second principal, one who actively encourages the commission of an act. Scant good will come from distinguishing between an accomplice and a principal. Current practice is to punish all direct participants as principals, as noted in Figure 2-6.

FIGURE 2-6   PRINCIPAL, AS DEFINED BY FEDERAL STATUTE

(a) Whoever commits an offense against the United States, or aids, abets, counsels, commands, induces or procures its commission, is punishable as a principal.

(b) Whoever willfully causes an act to be done, which if directly performed by him or another would be an offense against the United States, is punishable as a principal.

18. U.S.C. § 2

In the case of an accessory, a distinction must be drawn between an accessory before the fact, who is generally treated as a principal, and an accessory after the fact, who is ordinarily punished less severely than a principal. An **accessory before the fact** is a person who contributes as an assistant or instigator to the commission of an offence. An **accessory after the fact** is one who gives aid and support to the principal after the crime has been committed. It should be noted that a person cannot be found guilty as an accessory after the fact unless the principal has been convicted of a substantive crime.

At this point, we discontinue our discussion of the elemental properties of substantive criminal law. It would require far too much time to examine the individual criminal laws of even one jurisdiction to determine their constituent elements. Even if circumstances permitted, such an undertaking would be of questionable value, unless, by chance, we settled upon the specific jurisdiction in which you have an interest.

What we have learned in this chapter has universal application. If you keep in mind the general principles we have considered, you should experience little difficulty analyzing and understanding criminal law, no matter the jurisdiction. Besides, analysis of the law is only part of the job you will be expected to perform. What you do with your analysis and how you go about obtaining relief when you discover a problem are at least as important to you as a paralegal as discovering the problem in the first place. We will cover that subject of obtaining relief and other matters of importance as we proceed through this course.

3 BURDEN OF PROOF

THE OTHER ELEMENTS

In the previous chapter, we identified the elements of a crime as *mens rea* and *actus reus*. At that point in our discussion, we were considering crime as a universal concept. However, in the work-a-day world of criminal law, another more particular meaning is given to the phrase *elements of a crime*.

In this chapter we will be dealing with the duties of the attorneys and paralegals who are in charge of the prosecution for the government. In order to better understand those duties, we must first begin with an explanation of the other meanings for *elements*.

Elements of the Crime

Around the office and the courthouse, when lawyers speak of the **elements of a crime**, they are usually not referring to *mens rea* and *actus reus*. When they talk of elements, lawyers are probably referring to the constituent factors that make up a specific crime. For example, in the common law the crime of theft is known as larceny. The elements (constituent factors) of the crime of larceny are generally thought of as consisting of the following:

1. A trespassory taking and
2. Carrying away of
3. The property
4. Of another person
5. With the intent to permanently deprive

What this means is that all five of the factors making up the offense of larceny (theft) must be present for a crime to have occurred. Further, every element of the crime must be proved by clear and convincing evidence in order to convict an accused of larceny. The burden of producing such evidence rests squarely upon the prosecuting authority. When we say that the **burden of proof** is on the prosecution, we mean that the prosecution is responsible for proving each element of a crime.

Beyond a Reasonable Doubt

At a criminal trial, it is the prosecutor who must prove each and every element of the offense beyond a reasonable doubt. Proof **beyond a reasonable doubt** constitutes the highest standard of proof required in any legal proceeding. It is the standard of proof required to substantiate each element of a criminal charge in order to support a conviction. We emphasize the standard of proof because it is the heaviest burden borne by any party in any court proceeding in this country.

In other paralegal courses, you will consider evidence, its types and quality, and the rules that govern its admissibility. It is sufficient for our present purpose to note that, in criminal law, the accused is never required to prove his or her innocence. *The government always bears the burden of proof.*

MULTIPLE SOVEREIGNS

One more topic must be mentioned before we look at the duties of the prosecution in detail. This is as good a place as any to point out just who are the prosecutors.

By now you should be aware that in the United States there are more than fifty sovereign jurisdictions that possess the authority to charge and punish individuals for criminal conduct. Those jurisdictions are the federal government and the governments of the fifty states. If we add to that list the District of Columbia, Puerto Rico, other territorial entities, as well as the municipal subdivisions of the states, the number of sovereignties to which a person may be answerable becomes almost incalculable.

It may be of some value to consider how so many governmental entities interrelate, where jurisdictional lines are drawn, and what the areas of special concern are for each. The discussion that follows is not intended to be a complete treatment of the relationship between all the various law enforcement agencies, it is merely illustrative and is, perhaps, overly generalized. But it can be helpful to your understanding of the arena in which you will one day work if you concentrate your interest in the field of criminal law.

Local Jurisdictions

Local or municipal governments exercise a level of criminal authority that occasionally touches even law-abiding persons. Most traffic and public order–type crimes are enforced on a local level. Ordinances prohibiting petty offenses, such as public drunkenness, rowdiness, unsanitary health conditions, and noise and nuisance transgressions are typical of the laws enforced by local or municipal court systems.

Much of the formality we normally associate with judicial proceedings is missing at the municipal level, but the rules of validity we have considered apply to local ordinances just as they apply to statutes proscribing more serious evils. However, because of the inconsequential nature of the penalties likely to be imposed, an accused will be less inclined to underwrite the cost of waging serious legal battles over technicalities when a local ordinance is involved.

State Jurisdictions

The level above the local level is generally thought of as the felony level, the forum in which prosecutions for all serious state offenses originate. The courts at this level are frequently called district courts, but designations vary from state to state. In California, for example, state felony offenses are tried in superior court. Many states refer to their courts of original felony jurisdiction as county courts. Whatever the name, these courts are tribunals with jurisdiction spreading throughout a designated geographic area, such as a county. In less populated areas, a district comprises more than one county.

Crimes are prosecuted at this level by a state official, usually called the district attorney or the state's attorney. The authority of this officeholder is generally districtwide, but some states employ separate prosecuting attorneys for each county within a multicounty district.

In general, state criminal prosecutions involve crimes of the classic common law variety. We have already noted that most states have codified their criminal laws so that even when dealing with common law crimes the courts and attorneys have written statutes to guide their efforts.

When we speak of classic offenses, we are speaking of crimes such as arson, assault, burglary, battery, kidnapping, murder, rape, robbery, theft, and trespass. State prosecutions also extend to the so-called victimless crimes, gambling, prostitution, and narcotic offenses.

Many subdivisions of offenses are found in state penal codes. For example, homicide may be subdivided into first-degree murder, second-degree murder, manslaughter, and negligent homicide. Theft may be called grand larceny, embezzlement, theft by fraud, petty theft, or a variety of other names.

Though the terminology may vary from jurisdiction to jurisdiction, there is very little difference among the type of crimes prosecuted at the state level. It is hard to think of an example of an offense punishable in one state that is not punishable in every other jurisdiction. Activity constituting a crime in one state usually constitutes a crime in every other state, although the offense may be called by a different name.

Federal Jurisdictions

Throughout the country, there are eighty-one federal districts. Each state has at least one federal district; many have more than one. Federal districts are denominated geographically within a state, leading to such designation as the Northern District of Illinois or the Middle District of Florida. Within a federal district, there are frequently subdivisions (e.g., the Middle District of Florida, Tampa Division, and there are other divisions of the Middle District of Florida at Jacksonville and Orlando).

As we learned earlier in our consideration of common law crimes, federal courts do not enforce unwritten criminal laws. The bulk of federal criminal law is found in Title 18 of the *United States Code.* Title 26 of the code (26 U.S.C.) contains the federal tax laws, many of which carry criminal sanctions for their violation. Title 21 (21 U.S.C.) is the location of most federal narcotic laws. Other federal criminal statutes are spread throughout other sections of the code.

The chief federal law enforcement authority in each federal district is the U.S. attorney. With only limited interference from the Department of Justice, U.S. attorneys have broad authority over what crimes are prosecuted in their districts.

Federal criminal law enforcers, like their state counterparts, follow a pattern with respect to the type of crimes that they ordinarily prosecute. The normal pattern of federal prosecutions can be more easily understood if it is thought of in the negative. The rule, which admits many exceptions, is that federal authorities do not intrude into areas where there is ample local control.

For example, in the case of bank robbery, there is a specific federal statute, 18 U.S.C. § 2113. However, in every state, laws that penalize for the offense of robbery exist. Because state authorities are eager to prosecute such violent offenders and since most state laws carry very onerous penalties for conviction of bank robbery, federal officials frequently take no action themselves and allow the local authority to prosecute.

Notwithstanding the general rule, federal prosecutors usually pursue offenders when a crime has a peculiarly federal quality, even if state laws might also apply. For example, the theft of a Social Security check from a mail box is a state offense and a federal violation. Traditionally, the U.S. government will prosecute such a violation because it has a particularly federal relevance: a federally issued check has been taken from the federal mail service. Another example is in the area of narcotic violations. Even though there are state laws that can be evoked, federal prosecutors are quick to act.

A common characteristic of federal prosecutions is that they are usually more complex and lengthy than state cases. Whereas a typical state charge might be spelled out in a document of one page or less, it is not uncommon for federal indictments to exceed twenty pages in length. This is true because of the types of statutes that federal authorities have at their disposal. Another reason is that state authorities are usually inundated with the volume of cases that they must handle and are only too glad to defer complex prosecutions to the feds.

We have already mentioned the RICO statute as an example of the type of intricate and tangled federal law that is enforced in U.S. courts. For another example one might consider the anti–money laundering laws (18 U.S.C. §§ 1956–1957), which are grotesquely convoluted.

Double Jeopardy

While we are considering the overlap of federal and state jurisdictions, it may be a good time to bring up the notion of double jeopardy. When we discussed the Bill of Rights, we noted that the Fifth Amendment forbids trying a person twice for the same crime. Being twice put in jeopardy is called **double jeopardy**. The prohibition against double jeopardy does not apply to situations involving dual sovereignties; that is to say, if the crime is penalized by both federal and state law, an offender can be tried, convicted, and sentenced in both jurisdictions. Thus, in our bank robbery example, the robber could be tried in federal court and in state court for the same transgression.

The protection against double jeopardy only applies to situations in which a person is subjected to prosecution for the same crime more than once *by the same sovereignty*. The Constitution does not allow that to happen.

Equal Dignity

One final point should be made before we close out this section. Occasionally, the relationship between state and federal courts can be confusing. In fact, it is so often misunderstood that it warrants clarification in a section of its own. **Equal dignity** is the term used to refer to the parity between federal and state courts of comparable levels.

Federal district courts do not possess appellate authority over state district courts. The U.S. district court and a state district court have the same hierarchical dignity. The federal courts and the state courts are parallel systems. Except for constitutional issues that may arise during state prosecutions, the federal courts have no authority over state criminal proceedings.

CHRONOLOGY OF A PROSECUTION

We have seen that the burden of proof, at the time of trial, rests with the prosecuting authority. However, the job of the prosecutor does not begin when the trial starts. Usually the trial is one of the final stages in a process that may extend over many months.

In the remainder of this chapter we will examine the job of an attorney working in the office of the prosecution, beginning at the point where a case first surfaces. We will end with a survey of the assignments that may be handled by a paralegal.

Because we want our review to have the broadest applicability, we will survey the federal system. Keep in mind that the job of an attorney and a paralegal working in the office of a state prosecutor will be very similar to that of their federal counterparts. Keep in mind also that a paralegal can be called upon to perform most of the tasks that an attorney must perform, except for court or grand jury appearances and counseling and giving advice or opinions on the law.

Overview of a Prosecutor's Office

It might be helpful to begin our survey by taking a bird's-eye view of a prosecutor's office. It should be understood that no single model exists after which all offices are patterned. However, there are enough similarities among prosecution offices to make an overview worthwhile.

The Prosecutor. In state jurisdictions, the prosecutor is usually called the district attorney or state's attorney. The position is usually an elected one; that is, it is filled by a vote of the people of the district.

In the federal system, the prosecutor is the U.S. attorney for the federal district. This is not an elected position but one appointed by the president.

Depending on the size of the office over which they preside and depending on their individual personalities, district attorneys or U.S. attorneys may be personally very active in handling the cases that flow through their offices, or they may be chiefly administrators. The larger the office, the more likely that its head will be administrative and policy-oriented and less involved in hands-on prosecutions.

The First Assistant. Immediately under the district attorney and U.S. attorney is usually a position for a first assistant. This position may be mainly managerial if the subordinate staff is a large one. However, the personality of the individual and the work load of the district may allow the first assistant to be active in the handling of cases.

Department Heads and Other Organizational Structures of the Prosecutor's Office. Below the first assistant are department heads and other assistants. At this point, generalities become difficult. The subdivisions of a prosecution office, including department heads and below, may take any number of forms.

Some offices are organized along the lines of docket assignments. If so, department heads are usually assistant prosecutors, with supervisory authority, in charge of various dockets. A docket is a calendar of cases to be handled.

In offices organized along docket lines, the calendar for each docket contains cases of a similar nature or type. For example, separate dockets may be established for homicide, narcotics, and child abuse cases. A complaint involving one of these crimes would come into the prosecution office through the appropriate docket. It would be screened, investigated, charged or rejected, and maybe even tried by personnel assigned to that division.

Some offices are organized differently. For example, the prosecution staff may be divided according to job assignments. There may be a screening division, a trials division, a grand jury division, and an appeals division. Attorneys from those divisions work on all types of cases but only at a specific stage in the case's development.

In larger districts where there are multiple court sections, the organization of the prosecutor's office must accommodate each section of the court. In some instances, specific assistant prosecutors might be assigned to handle all cases coming before each particular section of the court. In other instances, an office may be organized so that each case is handled by an assistant from the docket where the case arose without regard for the allotment or court section. That is, a drug case would be handled and tried by a prosecutor from the narcotics docket no matter the court section.

The point here is that there is no general rule for the organization of prosecution operations. There is no typical setup. The first accomplishment of anyone who accepts employment as a prosecutor or paralegal in a prosecution office is to learn the system. Likewise, it is very important that the defense counterparts know the organizational structure employed by the prosecutor.

The Paralegal. From what we have seen of office structure, it is easy to understand why it is impossible to generalize regarding the responsibilities of paralegals who work with the prosecution. The supervisor of the paralegal will be an attorney, but little more than that is certain. The specific chain of command will depend on the organization of the office. We will have more to say regarding specific assignments of the paralegal later.

What we have mentioned concerning the organization and command structure of the prosecution office will become clearer as we look at the duties of the persons working in that office. As mentioned above, our discussion will focus mainly on a U.S. attorney's office in the federal system.

The Prosecutor as Legal Adviser

As a rule, the prosecutor becomes involved in a case when he or she receives a report of a completed investigation prepared by a law enforcement agency. The Federal Bureau of Investigation (FBI), the Postal Inspector's Office, and the Drug Enforcement Administration are examples of agencies that report to the federal prosecutor. On the state level, the investigator will ordinarily be a police investigator.

It is not uncommon for an investigator to consult the prosecutor before completing an investigation. The reasons why an agent might confer with the prosecutor while an investigation is in progress are many. In the federal system and in almost all state systems, the prosecutor's office serves as legal advisor to the law enforcement agencies working within its jurisdictions.

The significance of the job as adviser becomes apparent when one considers some of the tasks that a legal advisor may be called upon to perform. For example, an agent may need a search warrant to explore for evidence. As we will discuss in greater detail later, such a warrant can be issued by a judge or magistrate only upon a showing of probable cause by the person seeking the authority to conduct the search. **Probable cause** is defined as evidence that constitutes more than suspicion but less than the amount of proof needed to convict.

In order to establish that there is probable cause to believe that evidence is being concealed at a particular location, the agent seeking the warrant presents a sworn statement to a judge who can issue the warrant. The sworn statement, usually referred to as the supporting affidavit, is frequently prepared, or at least reviewed, by a member of the prosecutor's legal staff.

The list of tasks that a prosecutor can be asked to perform during an investigation is extensive. In some instances, the attorney must prepare formal documents for submission to a judge or magistrate, as when a telephone tap is requested, or make a formal appearance before a court to obtain judicial authorization for such things as collecting biological evidence or handwriting samples.

It should be apparent that the attorney who counsels and advises investigating agents must be well informed about the substantive criminal law that underlies an alleged offense. It should be equally clear that the prosecutor must be knowledgeable about the rules of evidence and procedure to determine the fitness of the evidence and to make decisions regarding its sufficiency to prove a case against an accused. A prosecutor's expertise in the areas of procedure and evidence is an invaluable asset in carrying out duties as advisor and as counselor to law enforcement agents.

In U.S. district courts, the admissibility of evidence is controlled by the **Federal Rules of Evidence (FED. R. EVID.)**. Procedure in criminal cases is governed by the **Federal Rules of Criminal Procedure (FED. R. CRIM. P.)**. Also, Title 18 of the *United States Code* contains statutes that prescribe procedures and regulations for many prosecutorial functions. Most states have similar evidence and procedural codes. If you are to be proficient as a paralegal working in the office of a federal or state prosecutor, you must become familiar with all applicable standards for admissibility of evidence and courtroom procedure in the jurisdiction in which you will work.

The Screening Process

In the typical U.S. attorney's office, assistant prosecutors are assigned to handle cases by docket assignment as previously described. Investigators or agents usually forward reports and requests for assistance directly to the assistant U.S. attorney who has the docket assignment covering the crime that is being investigated. The prosecutor who receives the report must perform a function called screening.

Screening cases for prosecution, an evaluation process, involves reviewing the material presented by the case agent to determine if a crime has been committed. During screening, the attorney must evaluate the available evidence and decide if it is admissible at trial and if it is sufficient to prove the elements of the crime beyond a reasonable doubt.

Lodging Formal Charges

If the screening assistant U.S. attorney believes that the case presented by the agent is worthy of prosecution, the case will be accepted for prosecution. If the case lacks merit, the screening attorney may reject it, that is, decline prosecution.

When the case is accepted for prosecution, the assistant U.S. attorney or someone working on the staff, such as a paralegal, must prepare the case for presentation to the grand jury in order to obtain an indictment. In the case of a misdemeanor, someone in the prosecutor's office must prepare a bill of information. The place (location) where a criminal charge is lodged is called the **venue**.

As we learned in Chapter 1, an indictment and a bill of information are formal charges of criminal wrongdoing. The chief difference between the two is that an indictment can only be made by a grand jury and a bill of information is filed by the U.S. attorney acting on his inherent authority.

Neither an indictment nor a bill of information is proof of a crime. An indictment is simply a finding by a grand jury that there is probable cause to believe that a crime has been committed by the named accused. A bill of information is an accusation by the prosecuting authority. Standing alone, neither will convict an accused. The allegations contained in each must be proved at trial by clear and convincing evidence that establishes each element of the crime beyond a reasonable doubt.

You will recall from our discourse on the Bill of Rights that one of the rights guaranteed all persons by the U.S. Constitution (Fifth Amendment) is to have all charges of serious crimes emanate from a grand jury. In the federal system, that has been interpreted to mean that all felony charges require grand jury approval. The approval comes in the form of an indictment.

THE GRAND JURY

The **grand jury**, a body of citizens that may investigate crimes and return formal charges in the form of an indictment, should not be confused with the jury that sits in judgment during a trial. A trial jury is usually referred to as a **petit jury**. The functions of these two types of juries are vastly different. You cannot know how a prosecutor's office works unless you know something about the functions of a grand jury.

The grand jury, as it is employed in the federal system, serves two functions. Its first function is accusatory; that is, the grand jury is the originator of formal charges in all felony cases. The second function is investigatory. A grand jury has the authority to command appearances of witnesses and production of evidence.

The Grand Jury as Accuser

As originally conceived, the grand jury acted as a buffer between an overlord and the people. In the fourteenth century, the function of the English grand jury was separated from that of the petit jury. It became a special body of citizens, laymen and neighbors, who had to give its consent before the sovereign could hold a person to answer for criminal charges. The concept of a grand jury and of its responsibility for returning indictments moved to this country with the common law and has been embodied in the laws of this nation, as illustrated in Figures 3-1 and 3-2.

FIGURE 3-1   THE GRAND JURY, AS CODIFIED IN THE FEDERAL RULES OF CRIMINAL PROCEDURE

The court shall order one or more grand juries to be summoned at such time as the public interest requires. The grand jury shall consist of not less than 16 nor more than 23 members. The court shall direct that a sufficient number of legally qualified persons be summoned to meet this requirement.

FED. R. CRIM. P. 6(a)

FIGURE 3-2   AN INDICTMENT, AS CODIFIED IN THE FEDERAL RULES OF CRIMINAL PROCEDURE

> An indictment may be found only upon the concurrence of 12 or more jurors. The indictment shall be returned by the grand jury to a federal magistrate in open court . . .
>
> FED. R. CRIM. P. 6(f)

A defendant is entitled to know if there has been compliance with the rule, as stated in Figure 3-2, calling for the concurrence of twelve or more grand jurors. To that end, the record will contain a disclosure, usually in the form of an attestation of the grand jury foreperson, indicating how many jurors concurred in the indictment. (See Figure 3-3).

As we have indicated above, the function of the grand jury when it sits as an accusatory body is to determine if there is probable cause to hold a person answerable for criminal conduct. The indictment is not proof of guilt. The charges must still be proved beyond a reasonable doubt to a judge or petit jury.

Two things should be remembered about the actions of a grand jury when it sits as an accuser. First, the accused is not entitled as a matter of right to appear and offer a defense to the accusations of the grand jury. Second, even if the grand jury refuses to issue an indictment, the party may later be charged by the same jury or by a different one. In other words, though the grand jury can initiate criminal charges, *it has no authority to acquit the accused.*

Some scholars believe that the grand jury, as it is presently employed, has outlived its usefulness. The complaint most frequently heard is that grand jury approval of indictments is a perfunctory process because the prosecutor is virtually certain to obtain an indictment anytime one is requested. Such criticism and the increased costs of court operations have caused some states to abolish the grand jury system within their jurisdictions.

The Grand Jury as Investigator

The second use for the grand jury is as an investigative body. We have seen that the prosecutor usually enters the picture after the criminal investigation is completed or during the course of an ongoing investigation. However, sometimes the prosecutor's office initiates and conducts its own criminal investigations. In such instances, the second function of the grand jury comes into play.

The *United States Code* contains a provision for calling special grand juries to probe into criminal activity within a federal district whenever the attorney general feels that it is warranted (18 U.S.C. § 3331). A federal judge can extend the term of such a special grand jury for up to thirty-six months and can impanel additional special grand juries if necessary.

FIGURE 3-3   RECORD OF GRAND JURORS CONCURRING

Record of Grand Jurors
concurring

United States District Court
FOR THE

_____

_____

UNITED STATES OF AMERICA
_v._

Criminal No. _____

I, the duly appointed foreman of the grand jury of this court, begun and held at
_____ on the _____ day of _____ , 19 ___ , do hereby file with the clerk
of the court as required by Rule 6(c), Federal Rules of Criminal Procedure, a record of the number of
grand jurors concurring in the finding of indictment in the above case, which record shall not be made
public except upon order of the court:

_____ grand jurors concurring.

_____   _____
Date   _Foreman._

Previous editions of this form should be used until exhausted.

The use of a grand jury as an investigating tool is significant because the U.S. attorney has no inherent subpoena powers or authority to command the cooperation of a witness. It is only through an investigating grand jury that the district's chief prosecutor can compel testimony and the production of evidence. At the conclusion of such an investigation, the prosecutor can ask for an indictment or advise the grand jury to issue a report of its findings that can be used to obtain indictments at a later date.

ENTER THE DEFENDANT

In many jurisdictions, and certainly in federal jurisdictions, the well-known movie scene—chase, shoot-out, and arrest—rarely occurs. It is becoming more probable that the defendant will be summoned to appear in court to answer charges that have grown out of a protracted investigation. (See Figure 3-4.) It is true that incidents in which a suspect is arrested at the scene of a crime before any knowledge of an investigation reaches the prosecutor still occur. This type of arrest is more likely to occur with violent crimes of the type usually prosecuted in state court. The federal complaint form illustrated in Figure 3-5 and the federal warrant form depicted in Figure 3-6 are characteristic of the forms used in both federal and state jurisdictions.

FIGURE 3-4   THE PROCESS OF ISSUING A WARRANT OR A SUMMONS FOR THE DEFENDANT, AS DEFINED BY THE FEDERAL RULES OF CRIMINAL PROCEDURE

> If it appears from the complaint, or from an affidavit or affidavits filed with the complaint, that there is probable cause to believe that an offense has been committed and that the defendant has committed it, a warrant for the arrest of the defendant shall issue to an officer authorized by law to execute it. *Upon the request of the attorney for the government a summons instead of a warrant shall issue.* (Emphasis added)
>
> *Fed R. Crim. P. 5(a)*

Initial Appearance

Whether it occurs as the result of an on-the-scene arrest or a summons following a lengthy investigation, the time comes when the defendant must make an initial appearance before a court to be advised of the charges being brought against him or her and to begin the process leading to trial.

When the defendant is arrested or summoned to answer to a felony charge, the initial appearance is conducted in accordance with the procedures set forth in Rule 5(c) of the Federal Rules of Criminal Procedure. (See Figure 3-7.) The **initial appearance** is the first formal appearance of a defendant before a judge or a magistrate so that the defendant may be apprised of the reason or reasons for the charges or for his or her arrest or detention.

In the case of an arrest on a complaint of a misdemeanor charge, the defendant may be called upon to enter a plea to the charge at the initial appearance. Rule 5(b) of the Federal Rules of Criminal Procedure provides that a magistrate conducting an initial hearing on a misdemeanor triable before a magistrate shall proceed in accordance with misdemeanor trial procedures. Thus, with the written concurrence of the defendant, the magistrate may even conduct a trial in place of a district judge. Except for the fact that the trier is a magistrate and not a judge, the procedures are identical to other criminal trials.

FIGURE 3-5   CRIMINAL COMPLAINT

United States District Court

_____ DISTRICT OF _____

UNITED STATES OF AMERICA
V.

CRIMINAL COMPLAINT

CASE NUMBER:

(Name and Address of Defendant)

I, the undersigned complainant being duly sworn state the following is true and correct to the best of my

knowledge and belief. On or about _____ in _____ county, in the

_____ District of _____ defendant(s) did, (Track Statutory Language of Offense)

in violation of Title _____ United States Code, Section(s) _____.

I further state that I am a(n) _____ and that this complaint is based on the following
                                          Official Title

facts:

Continued on the attached sheet and made a part hereof: ☐ Yes   ☐ No

_____
Signature of Complainant

Sworn to before me and subscribed in my presence,

_____   at   _____
Date   City and State

_____   _____
Name & Title of Judicial Officer   Signature of Judicial Officer

FIGURE 3-6   WARRANT FOR ARREST

United States District Court

_____ DISTRICT OF _____

UNITED STATES OF AMERICA
V.

WARRANT FOR ARREST

CASE NUMBER: _____

To: The United States Marshal
and any Authorized United States Officer

YOU ARE HEREBY COMMANDED to arrest _____
                                                                         Name

and bring him or her forthwith to the nearest magistrate to answer a(n)

☐ Indictment   ☐ Information   ☐ Complaint   ☐ Order of court   ☐ Violation Notice   ☐ Probation Violation Petition

charging him or her with (brief description of offense)

in violation of Title _____ United States Code, Section(s)_____

_____   _____
Name of Issuing Officer   Title of Issuing Officer

_____   _____
Signature of Issuing Officer   Date and Location

_____
(By) Deputy Clerk

Bail fixed at $_____   by_____
                                                                         Name of Judicial Officer

RETURN		
This warrant was received and executed with the arrest of the above-named defendant at _____		
DATE RECEIVED	NAME AND TITLE OF ARRESTING OFFICER	SIGNATURE OF ARRESTING OFFICER
DATE OF ARREST		

FIGURE 3-7   PROCEDURES SURROUNDING THE DEFENDANT'S INITIAL APPEARANCE

> If the charge against the defendant is not triable by the United States magistrate, the defendant shall not be called upon to plead. The magistrate shall inform the defendant of the complaint against the defendant and of any affidavit filed therewith, of the defendant's right to retain counsel or to request the assignment of counsel if the defendant is unable to obtain counsel, and of the general circumstances under which the defendant may secure pretrial release. The magistrate shall inform the defendant that he is not required to make a statement and that any statement made by the defendant may be used against the defendant. The magistrate shall also inform the defendant of the right to a preliminary examination. The magistrate shall allow the defendant reasonable time and opportunity to consult counsel and shall detain or conditionally release the defendant as provided by statute or in these rules.
>
> *FED. R. CRIM. P. 5(c)*

The initial appearance of the defendant serves to accomplish many purposes. Reproduced in Figure 3-8 is a form used by the federal court in the Eastern District of Louisiana to detail the matters covered at the initial appearance of the defendant. The completed form comprises the minute entry of the magistrate who presided at the hearing.

 POINTER: A minute entry is an official notation in the records of the court, made by the presiding judge (or clerk), of the proceedings held during a session of court.

Preliminary Examination

Following the lodging of a complaint, a defendant is entitled to a preliminary examination. A **preliminary examination** is a hearing held before a judicial officer to determine if there is probable cause to believe that a crime has been committed and that the defendant committed it. Figure 3-9 explains the procedures surrounding a preliminary examination.

At the preliminary examination, if there is a finding of probable cause to believe that the defendant committed a crime, the process continues, and "the federal magistrate shall forthwith hold the defendant to answer in district court" [FED. R. CRIM. P. 5.1(a)].

If there is no probable cause to believe that the defendant committed a crime, the magistrate will dismiss the complaint and discharge the defendant. Such a dismissal and discharge does not bar future prosecution for the same offense. [FED. R. CRIM. P. 5.1(c)].

Prosecutors hate preliminary examinations and do everything they can to avoid them. They view the process as little more than an opportunity for the defendant to discover the government's evidence. Of course, they are

FIGURE 3-8   FORM DETAILING THE PROCEEDINGS AT THE DEFENDANT'S INITIAL APPEARANCE

```
MINUTE ENTRY
MAGISTRATE:
DATE:
--------------------
          UNITED STATES  DISTRICT COURT
          EASTERN DISTRICT OF LOUISIANA

UNITED STATES OF AMERICA                CRIMINAL

     VERSUS                             NO.

_____           SECTION " "
                                        MAGISTRATE " "

                  INITIAL APPEARANCE

APPEARANCES: __¦ DEFENDANT:_____

             __¦ DEFENSE COUNSEL: _____

                 (ADDRESS) _____

             __¦ A.U.S.A.:_____

             __¦ INTERPRETER: _____

             __¦ OTHER: _____

__¦ DEFENDANT ADVISED OF HIS/HER RIGHTS

__¦ INDICTMENT READ/WAIVED

__¦ DEFENDANT INFORMED COURT THAT HE/SHE WILL RETAIN COUNSEL

__¦ DEFENDANT REQUESTED COURT APPOINTED COUNSEL

__¦ DEFENDANT SWORN & QUESTIONED  RE: FINANCIAL STATUS

__¦ FEDERAL PUBLIC DEFENDER APPOINTED

__¦ DEFENDANT FOUND NOT TO BE INDIGENT

__¦ BAIL SET AT: _____

__¦ DEFENDANT REMANDED TO CUSTODY OF U.S. MARSHAL

__¦ DEFENDANT RELEASED ON BOND

__¦ DEFENDANT NOTIFED OF ARRAIGNMENT SET FOR _____

__¦ DEFENDANT NOTIFIED DETENTION HEARING SET _____

__/ DEFENDANT ORDERED TO REAPPEAR WITH COUNSEL_____
-----------------------
CLERK TO NOTIFY:  U.S. ATTORNEY
                  ATTORNEY FOR DEFENDANT
                  U.S. MARSHAL
                  DEFENDANT
                  U.S. PROBATION/PRETRIAL SERVICES
```

FIGURE 3-9 PROCEDURE FOR HOLDING A PRELIMINARY EXAMINATION, AS DEFINED BY THE FEDERAL RULES OF CRIMINAL PROCEDURE

. . . Such examination shall be held within a reasonable time but in any event not later than 10 days following the initial appearance if the defendant is in custody and no later than 20 days if the defendant is not in custody, *provided, however, that the preliminary hearing shall not be held if the defendant is indicted or if any information against the defendant is filed in district court before the date set for the preliminary examination.* (Emphasis added)

Fed. R. Crim. P. 5(c)

correct: a preliminary examination is a discovery procedure. It is designed to apprise the defendant of the basis for the charges against him or her. Fortunately for the prosecution and unfortunately for the defendant, the preliminary examination is circumvented if the defendant is formally charged by indictment or by bill of information, which is what usually happens.

Detention Hearing

At some point during one of the appearances or perhaps as a separate proceeding, defendants are entitled to a hearing to determine if they are eligible for bail. The authority of the judicial officer to release or detain the defendant at a bail hearing, commonly referred to as a detention hearing, is contained in Title 18 of the *United States Code* (18 U.S.C. § 3142). A **detention hearing** is a formal hearing to consider if there is probable cause to hold a person in custody. The court may order the defendant

1. *Released on personal recognizance.* The defendant signs a bond assuring future appearances and is released from custody. **Personal recognizance** is a form of bail whereby defendants are allowed to remain free pending trial merely by giving written assurance that they will appear when requested.
2. *Released upon certain conditions.* The conditions may include posting a secured bond for future appearances; regularly reporting to a pretrial services officer; undergoing medical, psychological, or psychiatric treatment; or returning to custody during nonworking hours. Other conditions deemed necessary by the judge may be stipulated.
3. *Temporarily detained.* The defendant may be temporarily detained to allow other agencies and authorities to exercise control over the defendant for such things as revocation of probation or deportation.
4. *Detained pending trial.* No bail may be granted to the defendant.

At the detention hearing, the prosecutor takes an active role. If the crime charged is one of violence, if the possible sentence is lengthy, or if the defendant poses a danger to witnesses or is apt to flee, the government attorney must request conditions of release that eliminate these problems or must ask that the defendant be detained without bail. At that point, the prosecutor must be prepared to present evidence or information concerning the character of the defendant, the nature of the crime charged, the weight of the evidence of guilt, and other factors relative to the dangers posed by the defendant, such as the defendant's propensity to flee [18 U.S.C. § 3142(f)–§ 3142(g)].

Arraignment

Arraignment is the formal court proceeding at which a defendant is officially informed of the criminal charges against him or her and is called on to enter a plea of guilty, not guilty, or *nolo contendere* to the pending charges (FED. R. CRIM. P. 10). Figure 3-10 describes the proceedings of an arraignment.

FIGURE 3-10   ARRAIGNMENT, AS DESCRIBED IN THE FEDERAL RULES OF CRIMINAL PROCEDURE

Arraignment shall be conducted in open court and consist of reading the indictment or information to the defendant or stating to the defendant the substance of the charge and calling on the defendant to plead thereto. The defendant shall be given a copy of the indictment or information before being called upon to plead.

FED. R. CRIM. P. 10

If the defendant pleads guilty, skip to the chapter on posttrial. If the defendant pleads not guilty, you will need to know a few more things before you get to the point of sentencing. Forget about the plea of *nolo contendere*. *Nolo contendere* is a plea amounting to no contest. It is seldom attempted by the defendant in a criminal prosecution and is even less frequently accepted by the court. It is tantamount to a plea of guilty.

PROBABLE CAUSE AND THE QUALITY OF EVIDENCE

In this chapter, the term *probable cause* has been mentioned on several occasions. Rule 4 of the Federal Rules of Criminal Procedure provides that an arrest warrant or a summons may be issued upon a showing of probable cause. We have said that a grand jury indictment is based solely on probable cause that a crime has been committed. We have also mentioned probable cause in connection with the findings that can be made at a preliminary examination. But what is probable cause?

In *Brinegar v. United States*, 338 U.S. 160 (1949), the court had an opportunity to define the term. The best it could do was to explain that probable cause is more than suspicion but less than proof sufficient to convict. For our purposes, it may be best to think of the meaning in terms of probabilities. Thus, probable cause means that the finding is more likely to be true than

not true. So, when a warrant is issued for a search, it is based on the likelihood that evidence will be discovered. And, when an indictment is returned
by a grand jury, it is based on the likelihood that the defendant committed
the crime charged. In both instances, more than mere suspicion must exist.
The suspicion must have a perceptible factual basis.

Related to the question of probable cause is the issue of the *quality* of
proof that must be presented at the preliminary procedural stages discussed
in this section.

Rule 4 of the Federal Rules of Criminal Procedure declares that a finding of probable cause for the issuance of an arrest warrant or summons may
be based on hearsay evidence. At a preliminary examination, Rule 5.1 provides that a finding of probable cause may be based in whole or in part on
hearsay evidence and that objections to unlawfully acquired evidence may
not be made. The statute providing for detention hearings, 18 U.S.C. § 3142,
also provides that "[t]he rules concerning admissibility of evidence in criminal trials do not apply to the hearing."

What the above-cited rules mean is that the quality of evidence required to hold a defendant answerable for a crime is significantly less than
the quality of evidence required to convict. Thus, a person can be arrested,
charged, held without bail, and forced to trial on charges substantiated by
illegally obtained or hearsay evidence. The rules do not mean that at the
time of trial a defendant will be found guilty on such flimsy proof.

THE ROAD TO TRIAL

After the defendant is arraigned, the prosecutor must begin putting the case
in a posture to take it to trial. Actually, there may be other court proceedings
or hearings that intervene between the arraignment and trial, but the general rule is that the time constraints within which the case must be tried
begin to apply from the date of arraignment.

What follows is not intended to be an in-depth analysis of each chore
faced by a prosecutor leading up to a trial. It is designed to give you an
overview of the preparation that goes into getting a case ready for presentation. Many of the tasks can be accomplished by a paralegal working in the
office of the prosecutor.

While we are covering the material in this chapter dealing with the
prosecutor's duties, what we have to say about the road to trial applies with
equal force to the defense team. It will not be repeated in the next chapter
when we look at the job of the defense attorney and at the paralegal who
works for the defense. You should realize that there is but one trial, and the
same type preparation is made simultaneously by each side.

Speedy Trial

The right to a **speedy trial** (Bill of Rights—Sixth Amendment—remember?)
is vigorously safeguarded in the Federal Rules of Criminal Procedure and in
the statutory law of the *United States Code.* Strict criteria are in place limiting

the time delays between the lodging of a criminal charge and the trial. These time limits are more specifically discussed in Figures 3-11 and 3-12.

FIGURE 3-11   RIGHT TO A SPEEDY TRIAL, AS STIPULATED BY STATUTE

(c)(1) In any case in which a plea of not guilty is entered, the trial of a defendant charged in an information or indictment shall commence within seventy days from the filing date (and making public) of the information or indictment, or from the date the defendant has appeared before a judicial officer of the court in which such charge is pending, whichever date last occurs.

(2) Unless the defendant consents in writing to the contrary, the trial shall not commence less than thirty days from the date on which the defendant first appears.

18 U.S.C. § 3161

In addition to the time limits set out in Figure 3-11 each federal district is obligated to set up a system for the swift disposition of criminal charges. (See Figure 3-12.)

FIGURE 3-12   RIGHT TO THE PROMPT DISPOSITION OF CRIMINAL CASES, AS DEFINED BY THE FEDERAL RULES OF CRIMINAL PROCEDURE

To minimize undue delay and to further the prompt disposition of criminal cases, each district court shall conduct a continuing study of the administration of criminal justice in the district court and before the United States magistrates of the district and shall prepare plans for the prompt disposition of criminal cases in accordance with the provisions of Chapter 208 of Title 18, United States Code.

FED. R. CRIM. P. 50

As mentioned above, procedures and court appearances can take place and often do take place between the arraignment and the trial. Some of these occurrences may result in the delay of the trial beyond the seventy-day limit. However, the important thing to note, at this point, is that definite rules within the federal system (and in many states) mandate a speedy trial in all criminal cases.

Marshaling the Evidence

We have already spoken of the elements of the specific offense. Each crime has its elements. Each element requires categorical proof, evidence that will establish the existence of the fact beyond a reasonable doubt. Someone in the office of the prosecutor must analyze the indictment and collect evidence for each of the essential elements of the crime charged in the indictment or bill of information. The evidence can be in the form of documents, charts, photographs, tape recordings, testimony, or practically any other imaginable form. Someone has to locate, categorize, and prepare each exhibit.

Interviewing the Witnesses

Earlier in this chapter we noted that the quality of evidence allowed during an investigation and the preliminary proceedings is less than that which is required of trial evidence. Therefore, it may be that the indictment was obtained or that the bill of information was based on mere reports of witness statements and observations. Such reports are generally regarded as hearsay evidence. At trial, hearsay is usually not admissible. Someone has to contact and interview witnesses and perfect the testimony that will be introduced at trial.

Pretrial Motions

In later chapters we will look at the preparation of a defense. One of the topics we will cover in Chapter 5 concerns pretrial motions. Such motions can be used to seek all manner of relief. Most defense motions require a response from the prosecutor. The job of answering motions can be time-consuming and tedious. It is also very important.

In addition to defense motions, the prosecutor may wish to file some motions on behalf of the government, such as a motion to have a defendant examined for mental competence or a motion to resolve an apparent conflict of interest, when a defense attorney represents two or more defendants in the same case, for example. The person who responds to defense motions or who prepares the government's motions must be adept at research and writing. That person must work well under time limitations and be very familiar with the facts of the case.

Whether the preliminary motions are filed by the defense or by the prosecutor, they usually require a hearing before a judicial officer. Delay occasioned by the court taking such matters under advisement is one of the factors that can expand the time period between arraignment and trial.

Preparing to Select a Jury

The prosecutor and the defense counsel must submit to the court, prior to trial, a proposed set of *voir dire* questions that can be posed to the prospective jurors. ***Voir dire*** is the process of qualifying a person to serve on a petit jury. Submission of such questions is not mandatory in most jurisdictions, but it is generally done whenever the peculiarities in a case warrant special inquiry.

Opening Statement and Summation to the Jury

The prosecutor must make an opening statement to the jury outlining the proof that will be introduced during the trial. It was not too long ago that such statements were regarded as perfunctory. Today most prosecutors realize that the opening statement is very significant to the jury's understanding of the government's theory of the case. A great deal of effort is usually expended to assure that the opening statement is clear and as forceful as the court will allow.

At the close of the case, the government's attorney must summarize the evidence that was presented and show how that evidence proves each element of the crime. Most prosecutors have a summation prepared in advance of trial.

In the next chapter, we will look at the job of the defense counsel and at the paralegals who work for the defendant.

PARALEGAL'S ROLE AS AN AIDE TO THE PROSECUTOR

Although the task of preparing a case for prosecution is formidable, it is made easier by dividing the work among members of the prosecution team. Many of the jobs that have to be done on a case are assigned to the paralegals who are part of the government's team.

There is no way to give an overall job description for paralegals that will cover all their assignments in all prosecution offices. However, we can get a good idea of most of their duties by reviewing the jobs they perform in a typical job situation.

The job description presented in Figure 3-13 is taken from the position description on file with the U.S. Department of Justice, Executive Office for U.S. Attorneys. It pertains to the position of Paralegal Specialist GS-950-11 in the office of the U.S. attorney for the Eastern District of Louisiana. It presents a good model for reviewing typical job assignments of a paralegal in a typical prosecution office.

FIGURE 13-13   SAMPLE JOB DESCRIPTION FOR A PARALEGAL ON THE PROSECUTION TEAM

Paralegal Specialist GS-950-11

I. Introduction

This position is that of Paralegal Specialist in the Criminal Division of the United States Attorney's Office for the Eastern District of Louisiana. The incumbent is responsible for performing legal research, gathering and compiling statistical data and other factual information for use in the investigation and prosecution of criminal violations of Federal statutes. Incumbent is assigned to a group of Assistant U.S. Attorneys or an individual assistant depending upon the complexity of cases and the need for paralegal assistance. Specialist is key member of joint prosecutor/investigator team assigned to accomplish the Division's objectives.

II. Duties

1. Incumbent, on own initiative and responsibility and without specific supervision, originates and supervises the preparation and completion of legal, statistical, economic and other factual studies and analyses required in connection with the investigation and prosecution of criminal cases.

2. Analyzes and prepares for presentation in Court, tables, compilations, summaries and charts with respect to statistical information submitted to the Government voluntarily or obtained through investigation. Participates in interviewing witnesses and informants or representatives of Federal and local Government Agencies during the investigatory process. Prepares material relating to individual witnesses and organized crime defendants preparatory to trial. Compiles lists of names

FIGURE 3-13   SAMPLE JOB DESCRIPTION FOR A PARALEGAL ON THE PROSECUTION TEAM *(continued)*

showing relationship of witnesses and defendants with each other with pertinent organizations, thereby saving trial attorneys considerable time. Arranges transportation and accommodations for witnesses, as well as vouchers for expenses. Attends discussions and review of facts with witnesses to serve as witness to statements made during the interview. Also attends pre-trial hearings and conferences, taking notes and assisting in gathering necessary facts, e.g., for bills of particulars.

3. Analyzes records of numerous types obtained by the incumbent and the attorney-in-charge or furnished by other Federal or local Governmental Agencies. Assists in arranging and indexing such records. Reports results of analyses to attorney-in-charge indicating the apparent existence or non-existence of evidence or violations of Federal statutes or recommends additional data to be obtained and the specific type required. Shows initiative and imagination to help direct investigative efforts.

4. The incumbent must also assist in fulfilling discovery obligations pursuant to Rule 16 Fed. R. Crim. Pro. and 18 U.S.C. § 3500 et. seq. The incumbent prepares documents for production to defense counsel and maintains a filing system to keep track of those discovery obligations that have been met. The incumbent also drafts subpoenas duces tecum and ad testificandum. Exercises initiative, discretion and independence, contacting officials of Federal, State and Municipal Agencies to obtain information. Attends meetings and conferences with representatives of Governmental Agencies, private individuals, etc., on behalf of the United States Attorney, Eastern District of Louisiana. Researches statutes for applicability of Federal jurisdiction, extracts and summarizes pertinent references for use by the Attorney-in-charge. Prepares statistical tables and narrative analyses and reports on studies undertaken, presenting observations and conclusions.

5. Incumbent is custodian of and responsible for a variety of confidential records concerned with the particular cases to which assigned. Receives and analyzes documentary material. Prepares system of classification and classifies documents and evidentiary material according to plans of the Attorney-in-charge. Examines documents containing statistical studies and checks their accuracy in the light of information obtained from other sources. Arranges documents and excerpts there from under direction of the trial attorney for presentation in court and for printing in the record of the case. Assists in the development of computer programs for the automatic compilation and processing of data. Codifies documents, determines material essential to the study and coordinates with data processing representatives in the input of data to assure the accuracy and completeness of the end product. Reviews machine printouts and analyzes data to determine the value in the case and whether the data support the Government's position.

6. Has full responsibility for safeguarding classified material as well as material protected by Court orders against improper disclosure. Organizes documentary material for identification and marking as exhibits at trial. As required, may assist the attorney during trial with documents and witnesses, maintaining proper identification and organization and scheduling of witnesses for testimony. Takes notes on specific aspects of witnesses' testimony for later review and discussion with the Assistant U.S. Attorney.

7. May be called upon to testify at trial as to the data compiled, analyses performed, methods, and validity of conclusions.

8. Performs other duties as assigned, normally of a related nature.

4 THE DEFENDERS

WHO ARE DEFENSE COUNSEL?

Engraved on courthouses throughout the nation is a thought popularized by John Adams. It proclaims that ours is a "government of laws, not of men." High-sounding words, but do they have any relevance to our study of criminal law?

The answer, of course, is yes; they have monumental significance. The idea contained in that phrase is the cornerstone of our criminal justice system. Our method of administering justice is founded on the principle that the law is supreme, not the men who enforce the law, not those who would hide behind it nor those who would warp it to their advantage, and certainly not those who would disregard it and violate it. The law is the thing that must be preserved. It was his recognition of the law's priority that moved Samuel Johnson to observe, "The law is the last result of human wisdom acting upon human experience for the benefit of the public."[1]

It is easy to become poetic and wave the flag when one is serving as prosecutor, backed by all the majesty and authority of the government. In a criminal case, the government's attorney, representative of the forces of justice, defender of the law abiding, enters the scene wrapped in the mantle of lawfulness. But the prosecuting attorney has no greater claim to such titles than does the attorney for the defendant.

Not one criminal defense attorney has not been asked: "How can you defend such a person?" If you are ever employed in an office where attorneys engage in defending criminal defendants, you will almost certainly be asked the same question.

Many lawyers brush off the question. Many respond jokingly, "I only represent the innocent." Some answer cynically, "I do it for the money," but there is a real and valid answer to the question. It is most unfortunate, however, that many people, even lawyers, do not know it. The answer involves our adversarial system. Our criminal justice system was designed to work effectively only when each side acts as a guard against the other's zeal. When both attorneys do their jobs, they are making the system work. The adversarial system makes it less likely that an innocent person will lose life or liberty because of an unbalanced trial.

Many people, including attorneys and judges, have the mistaken notion that all persons charged with a crime are reprobates, shady, corrupt scoundrels. There may be some justification for such a belief, but it is not always accurate.

Everyone makes mistakes, even law enforcers. Many an innocent person has been arrested. Consider the civil rights demonstrators of only a few years ago. Our system of justice prevented grave miscarriages of justice in their cases.

We do a serious injustice when we characterize all defense attorneys as wheeler/dealers who help the guilty "beat the rap." We are all potential defendants, even those of us who are guilty of no crime. And since we are all vulnerable, we must have a system that guarantees the opportunity to avert injustice in those cases when a person is wrongly charged with a crime.

We have already seen that the Sixth Amendment guarantees the right to counsel in all federal criminal trials. All persons are entitled to representation by an attorney. It would be unrealistic to offer legal services only to those who are innocent. If that were the case, everyone who walks into a courtroom without an attorney would be confessing guilt.

Within our criminal justice system, laws and rules govern the collection of evidence, the admissibility of evidence, procedures for arrests, and the conduct of police, attorneys, judges, and jurors. As we noted when we considered the Bill of Rights, some of those guarantees have their basis in the Constitution. Others are statutory, and some have evolved from case law. Together they form an effective plan for the dispensation of justice.

The defense attorneys who represent an accused take it upon themselves to see to it that the rules are followed. No matter how ghastly or outrageous the alleged offense, the rules are the same. Those rules are not suspended for serial murderers or dope pushers or child molesters. Even against such defendants, the prosecutor has no right to use illegally obtained evidence nor an involuntarily extracted confession, and jurors are not allowed to consider unreliable evidence.

An attorney who guards against violation of the rules of evidence and procedure is not promoting rape, or murder, or any other crime. A lawyer who defends against abuse of the system is working to assure due process of law. The defense of an accused is no less than the defense of the rules of justice.

RIGHT TO COUNSEL

"Read 'em their rights!" It seems impossible to sit through a movie or tune in a television program without hearing those words. Furthermore, it is very likely that most of you can recite the rights to which the phrase refers:

You have a right to remain silent.

Anything you say can and will be used against you.

You have a right to an attorney.

If you cannot afford an attorney, one will be appointed to represent you at no cost to you.

In 1966 the Supreme Court decided the case entitled *Miranda v. Arizona*, 384 U.S. 436 (1966). The idea of reading a statement of rights to an arrestee grows out of that decision. Specifically, the *Miranda* case deals with the right of a suspect to confer with counsel before making a statement to criminal investigators. We cite the case here to emphasize the point that all persons suspected of criminal wrongdoing are entitled to an attorney even if the government has to supply the attorney because of the arrestee's indigence.

The right to appointed counsel has evolved steadily through this century. In *Powell v. Alabama*, 287 U.S. 45 (1932), the Supreme Court established that due process of law requires that a defendant who is illiterate and slow witted and who is charged with a capital offense should be assisted by counsel even if one has to be appointed. By 1938 the Court was ready to recognize that the Sixth Amendment required the appointment of counsel for all indigent defendants in federal felony cases. See *Johnson v. Zerbst*, 304 U.S. 458 (1938).

Twenty-four years after *Zerbst*, in a decision that can truly be called a landmark, the Court held that fundamental fairness required the states to provide attorneys for all indigent defendants in felony cases. See *Gideon v. Wainwright*, 372 U.S. 335 (1963).

We have noted that the right to appointed counsel now extends to defendants from the time of their arrest (*Miranda, supra*). See, also, *Escobedo v. Illinois*, 378 U.S. 478 (1964). There are other specific times during the pretrial process when an indigent suspect is entitled to free assistance of an attorney: for example, at a lineup, *United States v. Wade*, 388 U.S. 218 (1967); at a probable cause hearing, *Gerstein v. United States*, 420 U.S. 103 (1975); at a preliminary hearing, *Coleman v. Alabama*, 399 U.S. 1 (1970); in juvenile proceedings, *In re Gault*, 387 U.S. 1 (1967).

Interestingly, however, the court refused to extend the right to appointed counsel to an indigent "target" witness at a grand jury proceeding. In *United States v. Mandujano*, 425 U.S. 564 (1976), the court did not reach a majority opinion; four justices wrote that the Constitution does not require such an appointment. Apparently, the justices were impressed by the fact that Mandujano had been advised that he would be allowed to leave the grand jury room to confer with an attorney if he had been able to afford one.

Public Defenders

Today laws within the *United States Code* require the establishment of a plan within each federal district for providing legal representation to impoverished criminal defendants. (See Figure 4-1.)

FIGURE 4-1   LEGAL REPRESENTATION TO IMPOVERISHED CRIMINAL DEFENDANTS, AS ESTABLISHED BY THE *UNITED STATES CODE*

Each United States district court, with the approval of the judicial council of the circuit, shall place in operation throughout the district a plan for furnishing representation for any person unable to obtain adequate representation in accordance with this section. Representation under each plan shall include counsel and investigative, expert and other services necessary for adequate representation. Each plan shall provide the following:

(1) Representation shall be provided for any financially eligible person who—

(A) is charged with a felony or Class A misdemeanor;

(B) is a juvenile alleged to have committed an act of juvenile delinquency as defined in section 5031 of this title;

(C) is charged with a violation of probation;

(D) is under arrest when such representation is required by law;

(E) is charged with a violation of supervised release or faces modification, reduction, or enlargement of a condition or extension or revocation of a term of supervised release;

(F) is subject to a mental condition gearing under chapter 313 of this title;

(G) is in custody as a material witness;

(H) is entitled to appointment of counsel under the sixth amendment to the Constitution;

(I) faces loss of liberty in a case, and Federal law requires the appointment of counsel; or

(J) is entitled to the appointment of counsel under section 4109 of this title.

18 U.S.C. § 3006A

The federal defender programs are among the best funded and staffed in the nation. In addition to attorneys employed full time by the office of the public defender, each program utilizes the services of the local bar to supplement the number of professionals available to assist the indigent. Private attorneys employed by the public defender are reimbursed for expenses and are paid (modestly) for their time.

All state jurisdictions offer some form of public defender services for indigents charged with state offenses. In larger urban areas, public defender offices resemble their federal counterparts in range and scope of services. The principal difference between the two is funding. The federal system is generally much better financially supported.

In less populated areas, defense of indigents is frequently provided by direct appointment of attorneys by the court. In many instances, the appointed attorneys perform their services *pro bono* (for free).

If there is a drawback to the indigent defender programs offered by federal and state governments other than the low level of funding found in many jurisdictions, it is that the appointed attorney usually does not enter the case until after the arrest or the lodging of formal charges.

We noted in an earlier chapter that the prosecutor can and frequently does enter the case long before the filing of formal charges against an accused. In the case of the public defense attorney, it is unusual to become involved at such an early stage, even in instances in which the prospective defendant or suspect is alerted to an investigation before it reaches the point of formal charges or arrest. We have seen that the appointment of an indigent defender almost invariably comes after a suspect has been arrested or formally charged.

In the previous chapter, we learned that arrested defendants in federal criminal cases are entitled to be brought before a judicial officer for an initial appearance. The appearance mandated by the Federal Rules of Criminal Procedure requires prompt action by the arresting officer. (See Figure 4-2.)

FIGURE 4-2   AN INITIAL APPEARANCE MUST BE PROMPTLY HELD, AS MANDATED BY THE FEDERAL RULES OF CRIMINAL PROCEDURE

> An officer making an arrest under a warrant issued upon a complaint or any person making an arrest without a warrant shall take the arrested person *without unnecessary delay* before the nearest available federal magistrate or, in the event that a federal magistrate is not reasonably available, before a state or local judicial officer authorized by 18 U.S.C. Section 3041. (Emphasis added)
>
> *Fed. R. Crim. P. 5(a)*

It is common practice for an arrested person to be afforded an initial appearance within hours of his or her arrest. At that appearance, the rules call for assignment of counsel in the case of an indigent defendant. In the case of a defendant who is able to afford a private attorney, if he or she has not obtained counsel prior to the initial appearance, the law requires that the judicial officer advise that person of the right to retain counsel. (See Figure 3-9).

Retained Defense Counsel

There is no limitation on the right of a person to be represented by private counsel at any stage of a criminal proceeding or investigation. Because the principle is so clear, it has seldom been raised in the courts. That fact makes it virtually impossible to find any case law addressing the issue. On one occasion, the Supreme Court referred to the right as "unqualified." See *Chandler v. Fretag*, 348 U.S. 3 (1954). We may safely interpret the case to mean that there are no restrictions on a person's right to counsel (if he or she can afford to hire one) as guaranteed by the Sixth Amendment.

Persons who are financially able to hire a private attorney enjoy a distinct advantage over those who must wait to obtain appointed counsel. The suspect who can afford legal counsel at the early stages of an investigation may even be able to avert criminal charges because of the assistance of his or her attorney.

Although many persons are vaguely aware of the rights and safeguards available to a suspect, they are frequently unable to apply them to situations in which they are personally involved without an attorney present to offer advice. Just as the prosecutor advises investigators and agents in the preliminary stages of a case, so, too, can a defense attorney be of service to a client prior to arrest or lodging of formal charges. It is not difficult to conceive of situations in which a prospective defendant would benefit from legal advice in matters involving search and seizure, voluntarily turning over evidence, or making statements or confessions to investigators.

There is no usual point of entry where the privately retained defense counsel comes upon the scene. We have already noted that the earlier an attorney becomes involved, the more benefit a client will derive from the representation. However, it is impossible to generalize regarding when defendants or prospective defendants usually obtain counsel.

If you are curious about the business side of private law practice, you may well wonder how defendants seeking counsel are able to locate attorneys who are specialists in criminal law. This question is not as crucial as it once might have been. The advent of advertising for attorneys has reduced the significance of the problem for both client and counsel. However, most persons who are seeking the services of an attorney to represent them in matters involving criminal exposure do not rely on commercial advertising to help them locate representation. Criminal defense specialists derive much of their clientele from referrals. Former clients and other attorneys who do not engage in criminal defense work are usually the best sources for new clients. Also, criminal proceedings and trials usually generate significant news coverage. The reputation of an attorney as a defense specialist spreads quickly through media exposure.

DEFENSE COUNSEL'S TASKS BEFORE FORMAL CHARGES

Whether he or she is appointed or retained, the defense counsel faces a formidable task in representing someone who has been charged with violation of a criminal statute. Let's take a look at the job facing the defense team as it undertakes the representation of a defendant in a criminal case.

The Initial Interview

The time comes when a defendant or prospective defendant meets his or her attorney for the first time to discuss the situation that has brought them together. Under ordinary circumstances, the parties meet privately, at least for their first conference. This initial interview is an occasion for building confidence and trust. As a paralegal, it is doubtful that you will participate in many initial meetings between defense attorney and client. There is no strict prohibition against your presence; however, the normal situation would be for the principals to meet alone.

No scripted procedure must be followed during the initial stages of representation; however, certain areas of discussion are common to all such meetings. The attorney and the client must cover certain topics that are prevalent in all situations.

The lawyer is naturally interested in the factual situation that has resulted in the client's predicament. Also, the attorney is concerned about the identity of others who might be involved as participants or witnesses. Identification of other parties is important because the lawyer must avoid conflicts of interest. In the case of privately retained counsel, there is always the subject of the fee. The client's ability to afford the services being sought are of paramount importance to both parties.

Clients are entitled to the strictest confidentiality regarding their disclosures on all topics covered during an initial interview. Assuming that all goes well during the initial conference and that a representation agreement is struck, the parties will embark on a relationship that is one of the closest in the legal profession. Confidence and trust are the hallmarks of the association.

The private practitioner has a decided advantage over the public defender because the retained attorney has the luxury of time, the time to build the rapport and the accord that make the relationship effective. An attorney from a public defender program rarely has as much time to devote to individual clients as does private counsel.

Privileged Communications

It seems proper to note that the presence of the paralegal at an initial interview is not a fact that will destroy the confidentiality of the disclosures made by the client. All communications between a client and his or her attorney is privileged. The privilege belongs to the client; only the client can waive or abandon that right. This privilege attaches to communications made to the attorney and to the paralegal working in conjunction with the attorney. As a paralegal working in criminal defense, you are not allowed to divulge any information given to you by the client without the client's permission.

Alternatives to Prosecution

If an attorney becomes involved in a case early enough, before the client is formally charged with a criminal offense, the possibility exists of pursuing alternatives to prosecution. Naturally, cases occur in which no alternatives to formal charges can be pursued; however, in some instances, an attorney can avert an indictment or a bill of information by disclosing exculpatory circumstances to the prosecutor.

Obtaining a Refusal of Charges. The first possibility that must be considered concerns the substantive innocence of the client. If evidence or information is available that demonstrates that the client committed no offense, it is often beneficial to advise investigators of that evidence.

In most instances, prosecutors and investigators are very receptive to the idea of examining evidence that establishes the innocence of a suspect. It is a rare occurrence to find avenues of communication closed to defense counsel before formal charges are filed, especially if the attorney representing the suspect makes it known that evidence is available to show that the client is not guilty.

Of course, it is possible that the prosecutor will exercise a *nolle prosequi*, dismissing a case even after indictment or the filing of a bill of information should it become apparent that the defendant is not guilty. However, it is much more difficult to obtain a prosecutor's *nolle prosequi* than it is to obtain a refusal of charges. That fact alone demonstrates the importance of early involvement of defense counsel.

Obtaining a Grant of Immunity. Instances in which the prosecutor is in need of the assistance of witnesses often allow the attorney who represents a prospective defendant who may have some knowledge of the case being investigated and also some exposure to prosecution to trade upon this knowledge in order to secure a grant of immunity. A **grant of immunity** eliminates a person's Fifth Amendment right to remain silent in return for a binding commitment from authorities not to prosecute.

The federal law allows a prosecutor to grant a witness immunity from prosecution in exchange for his or her testimony before a court or grand jury. Laws in most states closely resemble this federal statute, an excerpt of which is shown in Figure 4-3.

FIGURE 4-3 GRANT OF IMMUNITY, AS DEFINED BY THE *UNITED STATES CODE*

(b) A United States Attorney may, with the approval of the Attorney General, the Deputy Attorney General, the Associate Attorney General, or any designated Assistant Attorney General or Deputy Attorney General, request an order [of immunity] under subsection (a) of this section when in his judgment—

(1) the testimony or other information from the individual may be necessary to the public interest; and

(2) such individual has refused or is likely to refuse to testify or provide other information on the basis of his privilege against self-incrimination.

18 U.S.C. § 6003

Obtaining Deferred Prosecution. Another possible alternative to prosecution is available to the potential defendant. In the case of persons suspected of nonviolent crimes, the prosecutor can agree to a form of precharge probation. Various names are employed for the process of obtaining deferred prosecution, but deferred prosecution, diversion, and pretrial intervention are the most common. Formally defined, **deferred prosecution** is an alternative to prosecution in which the defendant accepts a period of voluntary probation, which, if successfully completed, results in the dropping of criminal charges. **Diversion**, which has the same meaning as **pretrial intervention**, is a procedure by which a defendant is moved out of the criminal justice system into an alternative program designed to correct any behavior problems exhibited by the defendant.

No matter the name, the idea is the same in each case. The central feature of the program is that the defendant or suspect *agrees* to a term of probation prior to the lodging of formal charges, with supervision more or less stringent, depending on the jurisdiction and the nature of the offense. Upon successful completion of the probation, the charges are refused, and the person has no record of criminal conviction growing out of the offense.

It is essential that the suspect pursue this avenue early in the investigative process. A defense attorney who has a good working knowledge of the system can be of great service to a client who qualifies for deferred prosecution. We will have more to say about this subject and related topics in a later chapter concerning plea bargaining.

Representation before a Grand Jury

We have already seen that a person called before a grand jury is entitled to confer with his or her attorney outside of the presence of the grand jury during the course of the examination. We have also noted that the courts have refused to require the appointment of counsel for someone called as a grand jury witness even if the witness is indigent.

Prior to an appearance before a grand jury, the witness (client) can be counseled by his or her attorney on all aspects of the potential testimony. One area of concern involves the privilege against self-incrimination. We know that the Fifth Amendment protects all persons from having to give testimony that is self-incriminating or that even tends to be incriminating.

The decision to testify is one that should be made only after careful consideration of all factors. It is easy to understand how the advice of an experienced attorney can be of great benefit to one forced to make such a decision.

Representation at Lineups and Other Investigatory Procedures

In the previous chapter we noted that the prosecutor often advises investigating agents and police on the conduct of lineups and other preliminary investigative procedures. The suspect is entitled to the same type of advice and counsel. A lineup or a photo spread can be suggestive and unfairly conducted. On many occasions, the mere presence of defense counsel will cause the procedure to be conducted properly.

In instances when the agency conducting the preliminary procedure refuses to correct inequities, the defense attorney who observes the situation is in an enhanced position to seek and obtain proper relief. We shall delve more deeply into the subject of available relief later.

Confessions and Statements

It should be very clear by now that no one can be forced or coerced into giving self-incriminating statements to law enforcement personnel. However, as noted earlier, even though a suspect is aware of his or her rights, it is frequently difficult to make practical application of that knowledge without advice of counsel.

Many people think that speaking to an officer or an agent about a case is somehow different from making a formal confession. Many times incriminating statements are made in an informal context, even after a *Miranda* warning. A decision regarding speaking with investigators can be the most important choice made by a suspect. Statements to investigating agencies should only be made after consultation with an attorney.

Preparing for the Worst

In all instances, clients who are represented by counsel prior to the filing of formal charges or an arrest have a much better chance of having their rights safeguarded than are unrepresented suspects.

The defense team must weigh alternatives while guiding a client through the prearrest stages of an investigation. The ultimate outcome of a case can be, and usually is, greatly affected by what happens before formal charges are lodged.

When an attorney and those persons who work with the attorney embark on a representation, they must be ever mindful of the consequences that could befall their client. A legal representative must always keep in mind that most cases result in formal indictment or the filing of a bill of information. All of the advice and counsel imparted to the client must allow for the possibility that the person will be called to answer for the alleged offense. Nothing done preliminarily must compromise the position that will have to be taken if it becomes necessary to try a case.

DEFENSE COUNSEL'S JOB AFTER ARREST OR FORMAL CHARGES

POINTER: The student will do well to bear in mind that the material presented here is in serial form; that is, one procedure follows the other in neat order. It is the only possible way to put the information in writing. However, it is important to avoid the impression that events follow each other neatly, one completely concluding before the other begins. That is often not true. Things happen very rapidly at the beginning of a criminal case. Although some order is present in the midst of the chaos, it sometimes seems as though everything is going on at once.

The Call for Help

We know from our discussion in the previous chapter that certain formal stages are common to all criminal proceedings in all jurisdictions: initial appearance, detention hearing, preliminary examination, arraignment. Let's see how these procedures are accomplished in a typical single-incident-type offense such as a burglary.

Despite all of the advantages we have noted regarding early involvement of defense counsel, it is very likely that a defendant will not have an attorney on board prior to arrest. A defense attorney will most frequently be contacted by a family member of the defendant (typically in the middle of the night) who is very upset about the arrest of his or her relative. The first thing that an attorney must do in such a situation, after attempting to calm the caller, is to determine the nature of the charge and the location of the arrestee.

Usually little can be done until the arrested person is brought before a judicial officer for an initial appearance. A defense attorney can occasionally prevail upon a compassionate judge or magistrate to set bail or to permit release on recognizance before the usual court hour. If the charge is very serious, a midnight phone call, even to an ordinarily compassionate judge, is likely to be fruitless (it is difficult to arouse compassion at 2:00 A.M.), and the arrestee will probably remain confined until the initial appearance.

The Initial Appearance

We know that the defendant must be brought before a judicial officer without unreasonable delay to be formally apprised of the reasons for detention. Since the initial appearance and the detention are often combined, the attorney representative must be in a position to make a presentation regarding the client's suitability for bail. The factors that the judge or magistrate will weigh when considering bail include the probability (or lack of probability) that the accused will flee if released and whether the accused poses a threat to anyone, including himself or herself, while on bail.

The defense attorney's job at the initial appearance is not as easily accomplished as it is recited. Prior to the initial hearing, counsel must explore the background of the client, the nature of the charges, and the availability of security for a bond in the event that the court decides to require security or surety. All of this must be done in a very short period of time, and it may require in-depth discussions with family members, employers, and sometimes bail bondsmen.

If the attorney is not immediately successful in gaining the release of the defendant, there is the possibility of a later hearing on a motion to reduce bail. At such a hearing, information that was unavailable at the original proceeding may be presented.

The Preliminary Examination

At the initial appearance, the defense attorney may request that a preliminary examination be scheduled if the client has not already been indicted or named in a bill of information. There are advantages and disadvantages to such a request.

As discussed in the previous chapter, the preliminary examination is a hearing to determine the existence of probable cause for detaining the accused. At this hearing, the prosecution must present evidence to establish the likelihood of guilt. The defendant and defense counsel need do little other than listen and learn. However, though the issue is very limited, defense counsel can ordinarily question witnesses called to testify at a preliminary examination.

The revelations made at a preliminary examination are usually beneficial to the defense because they help identify the nature and strength of the evidence against the client. Also on the positive side, from the defense viewpoint, the preliminary examination could result in the release of the defendant if probable cause on which to base a belief of guilt is lacking.

On the negative side, requesting a preliminary examination could lead to a precipitous indictment or to the hasty filing of a bill of information. We know that prosecutors will go to great lengths to avoid a preliminary examination because it forces them to reveal evidence and other information about the case. We also know that the lodging of formal accusations eliminates the need for a probable cause hearing.

In actual practice, a defense attorney may decide to delay a preliminary examination so as not to force an indictment, using the time instead to gather information and evidence that may help convince the prosecutor to refuse the case. Remember, at this point, the prosecutor is probably gathering information to be used in the screening process.

The Arraignment

If all efforts to avoid formal charges fail and the defendant is indicted or named in a bill of information, the next stage is the arraignment. We know that a defendant can make several responses to a formal accusation: the not guilty plea, the response of *nolo contendere*, and the plea of guilty.

Why Plead Guilty? As a rule, defense counsel will recommend to the client that a not guilty plea be entered no matter what the circumstance. The plea of not guilty does not preclude a later change of mind or strategy, and it preserves all rights of the accused through this initial pretrial stage.

We learned that the arraignment of a defendant is usually scheduled within days of the filing of formal charges. In the usual case, during the very short interval between the lodging of charges and the arraignment, there is scarcely time for a defendant and defense counsel to review all avenues of defense. This time limitation is the chief reason for pleading not guilty at an arraignment.

If a client insists on pleading guilty at an arraignment, the guilty plea can be withdrawn in some cases, but it is a difficult process and one that ordinarily depends on the acquiescence of the court. (See Figure 4-4.) In other words, even if one attempts to withdraw a guilty plea, it is not easy to do and the judge may not allow it.

FIGURE 4-4 CIRCUMSTANCES SURROUNDING THE WITHDRAWAL OF A GUILTY PLEA

If a motion for withdrawal of a plea of guilty or nolo contendere is made before sentence is imposed, the court *may* permit withdrawal of the plea upon a showing by the defendant of any fair and just reason. At a later time, a plea may be set aside only on direct appeal or by motion under 28 U.S.C. section 2255. (Emphasis added)

Fed. R. Crim. P. 32(d)

There are few advantages to pleading guilty at the arraignment. If the defendant decides to plead guilty, he or she usually does so at a proceeding called a re-arraignment. A **re-arraignment**, a pretrial procedural device usually employed to allow a defendant to change a plea of not guilty to guilty, is scheduled only after the defendant has decided to plead guilty. It is not a required process unless a change of plea is to be made.

Boykinization. Since we are considering the arraignment process, this may be a good time to introduce a concept that you will be expected to know if you decide to work in this area of the law.

In 1969 the Supreme Court decided the case of *Boykin v. Alabama*, 395 U.S. 283 (1969). In *Boykin* the court declared that a plea of guilty must be knowingly and intelligently made because, in doing so, a defendant waives constitutionally protected rights. When the defendant Boykin pled guilty, the record of the arraignment in the district court contained no evidence that he was ever addressed by the judge or questioned about the voluntariness of his plea. The Supreme Court held that the defendant's silence could not substitute for an affirmative waiver of his rights to trial and to confront witnesses. Boykin's guilty plea was ordered withdrawn.

Since that decision, judges thoroughly Boykinize each defendant in state and federal court before a plea of guilty is accepted. To **Boykinize** means to judicially interrogate a defendant who has indicated an intention to plead guilty in order to determine that the plea is knowing and voluntary. The defendant is questioned about all aspects of the guilty plea and is called upon to affirm that the plea is voluntary and that he or she has had the opportunity to discuss the case and possible defenses with an attorney. In some instances, the defendant is asked, ''Are you satisfied with the services of your attorney?''

Knowing that the defendant will be questioned in detail about the voluntariness of the plea and the services of counsel, most attorneys are very reluctant to recommend a guilty plea until the client has been thoroughly counseled about the consequences of the plea and about the availability of possible defenses. This is another reason why guilty pleas are seldom entered at the first arraignment.

Mental Incapacity

A defendant's mental problems may form the basis of a defense to the charges or they may merely delay the proceedings. Misunderstanding among the public and even among some attorneys regarding the effect of the defendant's mental incapacity in a criminal case is widespread.

As a Defense. The plea of not guilty generally includes the concept of not guilty by reason of insanity. Some states require a specific plea of not guilty based on insanity; however, in most state jurisdictions and in the federal courts, a plea of not guilty encompasses all defenses, including the insanity defense. The defendant who intends to raise the question of mental incapacity at the time of the commission of the offense must give notice of that intention prior to trial, as provided in the Federal Rules of Criminal Procedure. (See Figure 4-5.)

FIGURE 4-5   PRETRIAL NOTICE OF THE INTENTION TO PLEAD GUILTY BY REASON OF INSANITY IS REQUIRED BY FEDERAL RULES

If a defendant intends to rely upon the defense of insanity at the time of the alleged offense, the defendant shall, within the time provided for the filing of pretrial motions or at such later time as the court may direct, notify the attorney for the government in writing of such intention and file a copy of such notice with the clerk.

FED. R. CRIM. P. 12.2

As a result of the notice, the court may order a medical examination of the defendant to determine competency. If the issue is properly noticed and the defense is raised during the trial, the jury or the judge (in a nonjury trial) may find the defendant guilty, not guilty, or not guilty by reason of insanity. See 18 U.S.C. § 4243(b).

We will deal with the consequences of a verdict of not guilty by reason of insanity later. The point to be remembered at this juncture is that nothing special is required to be done at an arraignment in order to raise the defense of insanity. It may be necessary after arraignment to notify the prosecution and the court of the intention to raise the issue.

As an Inability to Understand Proceedings or to Assist Counsel. We learned in a previous chapter that the question of a person's incompetence to stand trial or to assist in the preparation of a defense because of mental infirmity is quite different from the defense of insanity at the time the offense is committed. The defense attorney may raise the issue of mental incapacity that prevents assistance at trial at any time that it becomes necessary. The court will then order an examination of the defendant. A separate hearing is scheduled after the examination wherein a determination of competence is made. After a competency hearing, if the defendant is found to be unable to assist counsel or to understand the proceedings because of mental disorder, the court will order the defendant hospitalized until the condition is corrected or until the charges are disposed of according to law. See 18 U.S.C. § 4241. The examination for mental incapacity to stand trial may be requested by the defense counsel, by the prosecution, or by the court itself if it becomes apparent that the defendant is disabled.

Incapacity to stand trial is a condition that suspends all proceedings for as long as the condition exists. Insanity at the time of commission of the offense is a defense that must be ruled upon by the trier of fact, jury or judge.

The job of the defense counsel at an actual arraignment proceeding is not demanding. The entire procedure is brief and requires little from the attorney or defendant when the plea is not guilty. The *pro forma* nature of the court appearance, however, does not disclose the effort that has gone into the process leading up to the appearance.

Assuming that the plea is not guilty and that the defendant is mentally capable of assisting in the presentation of a defense, the case moves forward to the trial preparation stage.

PARALEGAL'S ROLE AS AN AIDE TO THE DEFENSE

Generalizing about the assignments given to a paralegal on the defense team is as speculative as doing so for his or her counterpart with the prosecution. The possible assignments are numerous and the situational changes are endless. When we looked at the job assignments for a paralegal in the prosecutor's office, we tried to get an idea of the tasks performed by examining a job description. Now we will examine a job description for a paralegal in the federal defender system. The example in Figure 4-6 is for a Paralegal Specialist JSP 11 working in the office of the Federal Indigent Defender Program in the Eastern District of Louisiana.

FIGURE 4-6   SAMPLE JOB DESCRIPTION FOR A PARALEGAL ON THE DEFENSE TEAM

U.S. PARALEGAL SPECIALIST JSP 11

CHARACTERISTICS OF THE POSITION

1) Applies a knowledge of the principles, concepts, legal requirements, and methodology of assigned areas of responsibility in order to perform independent assignments for which there are precedents or established procedures.

—Knowledge and skill in interpreting, explaining, and applying a body of law, regulations, and procedures.

—Skill in applying conventional fact finding, analytical, and problem solving methods.

continued

FIGURE 4-6   SAMPLE JOB DESCRIPTION FOR A PARALEGAL ON THE DEFENSE TEAM *(continued)*

—Knowledge of the common policies, practices, and operations of applicable institutions

—Knowledge and skill to analyze facts, identify problems, report findings, make conclusions, and recommend appropriate action.

2) The supervisory attorney defines objectives, priorities, and deadlines; advises on potential problems that may be anticipated; and assists the Paralegal with unusual situations for which there are no clear precedents.

3) The Paralegal executes projects or tasks according to accepted policies and practices. The Paralegal may alter the sequence of steps and coverage of fact finding to accomplish the project or task more adequately within established guidelines.

4) Completed work is reviewed for technical accuracy, appropriateness, and conformity to policies and requirements. The review focuses on the soundness of results rather than the adequacy of methods employed.

5) Specific guidelines are available to accomplish most assignments. Guidelines define what to do as opposed to how to do it (as in clerical/assistant positions). When situations not covered by established guidelines arise, the Paralegal consults with the supervisor.

6) The paralegal applies a methodology to solve legal problems or arrive at a conclusion. Problems are characterized by:

1) many inter-related facts;
2) facts obtainable from several sources;
3) some disputed facts;
4) facts accessible when a variety of standard fact finding techniques are employed;
5) one or a few related simple issues;
6) analysis requiring a determination of the relevance and importance of facts.

7) The effect of the work is to provide assistance to attorneys by relieving them of one or more routine work assignments concerning one or more aspects of litigation, and/or to facilitate investigation, review, or research performed by attorneys. Assignments are generally limited in scope.

ENDNOTES

1   *Anecdotes of Samuel Johnson (1786)*, ed. S. C. Roberts (New York: Macmillan Co., 1925), as cited in *Bartlett's Famous Quotations*, 15th ed. (Boston: Little, Brown & Co., 1980), 353.

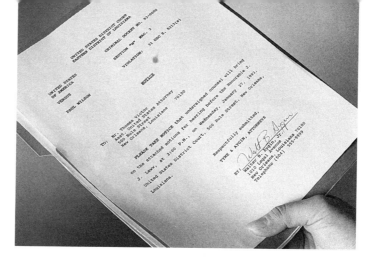

5 PRETRIAL MOTIONS

MOTION PRACTICE

We have seen that the guarantee of due process and the other safeguards built into the criminal justice system are directed toward striking a balance between individual freedoms and social order. The law does not allow enforcement practices that are so abusive as to destroy the fundamental fairness required by our Constitution. Likewise, an accused is required to submit to legitimate processes and cannot frustrate the government's permissible investigatory and accusatory activities.

What happens when the actions of the government extend beyond the limits allowed by law? How can prosecutors defend against conduct of the defendant designed to thwart the ends of justice? The answers to these questions are the focal points of this chapter. We will look at the remedies available to a party when the opposition attempts to gain illegal advantage, and we will consider the means available to secure those rights guaranteed by law.

When asked to enumerate the rights of an accused, most laypersons begin the list with the idea of a fair trial. All of us tend to think that way. The image in our minds is an attorney, cut from the cloth of Clarence Darrow, who jumps to his feet in the heat of battle and bellows an objection at any misrepresentation of justice. Obviously, the right to object at trial is one of the means used to prevent a miscarriage. But long before a trial begins, the defense and prosecution teams engage in the process of defending their side's rights and gathering the ammunition with which the battle will be fought. What happens at a trial is often anticlimactic—the results of a struggle that has raged for weeks.

Maybe the preceding imagery is a little dramatic. The idea of waging, raging, struggling, and battling may be somewhat overstated, but the impression is nonetheless accurate. What happens before a case makes its way to trial is often as significant as the trial itself. It is in the pretrial stage that many a case is won or lost. As a paralegal working on either side, much of your time will be spent preparing and responding to pretrial motions.

In Chapter 3 we noted that pretrial motions form an important part of the jobs of the prosecution and of the defense. To acquaint you with the dimensions of these tasks, we are going to take a look at the world of **motion practice**, as it is sometimes called, the manuevering of parties by the use of formal pleadings. Our treatment is not intended to be all inclusive. As you will come to understand, we cannot possibly cover all issues that may arise at the pretrial stage. Our objective is to be illustrative of this crucial aspect of the practice of criminal law.

As in previous chapters, for the sake of universality and to broaden the applicability of the lesson, our focus will be on the federal system. However, you should keep in mind that many state jurisdictions have requirements and rules closely resembling those covered here.

By concentrating on the system employed in federal courts, we do not mean to minimize the significance of procedures employed in state jurisdictions. You will be expected to know the requirements of your particular state regarding the filing of motions before trial.

If you know and understand the material covered in this chapter, you should have no trouble functioning effectively in any jurisdiction. Each court system has peculiarities. These variances are minor. The main points regarding pretrial matters are virtually identical in all jurisdictions.

ISSUES DECIDED BEFORE TRIAL

Many matters may be handled before trial; several can only be resolved at this stage. In the federal system, a single rule governs much of the pretrial activity in a criminal case. Similar regulations govern most state jurisdictions. Although they may not be grouped into one rule, state guidelines for pretrial resolution of issues closely parallel the federal standard.

Rule 12 of the Federal Rules of Criminal Procedure

In federal criminal practice, Rule 12 of the Federal Rules of Criminal Procedure encompasses the principal regulation of pretrial motion practice. It is divided into nine subsections, (a) through (i).

Subsection (a) substantially simplifies the terminology employed in federal courts. It abolishes all the archaic names for pleadings in criminal cases. Gone are demurrers, pleas in abatement, pleas in bar, and motions to quash. Though such terms were colorful and added something to the mystique of the practice of law, they were also confusing and frequently mixed up, even by the most seasoned attorneys. Issues and objections formerly raised through one or more of these pleadings are now brought before the court in a motion to dismiss or to gain other appropriate relief.

In other words, if some particular remedy is desired, the party seeking relief files a motion (not a demurrer, or a plea in abatement, or plea to quash). A **motion** is an application made to a court or to a judge to obtain a ruling. The title of the motion explains the relief sought; for example, *motion to dismiss the indictment* or *motion to dismiss count three of the indictment.*

The second subsection of the rule, Rule 12(b), defines two broad categories of issues that are properly considered prior to trial. (See Figure 5-1.) The first type *must* be brought by motion before trial. The other type *may* be disposed of by pretrial motion.

FIGURE 5-1   ISSUES PROPERLY CONSIDERED BEFORE TRIAL FALL INTO TWO BROAD CATEGORIES

Any defense, objection or request which is capable of determination without the trial of the general issue may be raised before trial by motion. Motions may be written or oral at the discretion of the judge. The following *must* be raised prior to trial:

(1) Defenses and objections based on defects in the institution of the prosecution; or

(2) Defenses and objections based on defects in the indictment or information (other than that it fails to show jurisdiction in the court or to charge an offense which objections shall be noticed by the court at any time during the pendency of the proceedings); or

(3) Motions to suppress evidence; or

(4) Requests for discovery under Rule 16; or

(5) Requests for severance of charges or defendants under Rule 14. (Emphasis Added)

Fed. R. Crim. P. 12(6)

The word *must* is key to understanding the significance of Rule 12(b). If the *must* issues are not raised *before* trial, they are considered abandoned or *waived*; thus they cannot be raised thereafter at trial or on appeal.

Format for Motions

Now that we know that the pretrial motion is the preferred manner, and in some instances the only manner, in which to raise certain issues, you may be wondering how motions are made and what form they take. Rule 47 of the Federal Rules of Criminal Procedure contains the general standard for content and form of motions. (See Figure 5-2.)

FIGURE 5-2   PROCEDURE FOR FILING A MOTION

An application to the court for an order shall be by motion. A motion other than one made during the trial or hearing shall be in writing unless the court permits it to be made orally. It shall state the grounds upon which it is made and shall set forth the relief or order sought. It may be supported by affidavit.

Fed. R. Crim. P. 47

The general rule is that motions, except under unusual circumstances, are made in writing and are submitted to the court and to opposing counsel with supporting documentation, authorities, and memoranda. The motion must also be specific regarding the relief sought, as is evident in Figures 5-2 and 5-3.

Local Rules. In addition to Rule 47, all districts have local rules that address the form and content of motions. In state systems, the format for motions is usually standard throughout the state. In some areas, it may vary from district to district.

It is not possible to summarize all rules for all jurisdictions, federal and state. It is possible, however, to generalize about one major point concerning requirements for pretrial motions. It is most unusual to find a court that does not require that a motion be supported by a memorandum detailing law and facts warranting the relief sought. The supporting memorandum of authorities must ordinarily be filed simultaneously with the motion. Because supporting memoranda are usually lengthy documents, we will not illustrate them. They generally carry the usual court heading and case caption and are titled for clear identification, Memorandum in Support of Motion to Suppress, for example.

Most jurisdictions, federal and state, have rules very similar to the rule cited in Figure 5-4. Figure 5-4, which reproduces Rule 2.05 from the Uniform District Court Rules for U.S. district courts in the Eastern, Middle, and Western districts of Louisiana, describes the process of filing a motion and its attendant memoranda according to a local rule.

Disposing of the Issues Raised by Motion. How does the court dispose of issues raised by pretrial motion? In other words, what happens after a motion is filed? Motions may be disposed of by the judge with or without a hearing. Most courts require that a motion be set for hearing at the time of its filing. Then, if the court determines that the hearing is unnecessary, it may cancel the hearing and issue its ruling without argument or presentation of evidence. (See Figures 5-5 and 5-6.)

At the motion hearing, if one is held, the parties may present evidence and argument in support of their positions. In essence, the hearing is a trial. It is held before a judge or, in some instances, before a magistrate, without a jury, and is confined to the specific issue presented in the motion.

The local rules and the sample notice for a hearing illustrated in Figure 5-6 are typical of those you will find in most federal and state district courts. The format for hearing and disposing of pretrial motions may vary in minor detail from district to district within the federal system and even from district to district within the various jurisdictions of a state, but the similarities in procedure are greater than the differences. If you are conversant with the rules of your local federal or state district, you will be able to adjust quite easily to the peculiarities of any other state or federal court. Now that we know something of the procedure that governs the filing, content, and

FIGURE 5-3   MOTION TO SUPPRESS

UNITED STATES DISTRICT COURT
EASTERN DISTRICT OF LOUISIANA

UNITED STATES OF AMERICA	**CRIMINAL NO. 93-00001**
VERSUS	**SECTION "W"**
ADAM A. ADAMS	

MOTION TO SUPRESS

NOW INTO COURT comes the defendant, Adam A. Adams, appearing herein through undersigned counsel, who, pursuant to the 4th and 14th Amendments to the Constitution of the United States and Rules 12(b)(3) and 41(e) of the Federal Rules of Criminal Procedure, moves to suppress and exclude from use as evidence numerous objects and items seized from him by federal agents on January 5, 1992 for the following reasons:

1.

The seizure was made pursuant to a search warrant issued by U.S. Magistrate Lester Grant supported by an affidavit of federal agent Will Dare. The affidavit is attached hereto as Exhibit "A". Likewise, the return on said warrant is attached as Exhibit "B". It contains a list of all items seized from defendant.

2.

The affidavit (Exhibit '"A") supporting issuance of the search warrant contains false statements which were recklessly and/or intentionally made; and if the affidavit were purged of its falsities, it would not be sufficient to support a finding of probable cause.

WHEREFORE DEFENDANT PRAYS that this Court conduct an evidentiary hearing on this motion to suppress and that in due course that an Order issue herein suppressing the items seized from defendant and prohibiting their use as evidence in any proceeding in this case.

Respectfully submitted,

TYME AND AYGIN

BY: _____

WALTER B. AYGIN, JR.
1010 Legal Avenue
New Orleans, Louisiana 70100
Telephone (504) 555-9999

CERTIFICATE OF SERVICE

I certify that a copy of the foregoing Motion To Suppress has been mailed to all counsel of record, on this 3d day January, 1993.

_____

Walter B. Aygin, Jr.

FIGURE 5-4 FILING A MOTION ACCORDING TO LOCAL RULE

The moving party shall submit and serve opposing parties with a copy of the motion and memorandum. Except as noted in Local Rule 2.06, all motions shall be accompanied by a memorandum commonly referred to as a "Memorandum in Support", which shall contain (1) a concise statement of the reasons in support of the motion, and (2) citations of authorities. If the motion requires the consideration of facts not appearing of record, the movant shall also file with the Clerk and serve upon opposing counsel a copy of all documentary evidence he or she intends to submit in support of the motion. Memoranda may not be supplemented except with leave of Court first obtained.

*UNIF. DIST. CT. R. 2.05
for the Eastern, Middle, and
Western Districts of Louisiana*

FIGURE 5-5 SETTING A MOTION FOR HEARING ACCORDING TO LOCAL RULE

Counsel filing a motion shall, at the time of filing, notice it for a hearing within a reasonable time thereafter.

*UNIF. DIST. CT. R. 2.02(e)
for the Eastern, Middle, and
Western Districts of Louisiana*

disposition of motions, it should be easier to understand the rules and procedures governing motion practice.

Defects in the Institution of the Prosecution

Rule 12 of the Federal Rules of Criminal Procedure speaks of five requests for relief (types of motions) that must be filed prior to trial:

1. Motion surrounding defects in the institution of the prosecution
2. Motion surrounding defects in the indictment or information
3. Motion to suppress evidence
4. Motion for discovery
5. Motion to sever charges or defendants

The first request listed concerns defects in the institution of the prosecution. This category of motion addresses the defendant's objections to the manner in which a charge originated.

Earlier we saw that the law governing federal procedure requires all felony charges to emanate from a grand jury in the form of an indictment. We now see what remedy a defendant has if that procedure is not followed. Should the prosecutor mistakenly file a bill of information charging a felony

FIGURE 5-6   NOTICE FOR A HEARING

UNITED STATES DISTRICT COURT
EASTERN DISTRICT OF LOUISIANA

UNITED STATES **OF AMERICA**	**CRIMINAL DOCKET NO. 93-0000**
VERSUS	**SECTION "W" MAG. 3**
PAUL WILSON	**VIOLATION: 31 USC S. 5313(a)**

NOTICE

TO: Mr. Tomas Velez
     Asst. United States Attorney
     500 Rule Street
     New Orleans, Louisiana   70100

    PLEASE TAKE NOTICE that undersigned counsel will bring on the attached motions for hearing before the Honorable Janice Liu at 2:00 P.M., on Wednesday, January 27, 1993, United States District Court, 500 Rule Street, New Orleans, Louisiana.

                             Respectfully submitted,

                             TYME & AYGIN, ATTORNEYS

                             BY: _____

                             Walter B. Aygin, Jr.
                             1010 Legal Avenue
                             New Orleans, Louisiana   70100
                             Telephone (504)   555-9999

without having obtained a waiver of indictment, the defendant could file a motion to dismiss the indictment. The motion would point to the prosecutor's lack of authority to file an information charging a felony and would request a dismissal of the charge. However, a motion to dismiss the indictment has to be filed before trial. The issue cannot be brought up after trial begins.

POINTER: Yes, instances occur in which a defendant will waive presentment to a grand jury and allow the prosecutor to file a bill of information. Such waivers are usually given when a plea agreement has been worked out in advance. A waiver of indictment is provided for by Rule 7(a) of the Federal Rules of Criminal Procedure.

Defects in the Indictment or Information

The second objection that can be raised only in pretrial motion is a complaint regarding a defect in the indictment or information. If the defendant believes that the grand jury that returned an indictment was improperly constituted, did not have a quorum present when the vote was taken, or was otherwise defective, he or she might file a motion to dismiss the indictment based on that ground, offering Rule 12(b)(2) as his or her authority. For the sake of emphasizing the point that motions must be filed timely, we must reiterate: no matter how grave the defect in the indictment or information, the motion to dismiss has to be filed before trial or it is waived.

Lack of Jurisdiction. Two additional objections are never waived even if they are not raised prior to trial. An objection to the court's jurisdiction or an objection that the formal charge fails to state an offense need not be raised by pretrial motion though they are directed at defects in the indictment or information. An objection to the court's jurisdiction is an objection to the power or authority of the court to interpret and apply the law within a given territory. This objection may be raised at any time during the pendency of the proceedings. It may even be raised by the court if the defendant fails to do so.

Failure to State an Offense. An objection that the formal charge fails to state an offense is an objection that points to a specific defect in the indictment or information: that it fails to properly charge the defendant with an offense. As noted in the preceding paragraph, although the court can take notice of its lack of jurisdiction and/or the failure of the indictment or information to state an offense, it is a wise and good practice for the defendant to raise this issue as soon as it becomes apparent, preferably prior to trial via a motion to dismiss.

Motion to Suppress Evidence

The motion to suppress is the third type of request for relief outlined in the Federal Rules of Criminal Procedure. It must be filed before trial if it is to be filed at all. Evidence, or more properly, information or material that the prosecutor would like to use as evidence, can come into possession of authorities in many ways. What happens when a defendant is confronted by evidence that he or she believes to have been unlawfully obtained? The answer is that the attorney for the defendant should file a motion to suppress such material. A **motion to suppress evidence** is a formal request of a party to prevent (or suppress) the use of certain evidence by another party. The motion is designed to allow a judge to rule on the admissibility of the evidence prior to trial.

All manner of evidence or proposed evidence is susceptible to suppression. Suppression means that the use of the material, document, report, testimony, or confession will not be allowed if it was gathered in an unlawful manner. We have already noted some of the practices that may give rise to a motion to suppress. A good example concerns the question of confessions and statements against self-interest made by a suspect or defendant. The *Miranda* case tells us that an arrestee has a right to confer with counsel before he or she makes any statement to investigators. If a statement is obtained without allowing the suspect to exercise his or her right to counsel or if the suspect is not advised of that right in the first place, a motion to suppress the statement may be well grounded.

In addition to confessions, material, that is, physical evidence, seized from a defendant may be suppressed if it was taken unlawfully. Generally speaking, the physical search of a person or the search of an area wherein a person has a reasonable expectation of privacy can be made only when authorized by a warrant, when incidental to a lawful arrest, or by consent of the suspect.

Earlier we noted that a search warrant can only issue on probable cause and that it must be supported by a sworn evidentiary statement. A motion to suppress can attack the sufficiency of the affidavit given in support of the warrant. (See Figure 3-4.)

The matter of improper searches and seizures raises a constitutional question. You will recall that the Fourth Amendment guarantees the right to be secure from unreasonable searches. In another landmark decision handed down in the case of *Mapp v. Ohio*, 367 U.S. 643 (1961), the Supreme Court ruled that the prohibition against unreasonable searches applies to state governments as well as to the federal. Thus, evidence unlawfully seized may not be used in state court prosecutions.

It was also pointed out earlier that lineups and other identification formats should not be suggestive or designed to unfairly single out a suspect. If a defendant feels that the process employed in his or her case was improperly conducted, the proper method to have the resulting identifications disallowed as evidence is to file a motion to suppress. We will have more to say about exclusion of evidence in Chapter 11; but we must remember that, in almost every jurisdiction, state as well as federal, an objection to the legality of evidence must be raised *before* trial via a motion to suppress. If an objection is not raised before trial, it could be waived!

The whole question of admissibility will be covered in more detail later. It is mentioned here to help you understand the significance of the motion to suppress.

Discovery

Knowing how to go about suppressing evidence does not answer all of the questions regarding the subject of evidence. Perhaps the idea has occurred to you that it would be impossible for a party to request suppression of evidence unless that party is aware of what evidence the opposition intends to use. To see how parties obtain knowledge of the opposition's evidence, we must look at the next category of pretrial motion covered in Rule 12.

Rule 12 states that discovery must be requested before trial. *Discovery* is a broad term used to describe the process by which a party attempts to ascertain (i.e., discover) the evidence that an opposing party will use to prove its case. Its focus is on preventing surprise by allowing opposing parties to determine what evidence is intended for use at trial.

Intent to Use Certain Evidence—Notice Required. Rule 12(d)(1) and Rule 12(d)(2) of the Federal Rules of Criminal Procedure form part of the pretrial discovery system. Subsection (d)(1) of Rule 12 allows the government to voluntarily give notice to the defendant of its intention to use specified evidence. Subsection (d)(2) authorizes the defense to request such notice if it is not voluntarily given. (See Figure 5-7.)

FIGURE 5-7   NOTICE MUST BE GIVEN OF INTENT TO USE CERTAIN EVIDENCE

(d)(1) At the arraignment or as soon thereafter as is practicable, the government may give notice to the defendant of its intention to use specified evidence at trial in order to afford the defendant an opportunity to raise objections to such evidence prior to trial under subdivision (b)(3) of this rule.

FED. R. CRIM. P. 12(d)(1)

(d)(2) At the arraignment or as soon thereafter as is practicable, the defendant may, in order to afford an opportunity to move to suppress evidence under subdivision (b)(3) of this rule, request notice of the government's intention to use (in its evidence in chief at trial) any evidence which the defendant may be entitled to discover under Rule 16 subject to any relevant limitations prescribed in Rule 16.

FED. R. CRIM. P. 12(d)(2)

Discovery under Rule 16. Rule 12(d) refers to another discovery rule, one that must be understood if any success is to be had in the discovery process. Far and away the most significant of the pretrial discovery rules is Rule 16 of the Federal Rules of Criminal Procedure. Most state jurisdictions have rules similar to this federal guideline, although some differ in one significant detail as we shall see later.

Discovery Allowed to the Defendant Rule 16 allows the defendant to request and be provided with a wide range of evidence prior to trial. It also denies access to certain other information and evidence in the possession of the government. The rule is quite extensive and is synopsized in Figure 5-8.

Discovery Denied to the Defendant We noted in the preceding paragraph that the rule also prevents the discovery of certain evidence in the hands of the government. The chief argument advanced by prosecutors for concealing information involves the danger that such disclosure may pose for government witnesses. Figure 5-9 summarizes the type of information denied the defendant during discovery.

Nearly half of the states require the prosecution to provide the defendant with a list of witnesses prior to trial. These states include Alaska, Arizona, Arkansas, California, Colorado, Florida, Idaho, Illinois, Indiana, Iowa, Kansas, Kentucky, Michigan, Minnesota, Missouri, Montana, Nebraska, Nevada, Oklahoma, Oregon, Tennessee, and Utah. There is no similar federal requirement. This is the major difference between federal and state discovery procedures referred to earlier.

FIGURE 5-8 DISCOVERY ALLOWED TO THE DEFENDANT

(a)(1)(A) Statements of Defendant

All written or transcribed statements;

All oral statements to be used at trial;

Recorded Grand Jury testimony of defendant;

Recorded Statements of Corporate Employees;
(When defendant is a corporation)

(B) A Copy of Defendant's Criminal Record

(C) Tangible Documents, Objects and Other

Evidence Which are Material to the Defense or Intended For Use as
Evidence by the Government

(D) Reports of Physical or Mental Examinations or Results of Scientific
Test

Source: FED. R. CRIM. P. 16

FIGURE 5-9 INFORMATION NOT DISCOVERABLE BY THE DEFENDANT

(2) Except as provided in paragraphs (A), (B), and (D) of subdivision (a)(1), this rule does not authorize the discovery or inspection of reports, memoranda, or other internal government documents made by the attorney for the government or other government agents in connection with the investigation or prosecution of the case, or of statements made by government witnesses or prospective government witnesses except as provided in 18 U.S.C. 3500.

FED. R. CRIM. P. 16(a)(2)

(3) Except as provided in Rule 6, 12(i) and 26.2, and subdivision (a)(1)(A) of this rule, these rules do not relate to discovery or inspection of recorded proceedings of a grand jury.

FED. R. CRIM. P. 16(a)(3)

Discovery by the Prosecution One important feature of Rule 16, the prosecution's right to obtain information from the defendant, is dependent upon the defendant's request for discovery. That is to say, the government is not entitled to discovery under Rule 16 unless the defendant first makes a request. (See Figure 5-10.)

Discovery Not Covered by Rule 16. Whether the defendant requests discovery under Rule 16 or not, certain disclosures must be made to the prosecution.

FIGURE 5-10   DISCOVERY AVAILABLE TO THE PROSECUTION IS DEPENDENT ON DEFENDANT'S REQUEST FOR DISCOVERY

(b)(1)(A) *If the defendant requests disclosure* under subdivision (a)(1)(C) or (D) of this rule, upon compliance with such request by the government, the defendant on request of the government, shall permit the government to inspect and copy or photograph books, papers, documents, photographs, tangible objects, or copies or portions thereof, which are within the possession, custody or control of the defendant and which the defendant intends to introduce as evidence in chief at the trial. (Emphasis added)

FED. R. CRIM. P. 16(b)(1)(A)

(b)(1)(B) *If the defendant requests disclosure* under subdivision (a)(1)(C) or (D) of this rule, upon compliance with such request by the government, the defendant, on request of the government, shall permit the government to inspect and copy or photograph any results or reports of physical or mental examinations and of scientific tests or experiments made in connection with the particular case, or copies thereof, within the possession or control of the defendant, which the defendant intends to introduce as evidence in chief at the trial or which were prepared by a witness whom the defendant intends to call at the trial when the results or reports relate to that witness's testimony. (Emphasis added)

FED. R. CRIM. P. 16(b)(1)(B)

Prior Notification of Special Defenses Previously, when we discussed the plea of not guilty, we noted that the defendant is obligated to advise the government of his or her intent to use the defense of insanity at the time of commission of the offense. This important procedural step is part of the discovery process. It is codified in Rule 12.1 of the Federal Rules of Criminal Procedure.

The requirements regarding prior notification can extend to other defenses. In the federal system, the defendant can be required to give prior notice if a defense based on alibi is contemplated. Most state systems have similar specifications. In a footnote annotation, the Supreme Court cited state court rules regarding notice of alibi as a defense. See *Williams v. Florida,* 399 U.S. 78 (1970).

Alibi Rule 12.1(a) provides that a defendant "shall" give notice of the intent to use an alibi defense. (See Figure 5-11.) For good cause, the court may, in its discretion, allow the defendant to impose an alibi defense even though pretrial notice was not given. See Rule 12.1(e) of the Federal Rules of Criminal Procedure.

Public Authority Another instance in which the defendant must grant pretrial discovery to the government is in the case of a defense based on public authority. That is, if the defendant claims to have been acting under

FIGURE 5-11   NOTICE OF DEFENDANT'S INTENTION TO OFFER AN ALIBI

> Upon written demand by the attorney for the government stating the time, date, and place at which the alleged offense was committed, the defendant shall serve within ten days, or at such different time as the court may direct, upon the attorney for the government, a written notice of the defendant's intention to offer a defense of alibi. The notice shall state the specific place or places at which the defendant claims to have been at the time of the alleged offense and the names and addresses of the witnesses upon whom the defendant intends to rely to establish such alibi
>
> *Fed. R. Crim. P. 12.1(a)*

authority of a law enforcement agency at the time of the alleged offense, notice of that claim must be given to the attorney for the government and filed with the clerk of courts. See Rule 12.3 of the Federal Rules of Criminal Procedure.

Disclosure of Evidence Favorable to the Defendant   The prosecution is obligated to disclose to the defendant, prior to trial, any information, tangible items, or other material evidence in its possession that is favorable to the defense. The prosecution's obligation to make such disclosures is not dependent upon a request from the defendant. In other words, the government must give the information to the defendant whether or not the defendant requests it.

This rule is known as the *Brady* rule because it was enunciated by the court in the case of *Brady v. Maryland*, 373 U.S. 83 (1963). The **Brady rule** is a rule of law that calls for the prosecution to disclose information to the defense that may be favorable to presenting a defense. In *Brady*, the court found that the requirement to disclose favorable evidence to the defendant is required by due process.

Since the decision was based on constitutional grounds, it is applicable to all state prosecutions as well as federal prosecutions. In fact, as the case caption suggests, the case out of which the rule derives originated in the state courts of Maryland.

In some instances, particularly where the evidence is fairly obvious and there is no particular need for requesting disclosure, a defendant may elect to forgo formal discovery allowed by Rule 16 and rely on the government's obligation to disclose favorable information under *Brady*. The defendant's obvious advantage in using such a tactic is that the government is then entitled to *no discovery* under Rule 16. Of course, the defendant is still obliged to give notice of an alibi defense or of a defense based on mental incompetency or public authority because such notice is not required by Rule 16 but rather by Rule 12.

Some defense counsel, presumably out of an abundance of caution, file a formal motion requesting that the government disclose all evidence favorable to the defendant and cite *Brady* as the authority for the request. Theoretically, the law does not require such a motion because the government's obligation to disclose exists whether or not the defendant makes a request. It may be a good practice to file a *Brady* motion, even though there is no strict requirement to do so, because it focuses the court's attention on the government's duty and may aid in clearing up questions regarding whether or not some particular piece of evidence must be disclosed.

Sometimes a question exists in the mind of the prosecutor as to whether certain evidence comes within the *Brady* rule. If there is a dispute or any uncertainty about the quality of the material, the defense or the government may ask the court to make a determination, *in camera*, prior to trial. When such a request is made, disclosures to the court are not revealed to the defense unless there is a finding that the evidence is favorable to the defendant.

The Jencks Act and Rule 26.2 Though it is technically not a pretrial discovery device, 18 U.S.C. § 3500, the so-called **Jencks Act**, may logically be considered at this juncture. The statute provides that no statement or report made by a government witness shall be discoverable until after the witness has testified.

Apparent from the language of the Jencks Act, the law benefits only the defendant because it requires delivery of a witness's statements only by the government after the witness has testified on direct examination at trial. (See Figure 5-12.)

FIGURE 5-12   EXCERPTS FROM THE JENCKS ACT

(b) After a witness called by the United States has testified on direct examination, the court shall on motion of the defendant, order the United States to produce any statement (as hereinafter defined) of the witness in the possession of the United States which relates to the subject matter to which the witness has testified. If the entire contents of any such statement relate to the subject matter of the testimony of the witness, the court shall order it to be delivered directly to the defendant for his examination and use.

18 U.S.C. § 3500(b)

(c) If the United States claims any portion of the statement ordered to be produced under this section contains matter which does not relate to the subject matter of the testimony of the witness, the court shall order the United States to deliver such statement for inspection of the court *in camera*. Upon delivery the court shall excise the portions of such statement which do not relate to the subject matter of the testimony of the witness. With such material excised, the court shall then direct delivery of the statement to the defendant for his use.

18 U.S.C. § 3500(c)

Rule 26.2 of the Federal Rules of Criminal Procedure extends the right to a witness's prior statements to both parties, the prosecution as well as the defense. (See Figure 5-13.)

FIGURE 5-13   THE RIGHTS TO A WITNESS'S PRIOR STATEMENTS

> After a witness other than the defendant has testified on direct examination, the court, on motion of a party who did not call the witness, shall order the attorney for the government or the defendant and the defendant's attorney, as the case may be, to produce for examination and use of the moving party, any statement of the witness that is in their possession and relates to the subject matter concerning which the witness has testified.
>
> *FED. R. CRIM. P. 26.2*

What makes the Jencks Act and Rule 26.2 relevant to our present discussion is that in practice many district courts make such material available prior to a witness's testimony and even prior to trial.

Amicable Discovery As a rule, if there are no extenuating circumstances such as safety of a witness, courts encourage the exchange of statements prior to trial. Some jurisdictions have local rules that require that the parties meet to discuss all discovery questions prior to the filing of discovery motions. Such rules may even provide for sanctions against an attorney who fails to participate in an amicable discovery conference.

The rule cited in Figure 5-14 is representative of those found in all federal jurisdictions and in many state jurisdictions. It is imperative that a paralegal intending to work in the area of criminal law become familiar with the rules governing amicable discovery in the state and federal jurisdictions in which he or she intends to practice.

FIGURE 5-14   AMICABLE DISCOVERY

> No motion relative to discovery shall be accepted for filing unless accompanied by a certificate of counsel for the moving party stating that counsel have conferred in person or by telephone for purposes of amicably resolving the issues and stating why they are unable to agree or stating that opposing counsel has refused to confer after reasonable notice. Counsel for the moving party shall arrange the conference. Any motion filed under this paragraph shall be noticed for hearing. If the Court finds that opposing counsel has willfully refused to meet and confer, or having met, willfully refused or failed to confer in good faith, the Court may impose such sanctions as it deems proper.
>
> *UNIF. DIST. CT. R. 2.05*
> *for the Eastern, Middle, and*
> *Western Districts of Louisiana*

Bill of Particulars. Like the Jencks Act, a bill of particulars is not, generally speaking, a discovery device. At least one appeals court decision—*United States v. Smith*, 776 F.2d 1104 (3d Cir. 1985), a decision by the U.S. Court of Appeals for the Third Circuit cited in the Federal Reporter, 2d series, has recognized that fact.

A **bill of particulars** is a clarification of an indictment or a bill of information, detailing the specifics of the alleged offense and making the charge more readily understood by the defendant. (See Figure 5-15.) Its purpose is to prevent surprise at the trial. *United States v. Diecidue*, 603 F.2d 535 (5th Cir. 1979). Whenever a formal charge is unclear, ambiguous, or stated with imprecision, the court may order the government to *particularize* the charges so that the court and the defendant are properly apprised of the specifics of the crime alleged.

FIGURE 5-15 BILL OF PARTICULARS

(f) The court may direct the filing of a bill of particulars. A motion for a bill of particulars may be made before arraignment or at such later time as the court may permit. A bill of particulars may be amended at any time subject to such conditions as justice requires.

FED. R. CRIM. P. 7(f)

Although it was not designed as a discovery tool, the bill of particulars can be the most informative disclosure made by the prosecution. The mere fact that an indictment contains all of the elements required to make it legally sufficient does not mean that it sets out all of the specifics needed for a defendant to fully understand the charge that he or she is facing. A court can order the government to give further details of the offense if the indictment or bill of information is not sufficiently clear. The defendant must request such an order by filing a motion for bill of particulars.

So what does all of this mean? Let's try to explain by use of an example. For the purposes of our example, we will assume that the language of the indictment set out in Figure 5-16 contains all of the elements required to be legally sufficient.

FIGURE 5-16 SAMPLE INDICTMENT

THE GRAND JURY CHARGES, that on or about January 1, 1993, in the Northern District of Illinois, John Smith, having devised a scheme or artifice to defraud, did knowingly and willfully use, or cause to be used, the United States mail to obtain money or property, by means of the said scheme or artifice to defraud, by placing, or causing to be placed, in an authorized depository for United States mail, and causing to be delivered by the United States mail, a writing containing false and fraudulent pretenses, representations, or promises, all in violation of Title 18, United States Code, Section 1341.

Though the sample indictment contains all the required elements, it is not very informative. It does not specify what type of fraudulent writing is involved nor does it identify the victim or intended victim of the plot.

Relying solely on the language of the indictment, it is possible that the defendant could arrive at trial believing that he had to explain an inflated damage claim that he had sent to an insurance company. However, the prosecutor could prove a case of fraud involving a credit card application containing false information. Neither situation is precluded by the language of the indictment. To clear up the confusion and to be fully apprised of the charges confronting him, the defendant could have filed a motion for a bill of particulars asking for specifics of the offense.

A bill of particulars is a very important remedy available to the defendant, but it is a motion for relief that addresses itself to the discretion of the court. A denial of a bill of particulars by a trial judge is not easily overturned in an appeals court. The defendant must not only show that the trial judge abused discretion but also that the abuse prejudiced the defendant at trial.

Three additional points must be made regarding a bill of particulars. First, a defective indictment or bill of information cannot be cured by supplying particulars. What this means is that, if an indictment does not contain all the requisites for formal sufficiency, those requisites cannot be supplied by answering a request for particulars.

The second point concerns the form of the request for relief. A request for a bill of particulars must include a specific reference to the parts of the indictment or information that require clarification or enlargement. In other words, a defendant has to be as particular in the request as he or she expects the government to be in response.

Finally, even though the request for particulars is not technically a pretrial discovery motion referred to in Rule 12, *it must be filed before trial. Kramer v. United States*, 166 F.2d 515 (9th Cir. 1948).

Depositions. The final item we will look at in our consideration of discovery is one that is not frequently used in a criminal case, but it is available if circumstances require it. A deposition, as it is used in civil cases, is generally thought of as a discovery device. In the context of a criminal case, it may be more properly regarded as a perpetuation technique, but it is still a means of uncovering information before trial.

FIGURE 5-17 EXCERPT CONCERNING DEPOSITIONS

(a) Whenever due to exceptional circumstances of the case it is in the interest of justice that the testimony of a prospective witness of a party be taken and preserved for use at trial, the court may upon motion of such party and notice to the parties order that testimony of such witness be taken by deposition and that any designated book, paper, document, record, recording, or other material not privileged, be produced at the same time and place.

Fed. R. Crim. P. 15(a) [in part]

A peculiarity about Rule 15 is worthy of our attention. The language of the rule allows a party to take a deposition only of its own witness. The rule states that a party's witness may be deposed "upon motion of such party." Thus, on its face, it would appear that the rule cannot be used as a discovery device because it does not allow the government or the defense to question a witness of the other side. However, it is not difficult to imagine circumstances in which a party (e.g., the defendant) might want the deposition of a witness who could be called by either side depending on the testimony derived at deposition. Therefore, a deposition may be ordered upon a defense motion that claims that a government witness is a prospective defense witness.

Through the subpoena power of a grand jury and the compelling authority of the office of the prosecutor and its investigators and agents, it is generally the government who has the upper hand in obtaining pretrial statements of witnesses. Through the deposition available via Rule 15, a defendant is given some (very limited) ability to demand a witness's presence for questioning before trial.

As additional authority for deposing witnesses prior to trial, Congress has enacted statutory legislation that essentially restates the language of Rule 15. This legislation is part of the Organized Crime Control Act of 1970. It is codified at 18 U.S.C. § 3503.

Severance of Charges and Defendants

The final category of motion identified in Rule 12 that must be filed prior to trial is the motion to sever defendants or charges. **Severance** is the separation of codefendants or counts of a formal charge for separate trials. A problem sometimes arises because, according to Rule 8, the government has a right to join offenses and defendants in the same indictment or information. (See Figure 5-18.) Almost without exception, it is the defendant who brings a motion to sever counts or defendants. However, the rule allows the motion to be brought by either side, prosecution or defense if the situation warrants. (See Figure 5-19.)

If two or more defendants are charged in the same indictment or information, the defense team must examine the case closely to determine what prejudice such joinder might produce for its client. A typical problem that might require severance involves a situation in which **A** and **B** are charged in the same indictment as codefendants. If **A** has made a confession that also incriminates **B**, it may be necessary to separate, or sever, the defendants for trial.

The situation in our example involves some of the fundamental rights we discussed earlier. In a criminal case, a defendant has the option to testify or not to testify. He or she cannot be forced to testify because of the Fifth Amendment right against self-incrimination. *This right means that the government cannot call a defendant to testify. It also means that another defendant in the same trial cannot call a codefendant to testify.* If you did not already know that a

FIGURE 5-18   THE RIGHT TO JOIN OFFENSES AND DEFENDANTS

(a) Joinder of Offenses.   Two or more offenses may be charged in the same indictment or information in a separate count for each offense if the offenses charged, whether felonies or misdemeanors or both, are of the same or similar character or are based on the same act or transaction or on two or more acts or transactions connected together or constituting parts of a common scheme or plan.

Fed. R. Crim. P. 8(a)

(b) Joinder of Defendants.   Two or more defendants may be charged in the same indictment or information if they are alleged to have participated in the same act or transaction or in the same series of acts or transactions connected together or constituting an offense or offenses. Such defendants may be charged in one or more counts together or separately and all of the defendants need not be charged in each count.

Fed. R. Crim. P. 8(b)

FIGURE 5-19   THE RIGHT TO SEVER OFFENSES OR DEFENDANTS

If it appears that a defendant or the government is prejudiced by a joinder of offenses or of defendants in an indictment or information or by such joinder by trial together, the court may order an election of separate trials of counts, grant a severance of defendants or provide whatever other relief justice requires. In ruling on a motion by a defendant for severance the court may order the attorney for the government to deliver to the court for inspection in camera any statements or confessions made by the defendants which the government intends to introduce in evidence at trial.

Fed. R. Crim. P. 14

defendant cannot be called to testify at his or her trial by the government, make a note of this bit of information and commit it to memory!

So, what happens to **B** in the example given above? Assuming that the confession is admissible against **A** and that **A** elects not to testify at trial, how can **B** confront and cross-examine **A**? The answer is **B** cannot, under those circumstances, confront or cross-examine **A** because **A** is a defendant and cannot be called to testify by any other party.

In the example, we see a conflict of two guaranteed rights, **A**'s right not to be a witness (Fifth Amendment) and **B**'s right to confront witnesses (Sixth Amendment). One way to resolve the problem is to sever the defendants for trial.

At **B**'s separate trial, **A**'s statement would not be admissible, but **A** could be called as a witness by the government to repeat allegations against **B**. If **A** testified, **B** could cross-examine. If **A** did not testify, the incriminating information against **B** would not go into evidence. You can see why defendant **B** would request a severance.

Of course, a severance is not automatic. It must be requested by motion *prior* to trial. The motion addresses itself to the discretion of the judge, who may grant a severance or order other relief.

An example of other relief is an order to the government to excise (remove) all reference to **B** from **A**'s statement. If, even after excision, an inference of prejudice to codefendant **B** remains, the judge can instruct the jury that the confession is only evidence against the party who made the statement and cannot be considered as evidence against any other party. This remedial jury instruction is seldom considered sufficient by defense counsel.

In *Bruton v. United States*, 391 U.S. 123 (1968), the Supreme Court declared that a mere jury instruction will not cure a confrontation problem similar to the one set out in our example; rather, the reference to the codefendant must be deleted from the confession in order to avoid reversible error. Sometimes the deletion severely impairs the usefulness of the confession. In that case, it may be the government who elects to sever the defendants for trial.

Bruton is an important case in this area of the law. The **Bruton rule** mandates separate trials for codefendants in situations in which one defendant's statements incriminate another defendant. Many defense attorneys and prosecutors refer to codefendant confession situations as *Bruton* problems. If you do not acquaint yourself with the decision, you may be embarrassed when a confession problem arises.

Another significant case in this field is *Dutton, Warden v. Evans*, 400 U.S. 74 (1970). In the *Dutton* decision, the court held that the statement of a coconspirator that implicates another coconspirator does *not* violate the confrontation clause. In other words, where the offense is conspiracy, the statement of one conspirator that implicates another conspirator is admissible into evidence.

The purpose of the rule regarding severance is to provide a means for solving prejudicial joinder problems prior to trial. It may be wise to note once again that Rule 12 requires that a motion seeking severance must be filed *prior* to trial. Neither the defendant nor the government can wait until trial begins to confront this issue.

OTHER PRETRIAL MOTIONS

The array of issues that may be settled by motion before trial is imposing. Now we will consider some of the maneuvers that are not covered by Rules 12 or 16.

Motion to Transfer the Case for Trial

As the title to this section suggests, some pretrial motions do not fall within the ambit of Rule 12. One of the more significant motions in that group is the motion to change the location of a trial.

Rule 21 of the Federal Rules of Criminal Procedure allows the court to shift the proceeding to a different district for trial if there is a danger that prejudice against the defendant will prevent a fair trial in the district of origin. It also allows a change of district if it is demanded by the interest of justice. (See Figure 5-20.)

FIGURE 5-20   RIGHT TO TRANSFER A CASE FOR TRIAL

(a) The court upon motion of the defendant shall transfer the proceeding as to that defendant to another district whether or not such district is specified in the defendant's motion if the court is satisfied that there exists in the district where the prosecution is pending so great a prejudice against the defendant that the defendant cannot obtain a fair and impartial trial at any place fixed by law for holding court in that district.

FED. R. CRIM. P. 21(a)

(b) For the convenience of parties and witnesses, and in the interest of justice, the court upon motion of the defendant may transfer the proceeding as to that defendant on any one or more of the counts thereof to another district.

FED. R. CRIM. P. 21(b)

Rule 21 authorizes the court to transfer a case *but only upon motion of the defendant.* We have already learned the reason why the court cannot transfer the case on its own motion or on the motion of the prosecutor. The defendant's right to be tried "by an impartial jury of the State and district wherein the crime shall have been committed" is guaranteed by the Sixth Amendment. The right belongs exclusively to the defendant; that is, neither the court nor the prosecution is empowered to set aside that privilege.

The idea of prejudice as grounds for transfer of a case is easy to grasp. Every state has a rule of procedure or a law that allows for transfer within the state for similar reasons. If a crime receives a great deal of notoriety, it is very possible that, with so much community interest, it would be impossible to find an impartial jury.

However, Rule 21(b) also allows for a transfer (on the defendant's motion) if such a move conveniences the parties or the witnesses and is in the interest of justice. Some state jurisdictions have rules similar to Rule 21(b), but the situation arises more frequently in federal prosecutions. When criminal activity spreads over a wide area, including several states, more witnesses may be located outside than within a district. The defendant may also live outside of the district, even in another state. In such a situation, it may be more convenient to hold the trial in the area where the witnesses and the defendant reside.

Motion to Disqualify the Judge

Here's a motion that will cause you to think. It is seldom used for obvious reasons. If a party (any party) believes that the judge before whom the case is to be tried is personally biased or prejudiced against him or her, that party may move to have the judge removed. The motion requires an affidavit from the moving party stating the facts and circumstances upon which the claim of bias is based.

The judge (yes, the one sought to be removed) must then review the motion and affidavit and determine if grounds for disqualification exist. If the judge feels that prejudice has been established, the case will be reassigned. If the judge does not find reason to excuse himself or herself, the case and all parties stay put.

The motion to disqualify a judge must be filed before trial. Once the trial has begun, all objections to the judge are waived. The motion is usually based on 28 U.S.C. § 144.

Motion to Strike Surplusage

An indictment or information must be stated in plain, concise, and definite language. According to Rule 7(c)(1) of the Federal Rules of Criminal Procedure, it must clearly spell out the offense and the essential facts of the offense. (See Figure 5-21.)

FIGURE 5-21   LANGUAGE IN AN INDICTMENT OR INFORMATION MUST BE SPECIFIC

(c)(1) The indictment or the information shall be a plain, concise and definite written statement of the essential facts constituting the offense charged.

FED. R. CRIM. P. 7(c)(1)

If the defendant feels that the language of the indictment contains assertions, allegations, or prejudicial statements that are unnecessary to a clear and concise declaration of the facts and charges, he or she may move to have the offensive language stricken from the charge. (See Figure 5-22.) Such extraneous, unnecessary, and often inflammatory language is called **indictment surplusage**.

FIGURE 5-22   RIGHT TO STRIKE SURPLUSAGE

(d) The court upon motion of the defendant may strike surplusage from the indictment or information.

FED. R. CRIM. P. 7(d)

The motion to strike surplusage is also exclusively a defense motion. This should not be a surprising revelation since it is the prosecution who drafts the indictment or information; consequently, any language contained in the charge was placed there by the drafter.

Rule 7 contains no provision that a motion to strike surplusage must be filed in advance of trial. However, in order for the remedy to be meaningful, the offensive language must be removed before the indictment or information is read to the jury at the beginning of a trial.

Motion to Consolidate

The purpose of the motion to consolidate is to economize time, effort, and expense. Rule 13 of the Federal Rules of Criminal Procedure allows the court to order consolidation of defendants and charges for trial. (See Figure 5-23.)

FIGURE 5-23   RIGHT TO CONSOLIDATE

The court may order two or more indictments or informations or both to be tried together if the offenses and the defendants, if there is more than one, could have been joined in a single indictment or information. The procedure shall be the same as if the prosecution were under such single indictment or information.

FED. R. CRIM. P. 13

The motion to consolidate is most frequently filed by the prosecutor; however, there is no restriction within its language limiting the availability to either party. Since the relief sought is a joint trial of charges and/or defendants, it must, of course, be filed before trial begins.

Motion to Continue

The motion to continue a trial is one that is available to either party. In an earlier chapter, we learned that in federal cases the trial must begin within seventy days of the arraignment. That time frame is frequently too optimistic for the circumstances surrounding a given case.

The mandate to try a case within seventy days and the excludable delays are all contained in 18 U.S.C. § 3161. Within that statute, a list of circumstances allow for exclusions of certain periods from the calculation of the seventy days. A paralegal trying to accomplish all the tasks that must be completed before trial would be wise to become thoroughly familiar with these exclusions.

Of particular importance when considering the motion for continuance are the factors that the statute allows the court to consider in determining whether or not to grant a delay of trial. (See Figure 5-24.) These ought to be reviewed carefully by anyone who is contemplating a motion to continue the trial of a criminal case in federal court. They appear in 18 U.S.C. § 3161(h)(8)(B)(i), (ii), (iii), and (iv).

FIGURE 5-24   CONSIDERATIONS IN GRANTING A CONTINUANCE

(i) Will it be impossible to go forward with the proceeding without granting the continuance, or will a miscarriage of justice occur;

(ii) Is the case novel or complex due to the number of defendants or the issues of fact and law;

(iii) Have grand jury delays made the time frame unworkable;

(iv) Will it allow defendant or government to obtain counsel and a reasonable time for the attorneys to prepare given that they exercise due diligence.

18 U.S.C. § 3161(h)(8)(B)

Essentially the motion to continue can be granted if the court finds that a continuance is necessary to allow for proper preparation of the case. The judge has latitude in extending the time limitations if there is good reason to do so. However, delaying a trial is not favored in any jurisdiction. A motion to continue is a remedy that can be easily abused. Most judges will not extend the pretrial period without close scrutiny of the reasons given by counsel.

* * *

As mentioned earlier, it would be impossible to cover every motion that can be filed prior to trial. What is most important to understand is that the pretrial motion is the usual way, the best way, and often the required way to raise issues that can be disposed of prior to trial. The purpose of such motions is to clear away all extraneous matters so that the trial can focus on the substantive, evidentiary issues of the prosecution and the defense.

It should also be clear that the paralegal working with the prosecutor or defense counsel will have a big part to play in preparing and responding to pretrial motions. During the pretrial stage, the paralegal gets to show off his or her abilities as a student of the law.

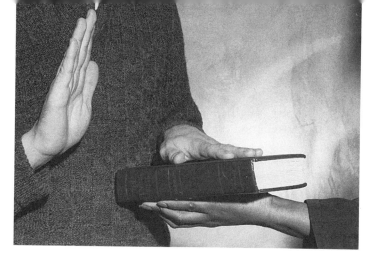

6 PRESENTING THE CASE

To reveal the truth, the whole truth, and nothing but the truth is the substance of the oath taken by every witness who testifies in a court of law. But the whole truth is far more than the obligation of a witness: it is the purpose and goal of the entire legal process. In the end, it is the truth that we seek. That fact is frequently overlooked because we have grown accustomed to using the word *justice* as a synonym for *truth*, but justice is a more abstract concept than truth.

The idea of pursuing truth is important to us at this point because we are about to consider the presentation of a case for trial. The trial, speedy, public, and fair, is the mechanism ordained by law to achieve justice.

THE THEORY OF THE CASE, OR THE CASE THEORY

Truth should be the goal of both prosecution and defense. The method of displaying the truth of a position taken by either party is what we call the **theory of the case**.

The Elements of Case Theory

Many attorneys and paralegals understate or fail to appreciate this most important part of preparation. If fully understood and properly appreciated, the theory of a case will affect the approach taken by a party from the very outset of a case. Formulating and developing a case's theory can provide opportunities for the paralegal to shine. As we shall come to understand, the theory of the case is the heart of the matter; everything we have covered and will cover can be related to the theory of the case. It may be helpful to think of the theory of the case as being made up of five elements: the *truth*, the *hypothesis*, the *supporting facts*, the *argument*, and the *conclusion*.

Truth is the proposition that explains a party's position. In a criminal case, the truth that the prosecution seeks to establish is always found in the indictment or information.

Example: John Doe did commit the crime of battery upon the person of Susan Smith.

For the defense, the truth is the reason that exonerates the accused.

Example: John Doe lacked the requisite criminal intent. The physical contact between John Doe and Susan Smith was merely accidental.

The **hypothesis** is the narration of circumstances that explains or validates the truth. It is the story line of the case as perceived by each party. The **supporting facts** are those that can be established through competent evidence to prove the hypothesis. The **argument** is the coherent presentation of the supporting facts that justifies the conclusion. The **conclusion** is the inescapable consequence of fitting all relevant, salient facts into the argument.

The Theory Must Be Reasonable

The theory must be reasonable. It should be apparent that a legitimate theory has to explain and account for all obvious facts and evidence. For example, if a person is charged with burglary, the defense theory cannot overlook evidence that the defendant's fingerprint was found at the scene. The theory must recognize that fact and offer an explanation consistent with innocence.

The Theory Must Have a Basis in Law

Finally, the theory must have a sound basis in law. As a defense against burglary, it does no good for a defendant to prove that he or she is addicted to narcotics since drug addiction is not a viable defense to the charge.

DEVELOPING THE THEORY

Now that we understand what is meant by the theory of the case, we are going to take a look at the process of its development. The theory of the case should be developed from the very beginning. It is virtually a truism to say that a case cannot be properly presented without a sound theory.

As mentioned at the outset of this chapter, some legal representatives never fully appreciate the importance of theory. However, whether or not they understand the concept or fully identify what they are doing as developing a theory, practitioners are successful only if they present a position justified by fact, logic, and law. This type of justification is what we mean by case theory.

The process of developing a case theory is very important to a paralegal helping to prepare a case for presentation. The paralegal whose duty it is to put the case together must have a plan for accomplishing his or her task. What follows is designed to help us learn how that is done.

* * *

At the end of this chapter, a sample case illustrates how the prosecution and the defense develop and present their respective theories.

Assembling the Facts

The first job of the paralegal whose duty is to help prepare for trial is to collect and examine as much factual material as possible. It makes little difference whether this task is performed for the prosecution or for the defense. Usually the only distinction is where the information originates.

The Prosecution. The first exposure to a case for a prosecutor usually comes from an agent, police officer, or investigator. The first objective of the screening attorney is to examine the report to determine whether a crime has been committed and whether the evidence is sufficient to identify the person who committed the offense. In short, the screening attorney must identify the truth, which is the cornerstone of the case.

At the time that the first report is made to the prosecuting attorney, the truth element may be obvious. For example, in the case of a bank robbery, the crime is evident, and the identity of the robber is certain if the robber is apprehended at the scene.

However, there are instances in which the truth is not so apparent. A police report of a homicide may indicate that a killing has taken place, but the circumstances surrounding that event will determine what crime, if any, the suspect has committed. The circumstances could indicate premeditated murder, they could indicate negligent homicide, or they might even indicate self-defense or justifiable homicide. The prosecuting authority must begin by sifting through the facts, evidence, and witness accounts to determine the truth of the situation.

To some extent, the prosecution has to begin developing a case theory with a slight disadvantage because the suspect cannot be forced to give an explanation of the circumstances (Fifth Amendment). However, if the suspect's right to remain silent causes any problem for the prosecuting authorities, that difficulty is usually overcome by the prosecution's superior investigative resources.

The Defense. Unlike the situation in the office of the prosecutor, most of the early information coming to the defense originates with the client. The defense team represents an individual. That fact creates some situations that are unique to the defense effort. It means that the defense team must deal not only with the facts of the case but also with managing the person who is the defendant.

Interviewing the Client

Though interviewing is an art, attorneys and their paralegals can employ some rules to advantage in developing rapport with a new or prospective client. Building a client's confidence in the people who will present his or her defense is the best way to get the whole truth. The following rules will help develop good client relationships:

1. *Proper appearance.* Dress should be appropriate by prevailing local standards.
2. *Proper setting.* If the client is not in jail, the meeting should be at a place where the attorney exercises control: his or her office is the obvious choice whenever possible. If the meeting is in a location where the attorney does not keep an office, a hotel or public facility with private accommodations is better than meeting at the client's home. House calls should be avoided. If an out-of-town client has an office or place of business offering a private setting, meeting there is preferable to meeting in a home setting.
3. *Proper language.* Do not speak down to or lecture a client. Use normal expressive language and avoid legalistic jargon.
4. *Explain confidentiality.* Make sure that the client is aware of your intent and responsibility to keep his or her disclosures confidential. This explanation should encourage openness.
5. *Proper technique.* Let the client express himself or herself. Ask questions that allow for expansive answers. Do not rely on questions that call for a single-word response. Let the new client know that you are interested in hearing what he or she has to say. Give indications that you are alert by maintaining good eye contact. Use expressive gestures and verbal acknowledgments to show you are following the story, but let the client speak. You can fill in the details by asking direct questions when the client has finished the narration. Be careful when asking leading questions so that you do not encourage the client to give answers that he or she thinks you want to hear.
6. *Be candid.* Do not avoid making observations. The client will ordinarily want input from his or her counselors. Point out problems that you recognize. Ask for clarification if it is needed.
7. *Encourage questions.* Let the client know that you want to have an open, clear relationship. If the client has questions about the role of defense counsel or what is expected of the client, do your best to give direct answers to those questions.

 POINTER: When a paralegal discusses a case with a client, two important things should be remembered. One is an ethical consideration; the other is a practical consideration:

Ethical: A paralegal cannot give legal advice or a legal opinion to a client. There will almost certainly be a time when the paralegal is asked for an opinion by a client. When that happens, it must be made clear to the client that limitations are placed on a paralegal by law and ethics. It is important that these limitations are understood by the client.

Practical: The paralegal must never upstage or derogate the lawyer handling the case. If a disagreement or question arises about the

way in which some matter is being handled, that issue must be
discussed privately with the supervising attorney. It is a mistake
to bring up the issue in the presence of the client. Such a mistake
is usually made only once at each place of employment.

We will have more to say about ethical matters in a later chapter.

EVIDENCE

After reviewing the reports or interviewing the client, the next consideration
facing attorneys and their paralegals is the evidence that supports the hypothesis that is being developed.

If you search very carefully through the codes and statutes of several
states and their federal equivalents, you will not find an all-embracing definition for the term *evidence*. Under the law, evidence means what it means in
every other context. Whether you are dealing with scientific research or the
law, the definition of evidence is the same: **evidence** is the information upon
which a conclusion or judgment can be based.

This definition does not mean that all information is admissible as evidence in a court proceeding. The keys to admissibility of evidence are relevance, competence, and the lawfulness of its seizure. We will have more to say
about competence and lawfulness in a later chapter; for the present, we must
look at the issue of relevance. The Federal Rules of Evidence concerning
relevance are typical of those found in most states. (See Figures 6-1 and 6-2.)

FIGURE 6-1   RELEVANT EVIDENCE, DEFINED

"Relevant evidence" means evidence having any tendency to make the
existence of any fact that is of consequence to the determination of the action
more probable or less probable than it would be without the evidence.

FED. R. EVID. 401

FIGURE 6-2   EXCEPTIONS TO THE ADMISSIBILITY OF RELEVANT EVIDENCE

All relevant evidence is admissible, except as otherwise provided by the
Constitution of the United States, by Act of Congress, by these rules, or by
other rules prescribed by the Supreme Court pursuant to statutory authority.
Evidence which is not relevant is not admissible.

FED. R. EVID. 402

Relevant Evidence and Testimonial Evidence

Several kinds of evidence can be used to prove the truth of a party's position.
At this point, we will focus on the types of evidence with which paralegals

deal and some of the terminology they confront. We have already introduced the term **relevant evidence**, evidence that pertains to a fact or an occurrence at issue. Now we will examine testimonial evidence.

Testimonial evidence—the name says it all—is evidence in the form of sworn testimony provided by a witness who appears in court during a trial to answer questions within his or her knowledge relating to a fact or a set of facts relevant to the matter being tried.

In just about every case, most of the evidence produced is testimonial. Testimony comes from witnesses. The requirement to properly prepare a presentation so that needed witnesses can be identified and secured is a skill that the paralegal must develop.

We would ordinarily think of the task of locating and identifying witnesses as a function of an investigator, not as a duty of a paralegal. In many offices, however, paralegals perform investigative functions. This situation is not only true in the private sector but occurs in some governmental offices as well.

Three kinds of witnesses can be important to the presentation of a criminal case: fact witnesses, expert witnesses, and character witnesses.

Fact Witnesses. As the name states, a **fact witness** possesses knowledge of specific factual data that should be revealed during the presentation of a case. In order to determine who those fact witnesses are, a legal representative must have a clear understanding of the case theory. Knowing the hypothesis (story line) enables the person preparing a presentation to determine what facts must be proved at trial. Once a decision is made regarding the facts to be presented, it becomes a matter of investigation and proper interviewing to identify the witnesses who can best deliver the needed testimony.

Expert Witnesses. We usually think of experts in terms of the type of testimony they give at trial. An **expert witness**, who by training, experience, or knowledge is allowed to give opinions about relevant issues at trial, can be very helpful in this regard since a nonexpert witness may be permitted to render an opinion in court only in very limited situations.

In a criminal case, experts are frequently brought in by the prosecution to testify as to technical facts, such as identifying fingerprints, making ballistic comparisons, analyzing suspected narcotic substances, and explaining the cause of death. Expert psychiatric witnesses are always used in cases where insanity is an issue.

An expert can be used in other ways. It is possible to use expert consultants in developing the theory of the case, and an expert may be used to examine or critique the theory of the opposing side. An expert can assist in the formulation of questions to be posed to witnesses. An expert can be useful in helping to direct discovery processes.

Locating an expert witness is becoming increasingly easier. Leads can be found through the suggestions and advertisements that are published in every legal periodical and bar association journal. Publications such as the *Expert Witness Index*, published by the Defense Research Institute, Milwaukee, Wisconsin, and a section in *American Jurisprudence Trials*, which is published by Lawyers Cooperative Publishers, entitled "Locating Scientific and Technical Experts" deal exclusively with locating experts. Electronic research services such as Lexis and Nexis are very helpful in locating experts in practically any field.

In the federal courts and in most state jurisdictions, rules of evidence affect the use of experts. In practically every jurisdiction, disclosure of experts and their reports must be made before trial. We shall have more to say on this subject in the chapter on evidence.

Character Witnesses. The reputation of a defendant can be a significant factor in a criminal trial. A defendant's reputation can be considered along with other evidence, and along with other evidence, it can form the basis of an acquittal. A **character witness** is a witness who is allowed to testify about the reputation of a defendant.

The general reputation of a defendant in the community as a law-abiding and honest person is always admissible. However, the presentation of such evidence remains at the discretion of the defendant; that is, the prosecution may not introduce general character evidence to prove that a defendant has a bad reputation.

Once the issue of character has been raised by the defendant, the prosecution may cross-examine the witness relative to specific prior offenses of the accused or concerning reports or rumors of such offenses. There are two reasons for allowing such cross-examination. First, the character witness's opinion may be of little value if he or she is not well enough acquainted with the defendant's reputation to have encountered the rumor. Second, the character witness's credibility may be flawed if he or she insists that a report of a prior offense does not damage the reputation of an accused.

Rule 404(b) of the Federal Rules of Evidence allows the prosecutor to introduce evidence of a defendant's specific prior crimes in order to establish such elements as motive, opportunity, intent, or absence of mistake. The rule does not allow the prosecution to produce such evidence in order to establish that the defendant has a bad reputation. (See Figure 6-3.)

FIGURE 6-3   THE ISSUE OF CHARACTER WITH RESPECT TO ITS ADMISSIBILITY AS EVIDENCE

Evidence of other crimes, wrongs, or acts is not admissible to prove the character of a person in order to show action to conformity therewith. It may, however, be admissible for other purposes, such as proof of motive, opportunity, intent, preparation, plan, knowledge, identity, or absence of mistake or accident.

FED. R. EVID. 404(b)

Evidence of Witnesses and Witness Preparation

There is an axiom popular among trial lawyers: Never ask a witness a question unless you know the answer. What this statement implies is that trials are no time for surprises. An attorney must be well prepared before he or she goes into the courtroom. Each witness's testimony should be planned in advance. Each question should be designed to elicit information that fits into the attorney's presentation, that is in accord with the theory of the case.

Of course, it is not always possible to know with certainty the answer that a witness will give. However, whenever possible, witnesses should be interviewed and their testimony reviewed before it is presented to a judge or jury. The following tips will be helpful in developing good habits in dealing with prospective witnesses:

- Explain the process to the prospective witness. Make certain the witness understands what the trial is about and what role he or she will play.
- Be certain that the witness understands that there is nothing improper about discussing his or her testimony with you prior to trial. Be equally certain to advise the witness to answer truthfully if questioned about having met or discussed the case with you.
- Explain that the witness will only be expected to testify about facts within his or her knowledge. No one will pressure him or her to say anything that is not the truth.
- Suggest means of improving delivery. If the witness has a problem with expression or language, it may be necessary to devote time and attention to rectifying those problems.
- Always let the witness tell his or her story. Never suggest an answer that does not conform to the witness's own recollection.
- Explain what objections are so that the witness will not become flustered if objections are made during his or her testimony.
- Explain about cross-examination so that the witness knows what to expect.
- Explain that the witness cannot be forced to testify to facts beyond his or her knowledge. If a question is asked and the witness does not know the answer, "I do not know" is a perfectly good response.
- Make sure that the witness understands that it is permissible for him or her to offer an explanation if the answer to a question requires one.
- Even though the witness can give explanations as needed, impress the fact that answers should be direct and not offer information not requested. For example, if the question is "Where do you work?" the only information requested is the name of the employer. There is no need to add, "I have worked there since I got out of prison ten years ago." (The example is not as far-fetched as it may seem!)

- If the witness's testimony will require identification of documents or other exhibits, make certain that the witness sees and can identify the material at the interview.
- Do not reveal a client's confidential disclosures to a witness. Also, remember, a witness's disclosures to you are not covered by attorney/client privilege.
- Give the witness the opportunity to ask questions regarding procedures, the trial, or any other matters that may be of concern.
- Make certain that the witness understands that you and the attorney for whom you work do not represent him or her (the witness). If the witness seeks advice or counsel beyond the area of procedure, explain that the advice should come from his or her own counsel.

Developing a System of Interviewing. It is important that you develop a system of your own for interviews. It may be wise to prepare a checklist of pointers to guide you through each interview. The key points of witness preparation are

1. Explain the process to the witness.
2. Build the witness's confidence.
3. Stress truthfulness.
4. Explore the witness's knowledge thoroughly.

POINTER: (Recording the Interview)
Considering Rule 26.2 of the Federal Rules of Criminal Procedure, a tape-recorded statement of a witness or a recorded interview of a witness's testimony is discoverable after the witness has testified.

Securing the Presence of a Witness at Trial. The attendance of a witness at trial can be assured only through the subpoena process. In many instances, a witness will voluntarily appear without the issuance of a subpoena; however, to protect against a last-minute change of heart by a prospective witness, a subpoena is required.

A **subpoena**, an order of the court commanding the person named in it to appear, must be obeyed under penalty (*sub poena*) of law. In state prosecutions, a court can usually order the appearance of any person who lives within the state. Under special circumstances, a court can issue a warrant for the arrest of a person who has fled the state in order to avoid testimony. This measure is somewhat extreme and is reserved for those instances in which the person has material evidence necessary to the prosecution or defense. The name by which such a warrant is known is either a material witness warrant or something very similar.

In federal jurisdictions, the general rule for witness attendance in criminal matters is that a subpoena may be served on a witness anywhere within the United States. If such service is made, the witness will be compelled to appear. Of course, the issuing party must advance travel expenses if the witness lives beyond the district within which the trial is scheduled.

Pretrial Cooperation of Witnesses. Securing the pretrial cooperation of a witness is a more difficult proposition than simply securing his or her appearance at trial. When discussing discovery devices in the previous chapter, we noted that the deposition of a witness can be ordered only under very limited circumstances. If a witness does not want to cooperate prior to trial, there is little either side can do.

The prosecution has something of an advantage in obtaining pretrial cooperation because of the persuasive effect of its authority. Yet even the prosecutor cannot force pretrial cooperation. The grand jury's investigative function cannot be used by the prosecutor to secure evidence once an indictment has been returned.

In the case of a reluctant witness, cooperation can sometimes be obtained by offering a full explanation of the witness's rights and why the testimony is required. Of course, it is better still to tender the explanation along with a subpoena for the witness's appearance at trial. Most reasonable persons would welcome the opportunity to discuss a matter being tried before being dragged into court.

If a witness is in possession of documents or other material needed as evidence, a subpoena duces tecum can be issued. **Subpoena duces tecum** literally means to appear and to have "documents with you."

Documentary Evidence

Documentary evidence refers to physical evidence in the form of papers, records, reports, letters, or other material that is relevant to the matter being tried. If you are planning to use documentary evidence, you must be prepared to prove its authenticity and its relevance. This type of evidence is usually identified and authenticated by a witness who has particular knowledge of the item. For example, you might want to use the minutes of a meeting of the board of directors of a corporation. In order to have the minutes introduced and admitted, you could call as a witness the secretary of the corporation who could identify the document as a record of the corporation, who could explain how it was prepared and how it is kept, and who could verify the authenticity of the material.

Once the authenticity of the document has been established, the issue of relevancy must be addressed. If the material is found to be authentic and relevant (by the judge), it may be admitted into the body of evidence and reviewed and examined by the jury.

Documentary evidence is conveniently defined for us in the Federal Rules of Evidence. The rules also define photographs. (See FED. R. EVID. 1001.) Rule 1002 of the Federal Rules of Evidence requires the use of originals for any writing, recording, or photograph; however, Rule 1003 allows for the use of duplicates unless a genuine question is raised as to the authenticity of the original or unless extraordinary circumstances make the use of a duplicate unfair.

Rule 1004 specifically allows proof of the contents of documents or recordings, without production of the original, if the original has been destroyed, is unobtainable, or is in the possession of an opposing party.

What all of this means is that the original document is preferred but a duplicate can be admitted unless there is a genuine dispute about its authenticity. And if the document, photo, or recording is not available or if it has been destroyed, testimony regarding its contents can be admitted into evidence.

Demonstrative Evidence

Demonstrative evidence, an evidence exhibit, consists of such material as photographs, diagrams, drawings, charts, graphs, and models that help to explain or graphically illustrate a characteristic, property, effect, or factual point. Demonstrative evidence means evidence that demonstrates. The judge retains a great deal of discretion in deciding whether or not to allow use and/or admission of demonstrative material into evidence.

Besides being relevant to the issues at hand, demonstrative material must be accurate in its depiction of a fact or condition, and it must be helpful to the jury (or judge) in understanding the testimony of a witness. Photographs must accurately depict the subject. For example, if the subject of the photograph is a crime scene, the witness who introduces the photo should testify that the picture shows the scene precisely as it appeared when the crime was committed. If there is no testimony to establish the accuracy of the depiction, the photo cannot be admitted into evidence.

It is usually *not* necessary to produce the photographer who took the photo or the person who developed the film. Testimony regarding the accuracy of the depiction is ordinarily sufficient.

Diagrams and charts are useful in many cases. The accuracy of the drawing or chart is of paramount importance. There is usually no requirement that the material be professionally produced. In fact, it usually falls to the paralegal to prepare charts and diagrams or, at the very least, to assist in their preparation.

A witness may illustrate with a drawing or chart made during the course of his or her testimony. In some instances, the drawing or chart need not be introduced into evidence. However, the better rule is to make an offer to introduce the item into evidence so that it can be referred to later in argument, examined by the jury, and used during deliberations.

Models and mechanical devices may be used if they can be helpful to the jury and if a witness can relate them to his or her testimony. The court retains discretion over the admission of such material into evidence. The witness may use a device or model to illustrate testimony without having the item introduced into evidence. Again, the better procedure would be to have the material introduced into evidence whenever possible.

OPENING STATEMENT

As the trial date nears, the focus of preparation shifts to those things that relate directly to the trial, and concerns become more directed toward presentation of the case. During the trial, the opening statement is the first order of business after the jury has been impaneled. It is not unusual for a paralegal to help prepare an opening statement. In fact, it is quite common that the preparation of an opening statement is a joint effort between the attorney and the paralegal.

More Than Just an Outline

In theory, the opening statement is not supposed to present argument or proof. It is designed to allow each party to outline the proof that it will present during the trial. As a practical matter, the opening statement is critical to the persuasion process and is much more than a mere outline of things to come.

The Jurors Do Not Wait for Evidence

As shown through studies, the people who comprise a jury do not wait for the evidence before making up their minds regarding guilt or innocence. What this means is that an opening statement is critical to the decision-making process. In many cases, a juror's decision flows from his or her subconscious. A juror's first choice regarding a verdict is usually the one he or she will stick with throughout a trial.

In the early 1960s, a study was performed at the University of Chicago Law School.[1] That study showed that had the jury voted immediately after the opening statements, the verdict would have been the same as it turned out after trial in 80 percent of the cases. This fact should point to the need to develop strong opening statements. A paralegal who is able to prepare good opening statements is a very valuable member of the trial team.

Never Waive an Opening Statement

In a criminal case, the prosecution *must* give an opening statement. The defense usually has an option: it may give a statement or pass over the opportunity. In most jurisdictions, the defense may defer its opening statement until the beginning of the defendant's presentation. Considering the material discussed in the preceding paragraphs, it should be apparent that an opening statement should never be waived. Although there may be a reason for deferring an opening statement, there is never a reason to waive one. Even postponing the opening address to the jury is risky business. It is very likely that jurors will have formulated firm opinions before the statement is made.

Prepare the Opening Statement Early

The paralegal who begins to think of an opening statement early is most likely to do the best job of preparation. It is no exaggeration to say that preparation of the opening statement should begin with the initial interview of the client or investigator. At that point, while considering the case theory, it is a good habit to mentally formulate the theory into a presentation for the jury. Much of the effort that goes into developing a theory of the case can be incorporated into the preparation of an opening statement. The five elements of the theory form a perfect framework for developing an opening statement. At the same time, the opening statement is a perfect vehicle for presentation of the theory of the case to the jury.

The First Minutes Are Critical

An audience remains alert for less than two minutes. After the first minute or so, the attention of your listeners diminishes. The primacy theory therefore asserts that the most important idea to be communicated to an audience should be the idea first enunciated to it. **Primacy** is a rhetorical technique that stresses the significance of the first position of an idea in an argument or a statement. Lead with your ace! Using our five elements of case theory, the ace is the *truth* that you want the jury to hear and remember.

Put Your Best Facts Forward

From the initial remarks, an opening statement must go on to explain all the supporting facts that the prosecution or defense will present. As mentioned earlier, it is better to use a narrative format to present these facts.

In detailing evidence to a jury, you should keep the primacy theory in mind. Remember, jurors will give their full attention to a presenter for only a short period of time. Consequently, it is imperative to drive home your biggest points while their attention is greatest.

Know the Players

It will be of great value in the preparation of an opening statement to know the tendencies and dispositions of the judge and the opposing attorney. There is no best way to obtain such information. Colleagues and associates can be very helpful in gathering impressions of the personnel who will participate in the trial.

CLOSING ARGUMENT

It must be recognized that a closing argument will not win a case that is beyond reach. An effective summation to the jury can tip the scale in situations where the strengths of a case are evenly divided between opposing parties.

If you have done a good job of preparing the opening statement, the closing argument will be much simpler to perfect. It is very difficult to accurately predict how the trial will unfold, thus allowing the paralegal to have the closing argument prepared before trial. To a large extent, the closing argument is prepared by the attorney who must deliver it.

Many attorneys will say that they want no assistance in preparing a closing argument, but some will admit that they require help. It matters little what the attorney says beforehand. The "thinking" paralegal working on the trial portion of a case must always be prepared to respond to this inevitable question: What do you think we should stress most?

When the question arises, some pointers can be helpful to the paralegal. All that has been discussed in relation to the opening statement applies with equal force to the closing argument.

- Place the strongest points for your side in a primary position.
- Relate the evidence to your theory of the case. Show how it logically supports the conclusion that you are asking the jury to draw.
- Anticipate the opposition's main points. Explain those points briefly and give your counterarguments fully.
- Do not try to cover every bit of evidence that has been produced during the trial. Stick to those facts that support a verdict favorable to your side.
- Emphasize the demonstrative evidence and photographs that support your theory.

As a rule, the paralegal will be expected to produce an outline for the closing argument. Most attorneys do not want a prepared speech to deliver to the jury. In preparing an outline, the paralegal will be able to rely heavily on the theory that was set out in the opening statement and developed throughout the trial.

SAMPLE CASE

In the following paragraphs, we develop a theory for a hypothetical case for both the prosecution and the defense for a routine criminal offense.

State v. John R. Williams

Johnny Williams was involved in a one-car accident. Late one evening he was driving home from the bowling alley where his team had just won the league championship. Johnny joined in the victory celebration following the match but cut short his participation because the hour was late and he had to be at work early the next morning.

During the festivities, everyone, including Johnny, was treated to beer by the establishment. A photograph of the champions shows the whole team lifting beer mugs in salute of their triumph.

None of the other participants recalls how much Johnny had to drink or if he had more than the one beer shown in the photo. Everyone remembered that he left soon after the party began and that he was not apparently intoxicated when he departed.

On the way home, Johnny's auto was forced off the road by a wild-driving motorist who did not stop to offer assistance. Johnny's car was disabled by

> ### *State v. John R. Williams (continued)*
>
> the accident, forcing him to walk to a nearby convenience store to call for road service. He was terribly discouraged by the damage to his new car and bought a six pack of beer to console himself.
>
> Johnny drank the beers on the walk back to the scene while waiting for the arrival of the tow truck. While he was waiting, the police patrolling the highway saw the troubled auto and stopped to investigate. They found Johnny sitting on the trunk of the car drinking beer and several empty beer cans in a bag next to the vehicle.
>
> When questioned, Johnny admitted that he had been driving the car and related his story to the officers. The police called an alcohol safety unit to the scene. Johnny tested over the legal limit for blood alcohol content. He was arrested for driving while intoxicated and now faces a trial on the charge.

The Prosecution's Theory of the Case

The Prosecution's Truth. The truth that the prosecutor seeks to establish is that Johnny drove his car while under the influence of alcohol.

The Prosecution's Hypothesis. Johnny began drinking at the bowling alley early in the evening and continued to drink through the victory celebration. When the hour got late, he had to get home and had no time to wait for someone to drive him; so he drove himself. An incident arose in which Johnny lost control of his vehicle, which proves his reflexes were impaired by alcohol.

Facts Relied on by the Prosecution. The supporting facts consist of the following:

- Johnny admitted to drinking beer before the incident.
- The photograph of the champs toasting their victory with beer was taken at least twenty-five minutes after the celebration began and immediately before Johnny drove off in his automobile.
- The police arrived on the scene within one hour after the accident.
- Johnny was legally drunk when the police arrived. It would be unlikely that the results of the breath test could reflect alcohol consumed only a short time before, as Johnny claims.
- Johnny admitted to swerving off the road while driving.
- Johnny was in possession of an open can of beer when first observed by the police.

The Argument of the Prosecution. The prosecution's argument takes the following form:

- John Williams did something before driving that could make him intoxicated: he drank beer at the victory party.
- He lost control of his vehicle while driving, as might be expected of an intoxicated driver.

- He was, in fact, legally intoxicated shortly after the incident.
- A reasonable inference would be that Johnny celebrated with his teammates for at least one-half hour and that the beer pictured in the photo was not his first.

The Conclusion Drawn by the Prosecution. Every known fact is consistent with the proposition that Johnny was driving his vehicle while under the influence of alcohol. Therefore, the logical conclusion is that he was in fact intoxicated while operating the vehicle.

The Defendant's Theory of the Case

The Defendant's Truth. The truth that the defense seeks to establish is that the prosecution's deduction is not the only one that can be drawn from the evidence. There is a reasonable conclusion that is consistent with innocence and that is supported by the facts of the case.

The Defendant's Hypothesis. Johnny acted responsibly all evening. He obviously was not drunk during the bowling match since he participated in a championship effort. He joined the victory party only long enough to appear in the traditional champions' photograph, after which he departed. Everyone who saw him prior to the incident says he did not appear intoxicated. There is no evidence that Johnny was drunk or even legally intoxicated at the time he left the party and began driving.

Facts Relied on by the Defendant. The supporting facts consist of the following:

- No one can swear that Johnny had more than one beer prior to driving.
- Johnny purchased and drank six beers after the incident, and he never drove again that evening.
- Johnny did not lose control of his vehicle; he was forced off the road by a reckless driver.
- Johnny's early departure from the party shows that he was acting responsibly when he began driving.
- Witnesses at the bowling alley state that Johnny did not appear to be drunk.

The Argument of the Defendant. The defense argument takes the following form:

- It is the responsibility of the prosecution to prove the case beyond a reasonable doubt. In this case, the prosecution did not carry out that burden.
- There is no direct evidence showing the level of alcohol in Johnny's blood before he began driving. The prosecution's theory relies entirely on circumstantial evidence.

■ The circumstantial evidence relied on by the state does not conclusively prove guilt because there is a plausible and reasonable conclusion that can be drawn from those facts that is consistent with Johnny's plea of not guilty.

■ Johnny's high blood/alcohol level was caused by the six beers he drank after the incident.

The Conclusion Drawn by the Defendant. The verdict must be not guilty because there is no direct evidence that Johnny drove his auto while intoxicated. The circumstantial evidence relied upon by the prosecution admits of another reasonable possibility, one consistent with innocence.

ENDNOTES

1   Richard J. Crawford, *The Persuasion Edge* (Eau Claire, Wis.: Professional Educational Systems, 1989), 104.

7 YOUR DAY IN COURT

The time comes when all pretrial preparations and preliminary maneuvering have been concluded, the case theory is fully developed, all the witnesses have been interviewed, and the day of trial arrives. It is then your day in court.

A trial has been compared to major surgery. If a similarity exists, it is only that both processes can have an immediate and dramatic effect upon the condition of the subject. For the trial participants, there is no restricted access. There are no off-limit areas providing the seclusion offered to the physician. When surgeons perform their life-altering operations, they work privately, surrounded by staff and life support specialists, all working toward the same goal. When the trial team operates, it does so publicly, with an assembly of adversaries contesting every move. The Sixth Amendment mandates that trials shall be public, open to all.

WHO WILL JUDGE THE FACTS, JUDGE OR JURY?

The verdict in a criminal trial is a question of fact. The facts are determined by a jury or a judge after hearing and considering all admissible evidence. In our criminal justice system, a trial may be conducted before a judge alone or before a judge and a jury.

In a judge-only trial, the presiding official (judge) is the arbiter of law and fact. In a trial with both a judge and a jury, the judge decides questions of law and procedure, but the jury decides issues of fact.

The difference between procedure and fact is easily demonstrated. Consider the hypothetical situation in which the prosecution calls a witness to explain the meaning of a document that has been admitted into evidence. The defense objects to the testimony by claiming that the document speaks

111

for itself and does not need interpretation. Two issues are presented by the situation:

1. *The first issue is one of procedure.* Should the testimony of the witness be admitted? This issue is decided by the judge.
2. *The second issue is one of fact.* How much weight and credibility should be given to the testimony? This issue is a question of fact and will be decided by the trier of fact (ordinarily a jury). The **trier of fact** is the entity, either a judge or a jury, that weighs evidence and determines the verdict. As noted above, in a criminal proceeding the jury is usually the trier of fact.

When Is a Jury Required?

The Constitution (Sixth Amendment) guarantees criminal defendants the right to trial by jury. The Supreme Court has recognized that the right to a jury trial extends to defendants charged in state court as well as to defendants in federal prosecutions. See *Duncan v. Louisiana*, 391 U.S. 145 (1968).

The guarantee of a trial by jury attaches whenever conviction subjects the defendant to possible imprisonment of six months or more. See *Baldwin v. New York*, 399 U.S. 66 (1968). There is no constitutional right to a jury trial for petty offenses (*Duncan v. Louisiana, supra*); however, some states do afford a jury trial for all cases where incarceration is possible, even for minimal sentences.

How Many Jurors?

The federal system provides that juries in all criminal cases be composed of twelve persons. The verdict in federal jury cases must be unanimous. If the parties agree in writing to a lesser number of jurors, the jury may have fewer than twelve members, but the verdict must still be unanimous.

The rule establishing a twelve-member jury has an interesting aspect. (See Figure 7-1.) If the court finds it necessary to excuse a juror after the jury has begun its deliberation, a valid verdict may be returned by the remaining eleven jurors.

FIGURE 7-1   RULE GOVERNING NUMBER OF JURY MEMBERS

(b) Jury of Less Than Twelve—Juries shall be of 12 but at any time before a verdict the parties may stipulate in writing with the approval of the court that the jury shall consist of any number less than 12 or that a valid verdict may be returned by a jury less than 12 should the court find it necessary to excuse one or more of the jurors for any just cause after the trial commences. *Even absent such stipulation, if the court finds it necessary to excuse a juror for just cause after the jury has retired to consider its verdict, in the discretion of the court a valid verdict may be returned by the remaining 11 jurors.* (Emphasis added)

FED. R. CRIM. P. 23(b)

In state court prosecutions, a twelve-person jury is not always required. In the case of *Williams v. Florida*, 399 U.S. 78 (1970), the Supreme Court held that a six-person jury fulfills the constitutional requirement of trial by jury. The reasoning of the Court in the *Williams* case stipulated that a six-member jury has the "essential feature of a jury." The opinion identified the essential feature as the "interposition between the accused and his accuser."

Though a six-member jury has been approved by the Supreme Court, a five-member jury has been held unconstitutional. See *Ballew v. Georgia*, 435 U.S. 323 (1978).

How Many Jurors Must Agree on a Verdict?

According to the Supreme Court, the verdict of a six-member jury must be unanimous. That opinion came in another of a stream of Louisiana cases that the court decided in the 1970s. See *Burch v. Louisiana*, 441 U.S. 130 (1979). However, the Court held that the Constitution does not require unanimity for a verdict in a twelve-member jury sitting in a state court prosecution. See *Johnson v. Louisiana*, 406 U.S. 356 (1972).

In order to determine the number of jurors required in various state court prosecutions, it is necessary to refer to local statutes. The size of a jury and the number who must concur for a valid verdict varies from state to state, but the jury size and concurrence requirements do not vary from district to district within a state. Generally, size and concurrence specifications are determined by the maximum penalty for the charged offense.

Waiver of a Jury

The federal rules and the rules pertaining in the several states allow for a waiver of a jury for most crimes. In the federal system, the defendant, the prosecutor, and the court must all agree to a waiver of the jury. (See Figure 7-2.) This rule is typical of the rules found in most state jurisdictions. Procedures surrounding a trial without a jury are also covered by the federal rules. (See Figure 7-3.)

FIGURE 7-2   WAIVER OF A TRIAL BY JURY

(a) Trial by Jury—Cases required to be tried by jury shall be so tried unless the defendant waives a jury trial in writing with the approval of the court and the consent of the government.

FED. R. CRIM. P. 23(a)

However, unlike the federal system, some states do not require the concurrence of the prosecution in the decision to waive a jury. Interestingly, the Supreme Court has held that there is no constitutionally protected right to a trial without a jury. See *Singer v. United States*, 380 U.S. 24 (1965).

In deciding to waive a jury, it is particularly important for the parties to know the disposition and propensities of the presiding judge. Some judges appreciate the waiver because it streamlines proceedings and leaves much less room for error. Other judges dislike the idea of presiding without a jury because of the added burden it places upon them.

FIGURE 7-3   A TRIAL WITHOUT A JURY PERMITS THE COURT TO MAKE A GENERAL FINDING

(c) **Trial Without a Jury**—In a case tried without a jury the court shall make a general finding and shall in addition, on request made before the general finding, find the facts specially. Such findings may be oral. If an opinion or memorandum of decision is filed, it will be sufficient if the findings appear therein.

FED. R. CRIM. P. 23(c)

Is Waiver of a Jury a Good Idea?

As alluded to earlier, a waiver of a jury can simplify and streamline a trial. If a general rule is possible regarding waiver of a jury, it is that a waiver is usually more advantageous to the prosecution than to the defense.

In a trial by jury, there are potential irregularities that do not exist in a trial by judge alone. Some of these irregularities may result in a mistrial or a reversal by the appeals court. And, too, there is always the possibility that one or more jurors will be reluctant to find a defendant guilty without the strongest possible proof. Most potential problems can be eliminated by the waiver of a jury trial, which is why it is generally regarded as a procedural device more favorable to the prosecution.

However, despite this general rule, a defendant may at times feel that he or she will receive a fairer trial from a judge sitting alone. If the case presents very complex issues, if the defense is a very technical one, if the case involves voluminous documentary evidence, or if the issue is a very emotional one, there may be good reason to consider waiver of a jury. A paralegal should *tactfully* encourage an attorney to make a decision regarding waiver of the jury as early as possible because trial preparation will be affected by this decision.

JURY SELECTION

If a case is to be tried by a jury, the first order of business on the day of trial is to select the persons who will make up the panel. Earlier we identified *voir dire* as the selection process for impaneling a jury. In theory, the parties use the selection process to choose jurors who will decide the case objectively, applying the law as disclosed by the judge to the facts as established by competent evidence. From the practical viewpoint, the parties use *voir dire* to select jurors who will be sympathetic to their positions. The rationale here is that objectivity is best when it is tempered with empathy.

During the selection process, prospective jurors are questioned to determine their attitudes and background. The cynic might conclude that jurors are selected for their ignorance. If a person knows anything of the history of the case or has any personal knowledge of the defendant or the attorneys, that person is ordinarily disqualified from service on the jury.

What Type of Person for the Jury?

The parties going into the selection process should have a clear idea of the type of person wanted to serve on the jury. It is becoming increasingly popular to use expert assistance in developing a profile for the most suitable juror. A psychological sketch of the ideal candidate can be formulated by professionals, such as a psychologist; and used to screen potential jurors.

Prior to the beginning of trial, it is often possible to obtain a list of the general venire. The **venire** is the larger array of persons from which the smaller jury pool will be assembled. Working with the list and public information available through public records and published guides such as city and suburban directories, a paralegal or investigator can turn up a great deal of information about prospective jurors before a case begins.

The Mock Jury

One of the newer developments in trial preparation is the use of mock juries. Prior to trial, a **mock** (simulated) **jury** can be assembled from persons in the same community from which the real jury will be picked. Its purpose is to review the evidence as though it were trying the case. The reactions of mock jurors to evidence and issues can be very helpful in profiling the type of person most desirable as a trial juror. Mock juries can also be helpful in planning for the real trial.

Contact with Prospective Jurors

Sometimes, out of zeal to thoroughly investigate prospective jurors, a paralegal may be inclined to contact members of the venire or their families. Even if the court allows the identities of prospective jurors to be known before trial, contact with potential jurors is not allowed. In fact, many courts will not allow the venire to be identified.

Every court, federal and state, has rules that limit contact between the parties, their attorneys, and prospective jurors prior to trial. See Figure 7-4 for an example of a state rule from the Eastern, Western, and Middle districts of Louisiana that limits this contact.

FIGURE 7-4   CONTACT WITH PROSPECTIVE JURORS PRIOR TO TRIAL IS LIMITED

Prospective jurors shall not be contacted, either directly or through any member of their immediate family, in an effort to secure information concerning the background of any member of the jury panel.

UNIF. DIST. CT. R. 13.04

Contact with Jurors after Trial

While we are discussing the subject of contacting prospective jurors, it may be wise to discuss the issue of contact with former jurors. Although it may be very informative and instructive to discuss a case with a person who served on the jury, great care must be taken to avoid violating court rules concerning such contact. Even after a trial has been concluded, the courts take particular interest in protecting the privacy and security of jurors, as seen in Figure 7-5, which is also taken from the local rules of the Eastern, Western, and Middle districts of Louisiana.

FIGURE 7-5   THE PRIVACY AND SECURITY OF JURORS IS PROTECTED

a. No juror has any obligation to speak to any person about any case and may refuse all interviews or comments.

b. No person may make repeated requests for interviews or questions after a juror has expressed his or her desire not to be interviewed.

UNIF. DIST. CT. R. 13.05

Some jurisdictions prohibit all contact between attorneys or parties and former jurors. The pertinent section of the local rules established for the U.S. district court in the Middle District of Florida (see Figure 7-6) is an example. *The point to be understood here is that precautions must be taken before a former juror is contacted. It is extremely important that attorneys and paralegals be aware of all rules covering the matter before an attempt is made to speak with a former juror.*

FIGURE 7-6   CONTACT WITH FORMER JURORS IS SOMETIMES PROHIBITED

No attorney or party shall undertake, directly or indirectly, to interview any juror after trial in any civil or criminal case except as permitted by this Rule. If a party believes that grounds for legal challenge to a verdict exists, he may move for an order permitting an interview of a juror or jurors to determine whether the verdict is subject to challenge.

U.S. DIST. CT. 5.01(d)

The Selection Process

The type of preparation required for *voir dire* is determined by the method the court uses to select the jury. A good overview of possible selection methods can be gathered by examining the federal rule. (See Figure 7-7.) In order to determine the selection process used in a particular jurisdiction, the local rules of court must be consulted.

FIGURE 7-7   POSSIBLE JURY SELECTION METHODS

> **(a) Examination**—The court may permit the defendant or the defendant's attorney and the attorney for the government to conduct the examination of prospective jurors or may itself conduct the examination. In the latter event the court shall permit the defendant or the defendant's attorney and the attorney for the government to supplement the examination by such further inquiry as it deems proper or shall itself submit to the prospective jurors such additional questions by the parties or their attorneys as it deems proper.
>
> FED. R. CRIM. P. 24(a)

Because it slows down the selection process, many courts are abandoning the practice of allowing attorneys to personally conduct *voir dire.* Instead, the examination of prospective jurors is performed by the presiding judge. But even if the judge conducts *voir dire,* parties are given the opportunity to suggest questions. Proposed questions usually must be submitted in writing before trial.

If written *voir dire* suggestions for the court are to be submitted, it is very likely that a paralegal will prepare the material. Usually the submission consists of a list of questions or a list of issues from which questions may be formulated.

Many jurisdictions still allow attorneys to conduct the examination of potential jurors. The *voir dire* process gives the attorney an opportunity to have two-way communication with the jurors. At no other time during the trial is either party able to elicit responses from members of the jury. This is the chief reason why many trial lawyers covet the opportunity to personally conduct the examination of jurors.

When paralegals are given an assignment to help prepare for the examination of prospective jurors, they must determine from the attorney exactly what is expected. Usually the attorney wants only a list of issues with which to work. Some attorneys prefer to have specific questions prepared.

 POINTER: The exchange between attorney and juror that occurs during *voir dire* affords an excellent opportunity to present the essentials of the case theory. Major factors important to the case should be worked into the questions and suggestions.

Rejection of Jurors

Prospects for jury duty may be rejected in two ways. The judge may eliminate prospects who are unqualified or for whom jury service may be a hardship. The parties may dismiss potential jurors by exercising peremptory challenges even if jurors possess all necessary qualifications for serving.

Dismissal, or Excuse, for Cause.   In ruling on the qualifications of prospective jurors, the court has the duty to dismiss any person who is unqualified for service on the jury. Dismissal by the court is referred to as dismissal for cause. **Dismissal, or excuse, for cause**, formally defined, is the rejection of a prospective juror by the court because he or she is in some manner unqualified to serve as a juror on the case. There is no limit to the number of persons who may be disqualified for cause in a particular trial.

Any number of factors may constitute cause to dismiss a prospective juror. If the person knows any of the parties or attorneys, if the person has preconceived ideas regarding the guilt or innocence of the defendant, if the person is biased in any way that will prevent objectivity, or if the prospect has a pressing personal problem, such as illness, the court may exercise its prerogative to discharge the person from serving on the jury.

Peremptory Challenges. Instances occur when the jury candidate meets all the qualifications for service but one of the parties, for any reason, *or for no apparent reason*, does not want the candidate to serve on the jury. Each side may dismiss prospective jurors peremptorily, without stating a reason, by exercising a peremptory challenge. A **peremptory challenge** is the dismissal of a prospective juror by a party. No cause needs to be stated by the dismissing party when rejecting a juror.

Unlike dismissal for cause, there is a limit to the number of peremptory challenges that a party may exercise. The number of peremptory challenges is set in the law and rules of each jurisdiction. In the federal system, the number of challenges allotted to each side is found in Rule 24 of the Federal Rules of Criminal Procedure. In an ordinary federal case, the prosecution may exercise six peremptory challenges and the defense may excuse ten persons peremptorily. If the case involves multiple defendants, the court may grant additional peremptory challenges to the defense to be exercised individually or jointly. In a capital case, each side is entitled to twenty challenges.

Jury Selection and Duties of the Paralegal

Paralegals can play an active role in the selection process. Paralegals usually assist by keeping track of potential jurors. The job entails noting the answers given to *voir dire* questions, checking jurors for desirable and undesirable traits, observing members of the pool to determine whether they fit the predetermined juror profile, and keeping records of the challenges used by each side.

Each judge may use a different method for calling and seating prospective jurors. There are times when the record-keeping process can be quite confusing. Some judges will speed through the selection process to get the trial started. The paralegal working on this phase of the case will find it intricate and demanding.

A simple but effective way to keep track of jurors as they are seated in the jury box is by chart. A sheet of paper can be sectioned into the appropriate number of spaces, usually twelve or six, corresponding numerically to the seat occupied by each prospective juror. As a candidate is called, his or her name is inserted in the appropriate section on the sheet. Notations can be made in the sections concerning answers given by the prospect and challenges can be marked in the section as they are used. (See Figure 7-8.)

FIGURE 7-8 JURY SELECTION CHART

POSITION 1	POSITION 2	POSITION 3	POSITION 4	POSITION 5	POSITION 6
POSITION 7	POSITION 8	POSITION 9	POSITION 10	POSITION 11	POSITION 12

CHALLENGES USED

Prosecution:

Defense:

Those paralegals who work with the defense may find that the most demanding aspect of the selection process is listening to and conferring with the client while the selection is being made. It will be helpful if *voir dire* is fully explained to the client before the selection process begins.

The Shadow Jury

Earlier we discussed the use of a mock jury during the preparation phase to help refine the presentation that will be made at the actual trial. When the trial begins, another device, which is gaining in popularity, may be implemented. It also involves the use of a group of people selected to simulate the jury. It is called a shadow jury. A shadow jury is different from a mock jury because it is employed while the trial is in progress. It makes good sense to explain the use of shadow juries while we are considering the subject of jurors.

The idea of a shadow jury is relatively new and must be researched thoroughly in each jurisdiction before it is attempted. A **shadow jury** is a privately hired group of individuals, having no official status, who are paid by a party to sit through a trial to hear and see the presentation in the same way that the real jury makes its observations. The group is selected to closely resemble the actual jury in demographic composition—sex, race, social status—and in as many other ways as possible to test the effectiveness of evidence and presentation.

After each day's presentation, the shadow jury may be consulted by the party who has hired it to determine the effect of evidence, issues, and other developments of the day. The information thus garnered may be used to shore up weakness in the case and to capitalize on strong points.

Several problems are obvious when considering a shadow jury. One of the more significant concerns is cost. The average defendant is not likely to be in a position to pay the substantial expense associated with the process. Then there is the problem of space. Since the likelihood exists that any case significant enough to warrant the use of a shadow jury will also attract great public attention, there is no way to assure the accommodation of the private panel at each session of trial unless the cooperation of the court is obtained.

Court approval is necessary because a shadow jury must be moved in and out of the courtroom, just as the real jury, so that it will not be influenced by material unknown to the real jury. Such a process can be disruptive and would be nearly impossible without the court's cooperation.

The shadow jury is currently being used most frequently in civil cases. However, it presents interesting possibilities for criminal trials. In some ways the concept is not at all new. The idea of having an observer sit through the trial and critique the evidence and issues has been around as long as the jury system. The new twist, added in the shadow jury concept, involves the notion of matching the features of the shadow observers to the characteristics of the jury. Even if a client cannot afford to hire a full shadow jury for an entire trial, a modified version of the concept could prove helpful in almost every case.

ORDER OF TRIAL

Criminal trials generally follow the same order whether they are conducted in state or federal court.

1. *Jury selection.* No limit is permitted on the number of prospective jurors who can be excused for cause.

    The number of peremptory challenges allowed to each party may change from state to state and court to court.

In federal district courts, the prosecution is ordinarily granted six peremptory challenges; the defense is granted ten.

The judge retains discretion to increase the number of peremptory challenges in multidefendant trials.

2. *Opening statements.* The prosecution is required to make an opening statement at the beginning of trial.

The defense may waive its opening statement or reserve its statement until the beginning of the defense portion of the trial.

3. *Case in chief.* The prosecution presents evidence first. It must produce proof of all elements of the offense beyond a reasonable doubt during the case in chief. *The prosecution may not call the defendant to testify.*

The **case in chief** is the first stage in the presentation of evidence at trial by the prosecution and the defense. It constitutes the portion of the trial when parties may present evidence on any and all relevant issues. It should be distinguished from the rebuttal or surrebuttal stage of trial when evidence may be presented only on specific issues that have been previously addressed by an opponent.

The defense may cross-examine prosecution witnesses and object to offers of evidence made by the prosecution, but it may not offer defense evidence during the prosecution's case in chief. The defense may, with leave of the court, introduce and offer as evidence exhibits that are used in cross-examination.

4. *Defense presentation.* The defense may offer evidence, including testimony of the defendant. *The defendant retains the right to remain silent and need not testify in his or her defense.*

The defense may elect to put on no evidence, in which case, the trial moves directly to closing arguments.

5. *Prosecution rebuttal.* The court may allow a rebuttal presentation by the prosecution. However, the evidence produced during rebuttal must truly rebut evidence that was produced by the defense. The prosecution cannot sandbag, that is, withhold evidence from the case in chief and introduce it late in the trial after the defense presentation.

6. *Defense surrebuttal.* If the defense needs a surrebuttal to confront evidence produced during rebuttal, the court can allow such a request. However, a judge may deny surrebuttal if the evidence to be offered is merely cumulative. Formally defined, a **surrebuttal** is that portion of a trial, coming after the prosecution's rebuttal, when the court may allow the defense to present additional evidence, usually on a narrowly defined issue or issues.

7. *Reopening the case.* The court may, in its discretion, allow a case to be reopened for additional evidence. This is not a favored practice among trial judges; however, it is not extraordinarily uncommon.

8. ***Prosecution closing argument.*** The prosecution must deliver the first closing argument. It should cover all evidence and issues raised during trial.
9. ***Defense closing argument.*** The defense's closing argument is delivered after the prosecution's argument. In addition to covering all evidence and issues, it should include whatever rebuttal the defense deems necessary because it is the defense's final opportunity to address the jury.
10. ***Prosecution's rebuttal argument.*** The prosecution is given the opportunity to address the jury in rebuttal of the arguments and issues raised by the defense during its closing argument. No new issues should be raised at this juncture.
11. ***Court's instruction to the jury.*** The court addresses the jury and instructs it on the law relevant to the issues raised during trial and on the duties and obligations of the jury during deliberations.
12. ***Jury deliberation.*** The jury retires from the courtroom and begins its deliberation. It may have access to the indictment or bill of information and all evidence exhibits.
13. ***Jury verdict.*** When the jury has reached a verdict, or if it is unable to reach a verdict, it notifies the judge and the outcome of deliberations is announced in open court with all parties present.

DUTIES OF THE PARALEGAL DURING TRIAL

The following paragraphs present explanations of the tasks that may be expected of a paralegal as a trial passes through its stages.

Opening Statements

The first order of business after the jury has been selected and sworn is the opening statement. In the previous chapter, we learned about the importance of the opening statement and some techniques regarding its preparation and presentation.

The prosecutor is the first to speak. The paralegal has obviously completed all of his or her work on the opening statement before the trial begins; however, two points should be kept in mind regarding the duties of the paralegal while the opening statements are in progress:

■ *First, if the paralegal sits at the counsel table during the trial, he or she should be (or appear to be) totally attentive.* It is very likely that the paralegal who has poured effort and soul into getting a case ready will be present when the opening statement is made. During the presentation of the opening statement, it is important for the paralegal to be attentive and alert. Sometimes a temptation arises to shuffle files or to engage in other activities in preparation for the upcoming witnesses. The jury, however, will detect a lack of interest if the paralegal is distracted by other activities.

■ *Second, the paralegal sitting in the courtroom near the jury has an opportunity to observe the jurors while opening statements are being made.* Often a juror will display an important sign: an involuntary nod of assent or dissent; a look of confusion or understanding; an indication of boredom or a lack of interest. Such observations can be helpful in shaping further presentations to suit the jury panel.

Presentation of Evidence

In the trial of a criminal case, the prosecution is first to present its case in chief. As noted earlier, this is the primary evidence presentation portion of the trial. It is called in chief to distinguish it from the rebuttal, when evidence may also be introduced. During the case in chief the prosecution must produce evidence proving all of the elements of the crime charged.

The prosecution will ordinarily be afforded the opportunity to present rebuttal evidence after the defense has presented its case in chief. At the discretion of the court, and if justice requires, the defense may be allowed a surrebuttal after the prosecution's rebuttal. In all of the evidence stages of the trial, the duties of the paralegal are the same.

As discussed in the preceding chapter, evidence can be in the form of testimony, documents, photographs, movies, physical evidence (the weapon, the narcotics, etc.), audio or videotape recordings or many forms of demonstrative exhibits. The paralegal must be prepared to deal with evidence of all types.

Witnesses

Testimony from witnesses forms the major part of the evidence in most cases. Paralegals assisting at trial will be expected to have folders prepared on each witness. The files should contain a list of the facts expected to be proved by the witness, any statements given by the witness, and research notes concerning possible objections to the witness's testimony.

If a witness has entered into a plea agreement with the prosecution or has been granted immunity in return for his or her testimony, the agreement and/or immunity order should be included in the folder. If the witness has a previous criminal record, that information should also be found in the witness's folder.

The paralegal will also be expected to keep tabs on witnesses who are waiting to testify. Usually a witness is not allowed in the courtroom prior to being called to give testimony. Scheduling the appearance of witnesses is part of the process. The paralegal and the attorney usually plan the presentation so that all witnesses do not have to be present during the entire proceeding. Getting witnesses into the courthouse on schedule is an important part of the paralegal's job. Scheduling can become cumbersome in cases that run more than a day or two.

In many cases, more than one lawyer represents each side. The prosecution almost always has more than one attorney. The presence of a second attorney gives the paralegal more time to schedule and coordinate appearances of witnesses. In those instances where only one attorney and one paralegal represent a party, the coordination of witness appearances must be carefully planned to avoid confusion.

Though the responsibility for a witness's presence at trial usually falls to the paralegal, in larger defense firms and in all prosecution offices, clerical help is available to coordinate travel and accommodations. Whenever possible, the paralegal should utilize the assistance of other office personnel to get witnesses to court on time.

Evidence Exhibits

A paralegal with the responsibility of keeping evidence exhibits in proper order should properly mark and list all exhibits prior to trial. Most courts require that evidence that will be offered at trial to have been marked, identified, and disclosed to the opposing party before the trial commences.

Local rules must be consulted concerning evidence exhibits because directives about their identification will be found there. Again, the rule from the U.S. District Court of the Middle District of Florida is a good example of how courts regulate this matter. (See Figure 7-9.)

FIGURE 7-9   LOCAL RULES DIRECT THE IDENTIFICATION PROCEDURES FOR EVIDENCE EXHIBITS

(a) Counsel for each party in any case shall obtain from the Clerk, in advance of trial, tabs or labels for the marking and identification of each exhibit proposed to be offered in evidence or otherwise tendered to any witness during trial.

(b) Upon marking the exhibits counsel shall also prepare a list of such exhibits, in sequence, with a descriptive notation sufficient to identify each separate numbered exhibit, and shall furnish copies of the list to opposing counsel and two copies to the Court at the commencement of trial.

U.S. Dist. Ct. Mid. Dist. of Fla. R. 301

Exhibits are usually marked in a manner that identifies the introducing party. Prosecution exhibits are commonly identified by the letters *S* or *G*, denoting *State* or *Government*. The letter is followed by a number. Thus, a typical prosecution exhibit would be identified as S-3 or G-5. Defense exhibits are marked D-1, D-2, etc. When more than one defendant is involved in a trial, the exhibit markings are chosen to reflect the identity of the defendant offering the item, such as W-7 (the seventh exhibit for defendant Williams). A typical exhibit list could look like the one depicted in Table 7-1.

The paralegal should keep a running list of exhibits offered by each side with appropriate notations to indicate whether or not the exhibit has been admitted into evidence by the court. By using a list as illustrated, a paralegal is able to note all objections and anticipated objections to exhibits.

TABLE 7-1 GOVERNMENT EXHIBIT LIST

Exhibit	Description	Anticipated Objection	Objection Raised	Offered	Admitted
G-1	Bag of white powder	improper evidence chain		yes	yes
G-2	Lab report	none		yes	yes
G-3	Videotape	none		yes	yes
G-4	Confession	*Miranda* not given			
G-5	Photo of defendant's apartment	irrelevant			

By anticipating objections likely to be made by the opposition and planning in advance objections to exhibits presented by the opposition, the attorney and paralegal will be able to devote more attention to other details of the trial. Also, the list makes a good reference document if and when an appeal is considered.

The columns for "Offered" and "Admitted" are extremely important in a long trial or in a trial with many documents or other exhibits. As unlikely as it may seem, it is easy to lose track of exhibits during the proceedings unless a system is in place to safeguard against such oversights.

Defense Presentation, Rebuttal, and Surrebuttal and the Motion for Judgment of Acquittal

The duties of paralegals regarding the handling and tracking of witnesses and evidence is generally the same whether working for the prosecution or the defense.

A procedural point of major significance to the conduct of the trial, the motion for judgment of acquittal, is a procedural move that helps demonstrate why good record keeping during a trial is a necessity. After the conclusion of the prosecution's case, if a deficit of evidence exists with respect to any of the elements of the offense, the trial can be terminated by the court's granting a judgment of acquittal. The judgment of acquittal is based on a finding by the court that a reasonable jury, relying solely on the evidence presented, would necessarily acquit the defendant.

The court may enter a judgment acquitting the defendant on the motion of the defense or on its own motion. The judgment may be on all counts of the indictment or information, or it may be on any number of the counts being tried.

Although the court may enter a judgment on its own (*sua sponte*), that is, without the urging of the defense, it is imperative that the defense be prepared to make and support such a motion.

A motion to acquit must not be made within the hearing of the jury. It may be made at the close of the government's case in chief or at the close of all evidence, that is, after the defense has rested. The court must rule on a motion made after the close of the prosecution's case in chief. It cannot reserve, withhold, or postpone its ruling until a later part of the trial. On a motion made after the close of all evidence, the court *may* reserve its ruling until the jury returns its verdict. If a verdict of guilty is returned, the court may set aside the verdict and enter a judgment of acquittal; however, a judgment of acquittal granted after the jury has returned a guilty verdict may be appealed by the prosecution.

In the federal system, the procedure for making and disposing of a motion for acquittal is contained in Rule 29 of the Federal Rules of Criminal Procedure. In deciding a motion for acquittal, the court must view the evidence in a light favorable to the government; that is, if two equally plausible conclusions can be drawn from the evidence, one consistent with guilt, the other consistent with innocence, the court must adopt the conclusion consistent with guilt and deny a motion for judgment of acquittal. See *United States v. Mundt*, 846 F.2d 1157 (8th Cir. 1988).

For the paralegal working with the prosecution, it is important to chart the presentation of evidence well in advance of trial so that no question surfaces about the proof for each essential element. Such preparation reflects back upon our discussion of the theory of the case. If the theory is well conceived and set out, there should be no problem in meeting the proof requirements of the case.

When the paralegal is part of the defense team, each element of the offense must be charted in advance of trial and careful notes kept regarding the evidence offered to prove each element. If the evidence is lacking or flimsy on any essential element of the crime, that fact could result in a judgment of acquittal.

Closing Arguments

The duties of the paralegal regarding closing arguments vary from assignment to assignment, depending on who tries the case. Some lawyers expect greater input from paralegals than others.

Generally speaking, the closing argument can be anticipated prior to trial, but it cannot be formally prepared until all the evidence is in. As discussed in the previous chapter, usually the attorney expects only an outline submission for the closing argument from the paralegal.

Possibly the outline may be done in advance of trial, especially for cases where discovery has been extensive. Even in those instances where an outline is prepared in advance and no surprises arise during the trial, the layout must be supplemented and augmented during trial to reference all evidence actually produced.

In every trial, some portion of the evidence takes on critical significance. In some instances, the evidence that proves to be critical at trial is not the same as that which was anticipated. In those instances, the meaningful evidence must be worked into the outline for the closing argument.

As in the case of the opening statement, the paralegal present in the courtroom during the closing argument must remain attentive and interested in the presentation. If the paralegal displays boredom or disinterest that is detected by the jury, the results could be ruinous.

Instructions to the Jury

The court has a duty to instruct the jury regarding the law and procedure prior to the beginning of its deliberations. **Jury instruction**, a statement of the law made to the jury before deliberations begin, is usually prepared by the court; however, some state jurisdictions require that the prosecution prepare the instructions, which will then be given to the jury by the judge.

Before the instructions are delivered to the jury by the judge, the parties must be given the opportunity to submit requested instructions, sometimes called charges, to the court. The court will then decide whether or not to include the requested charges in its jury instruction. The procedures followed by the courts in all federal districts and in state jurisdictions with respect to jury instructions is virtually identical. The federal rule is suitably instructive. (See Figure 7-10.)

FIGURE 7-10   PROCEDURE FOR DELIVERING JURY INSTRUCTIONS

At the close of the evidence or at such earlier time during the trial as the court reasonably directs, any party may file written requests that the court instruct the jury on the law as set forth in the requests. At the same time copies of such requests shall be furnished to all parties. The court shall inform counsel of its proposed action upon the requests prior to their arguments to the jury. The court may instruct the jury before or after the arguments are completed or at both times. No party may assign as error any portion of the charge or omission therefrom unless that party objects thereto before the jury retires to consider its verdict, stating distinctly the matter to which that party objects and the grounds of the objection. Opportunity shall be given to make the objection out of the hearing of the jury and, on request of either party, out of the presence of the jury.

FED. R. CRIM. P. 30

Requesting Special Charges. The responsibility for preparing jury instruction requests is often assigned to the trial paralegal. Most offices, prosecution and defense, have charges on file that courts have given in previous cases. Such files probably contain charges given by courts within the local area. Additionally, published jury instructions are available from every federal appeals circuit and from most state jurisdictions. Pattern instructions are charges that have been approved by the appellate courts.

Often a case has a unique aspect requiring special research to substantiate a point of law that a party wants to incorporate into an instruction. A **requested special charge** is an instruction of law made to the jury that has been requested by one of the parties. It usually involves an issue specific to the case that is not found in all cases. The court has the discretion to accept or reject the request for a special charge. For example, in a case involving intoxication as a defense to murder, a requested charge might take the form illustrated in Figure 7-11.

FIGURE 7-11   DEFENDANT'S REQUESTED JURY CHARGE NO. 1

If you find that the defendant's ability to formulate a specific intent was prevented by the fact that he was voluntarily or involuntarily intoxicated, you must find the defendant *not guilty* of the crime of first degree murder.

State v. Smith, *123 N.Rep 8th 456, 789 (1990)*

Format for Requesting Instructions. The form used in Figure 7-11 is typical of the form used in most courts. Each request is usually presented separately, identified as Prosecution Request or Defense Request and numbered. In the illustration, note that the authority upon which the request is based is given along with the suggested wording for the charge. Authority need not be case law, it may be statutory, definitional, etc. Most courts require that the authority for the requested charge be included with the request.

Although requested special charges are prepared in advance, the paralegal must be ready to perfect and submit instructions for those nuances of evidence that pop up during trial. The court gives each side the opportunity to submit charges on any issue that develops during trial.

Objections to the Charge. Before the jury is charged, the court rules on the requested charges and advises the parties of the instructions that will be given to the jury. The paralegal must carefully review the court's planned instructions and note objections to specific portions that are belived to be inappropriate. If the objections are not made at this juncture, they are waived.

It is very important to understand that objections to jury instructions *must* be lodged prior to the jury beginning its deliberations. Rule 30 (Figure 7-10) contains very specific language prohibiting a party from raising an objection to the jury instructions or using the objection on appeal if it is not raised before deliberations begin.

Deliberation and Decision

The last segment of the trial is the return of the jury after it has completed its deliberations. There is little that the paralegal can do while the jury is deliberating its verdict. However, it is important that all parties and the members of the prosecution and defense teams stay close to the courtroom during this period because the jury frequently poses questions to the court that may require their input.

The Hung Jury. Sometimes jurors are so divided in their opinions that they cannot muster enough votes to sustain a verdict of any kind. A **hung jury** is a jury unable to reach a verdict. If the jury notifies the court that it is deadlocked, the court may elect to further instruct the jury on its duties. The court may, in its discretion, give a version of the *Allen* charge. The ***Allen* charge**, sometimes referred to as the "dynamite charge" or the "hammer charge," is a jury instruction designed to avoid a hung jury by urging the jury to come to an agreement. The name derives from the case of *Allen v. United States*, 164 U.S. 492 (1896).

If the jury cannot be "dynamited" into a verdict, the result is commonly referred to as a hung jury, and a mistrial is declared. At the entry of a mistrial, the prosecution may elect to retry the case. A retrial is not double jeopardy.

Polling the Jury. If a verdict has been reached, it is returned to the judge in open court with all parties present. Upon the return of a verdict, the jury may be polled in open court to determine if the announced decision is the one actually reached by the jurors. A **poll of the jury** is an examination of each juror to determine if the verdict announced is the one actually reached during deliberations.

Either party or the court itself may request a poll. During the poll, each juror is required to openly acknowledge the accuracy of the verdict as reported.

If the poll indicates that the proper number of jurors needed to support the verdict was not achieved, the court may send the jury back to deliberate further or declare a mistrial. A **mistrial** is a ruling delivered during a trial or during jury deliberations that proceedings have been invalidated and the trial must be abandoned. A mistrial frequently occurs because a jury is unable to reach a verdict.

As previously noted, the requirement in federal court is that all verdicts, whether guilty or not guilty, must be unanimous. In state prosecutions, the number of concurring jurors necessary to sustain a verdict varies from jurisdiction to jurisdiction. Attorneys and paralegals must know how many votes are required in order to determine if a verdict has been properly reached.

The federal rule concerning verdicts gives a good summary of the law. Familiarity with Rule 31 of the Federal Rules of Criminal Procedure will stand the paralegal in good stead because the law is virtually identical in all jurisdictions. Much of the material presented in the following paragraphs can be found in Rule 31.

Responsive Verdicts. In a case with multiple defendants, a jury may return a verdict regarding one or several of the defendants without having reached a verdict on all defendants. Rule 31 also provides that a jury may return a verdict of guilt on a lesser charge, a charge necessarily included in the offense contained in the indictment.

The notion of a lesser included offense may be easier to understand by considering an example of a typical state felony charge. If a defendant is charged with assault with a weapon, the jury might find the defendant guilty of only simple assault. This verdict is possible because simple assault is included in the concept of assault with a weapon. Perhaps the jury was not satisfied that a dangerous weapon was employed, but it was convinced that an assault took place. Returning a verdict to a lesser offense, while permissible, is known as a **responsive verdict**.

Two-Phase Trials

A relatively recent development in the law is the two-phase trial. A **two-phase trial** is a trial in which the jury is required to reach a second verdict regarding the sentence. The second phase of the trial is conducted only if a guilty verdict is returned during the primary phase. As an example, consider the situation of a trial for first-degree murder in a state where the death penalty may be imposed. If the jury finds the defendant guilty as charged, it is then given the opportunity to decide on the sentence.

The jury may decide that the guilty defendant is deserving of the death penalty, or it may decide that life in prison is the appropriate sentence. In order to make that decision, the jury must be given the opportunity to consider the character of the defendant and the circumstances surrounding the offense.

In considering the circumstances, the jury must be allowed not only to consider those factors that make the offense more aggravated but also to consider those factors that mitigate the defendant's crime. The law evolves from two Supreme Court decisions emanating from the state of Georgia.

In 1972 the Court decided *Furman v. Georgia*, 408 U.S. 238 (1972). In that case, the Court held that the death penalty, as it was applied in most states, was unconstitutional because it was cruel and unusual punishment.

There was no majority opinion in *Furman*. The decision came from a combination of concurring opinions. In one of the concurring opinions, two justices felt that the death penalty violated the Eighth Amendment because it was infrequently and arbitrarily applied. To circumvent that objection, some states have enacted laws that make the death penalty mandatory in situations containing certain aggravating circumstances. The Supreme Court struck down the mandatory death penalty in 1976.

In the case of *Gregg v. Georgia,* 428 U.S. 153 (1976), the Court approved of an approach to the death penalty that involved a bifurcated trial. In such a trial, the penalty is considered separately from the substantive offense. During the second (i.e., penalty) phase of the trial, the jury is given the opportunity to consider not only the aggravating circumstances of the offense but the mitigating circumstances as well.

In a two-phase trial, both sides must be prepared to go forward with the sentencing portion of the trial immediately after a finding of guilt. In such a case, all evidence of a mitigating and aggravating nature must be presented.

The paralegal working for either side must have the witnesses and evidence needed for the sentencing phase prepared and ready for presentation after the first phase is concluded. The preparation should be every bit as thorough as the preparation done for the first phase of the trial. Of course, if the jury acquits the defendant or finds the defendant guilty of a lesser offense not requiring a second hearing, the evidence will not be presented.

In states employing the two-phase trial, the aggravating and mitigating circumstances to be considered by the jury are most frequently contained in the criminal procedure statutes of that state.

Mitigating Circumstances. Mitigating factors may relate to the mentality of the defendant, the circumstances of his or her state of mind at the time of commission, the conditions of the defendant's life that led him or her to the commission of the offense, the role of the defendant in the offense, the defendant's lack of criminal history, the age of the defendant, or any other important factor that tends to explain and mitigate the offense.

Aggravating Circumstances. Circumstances that aggravate the offense will be presented by the prosecution. Aggravating factors may include proof that the defendant has previously been convicted of other significant crimes; evidence that the offense occurred in perpetration of a rape, kidnapping, or armed robbery: evidence that the victim was a police officer or that the crime was committed in a particularly heinous manner. This enumeration is merely illustrative. Other aggravating factors can be proved during the second phase of a two-phase trial.

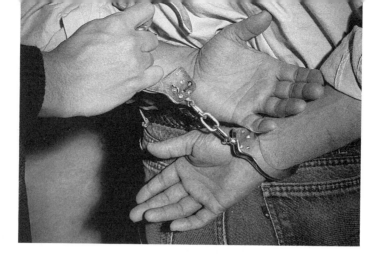

8 GUILTY VERDICT: THE AFTERMATH

In the preceding chapter, we touched upon the possible results of a criminal trial. The return of a verdict is not a perfunctory event. The jury's decision must be returned in open court. The defendant must be present. Rules cover the presentment of the verdict and its public verification by the jurors themselves.

In this chapter, we will concern ourselves with the aftermath of a guilty verdict. If the verdict is not guilty, the case is concluded. If the jury is unable to reach a proper verdict, the case is retried or dismissed. It is only after a verdict of guilty that the justice process enters advanced stages.

RENEWING THE MOTION FOR ACQUITTAL— A JUDGMENT N.O.V.

The **motion for judgment of acquittal** is a request that the court enter a judgment of not guilty. The motion may be made at two times during the trial: at the close of the prosecution's case in chief and again after the defense has presented its evidence. We now consider the fact that the motion may be made one final time after a return of a guilty verdict.

In the parlance of the criminal bar, the entry of a judgment of acquittal by the court after the jury has returned a guilty verdict is referred to as a **judgment n.o.v.**, or a **judgment notwithstanding the verdict**. The letters *n. o. v.* come from the Latin phrase *non obstante verdicto*, which may be literally translated as "the verdict being no obstacle," or more frequently, "notwithstanding the verdict." A judgment of not guilty entered by the court when the jury is unable to reach a verdict is also termed a judgment n.o.v.

Figure 8-1 illustrates the appropriate passage concerning a judgment n.o.v., which appears in the Federal Rules of Criminal Procedure.

FIGURE 8-1   A MOTION FOR ACQUITTAL MAY BE MADE AFTER A GUILTY VERDICT IS RETURNED

> **(c) Motion After Discharge of Jury**—If the jury returns a verdict of guilty or is discharged without having returned a verdict, a motion for judgment of acquittal may be made or renewed within 7 days after the jury is discharged or within such further time as the court may fix during the 7 day period. If a verdict of guilty is returned, the court may on such motion set aside the verdict and enter judgment of acquittal. If no verdict is returned, the court may enter judgment of acquittal. It shall not be necessary to the making of such a motion that a similar motion has been made prior to the submission of the case to the jury.
>
> FED. R. CRIM. P. 29(c)

A judgment n.o.v. is rarely granted. The fact that the court may have previously denied a motion for a judgment of acquittal does not bar the granting of such a judgment after the verdict. However, in order to grant the motion for an acquittal after the jury has returned a guilty verdict, the court must find that no credible evidence sustains the guilty verdict. Since a judgment n.o.v. must be granted by the same judge who allowed the case to go to the jury, it is easy to see why it is so rarely encountered.

In support of the motion for acquittal after the verdict, the defendant relies on much the same argument made in support of the motion put forth during trial. The request for a judgment n.o.v. addresses the lack of evidence produced by the prosecution.

The paralegal asked to assist in the preparation of a motion to acquit should rely on the notes and records he or she made during the trial. The paralegal working with the prosecution whose assignment is to prepare a response to the motion for judgment n.o.v. must also rely on the work product produced during trial.

Strict time limitations are placed on the motion for an acquittal after the verdict has been returned. Local rules must be studied carefully and strictly complied with when a trial court is asked to disregard a jury's pronouncement.

Sufficient time to obtain a transcript of the trial proceedings will rarely be available before the motion must be filed. In those instances where the weakness of the prosecution's evidence is suspected before trial and where there is substantial reason to feel that the court may grant the motion for acquittal, the parties may want to consider ordering a daily transcript of the testimony.

Recording testimony in the computer age has reached the point where producing daily transcripts is not as demanding upon the court reporter as it once was; however, the cost of the service is quite expensive. Attorneys and paralegals may find the expense warranted if the client can afford the cost. This expense is frequently a bigger problem for the defendant than it is for the prosecution. However, if a substantial question regarding evidence remains unsettled, the paralegal may want to broach the subject of a daily transcript with the attorney.

THE MOTION FOR A NEW TRIAL

Closely associated with the motion for a judgment n.o.v. is the motion for a new trial. The two motions are distinct, and the remedies they afford are quite different. In a judgment n.o.v., the court actually enters a verdict of not guilty in favor of the defendant. In the case of a motion for a new trial, the defense does not request a verdict of not guilty but instead asks that the case be retried. A **motion for a new trial** is a procedural device available only to defendants. It enables them to request that a case be retried after a verdict of guilty has been issued by a jury or after a finding of guilty has been made by the court. (See Figure 8-2).

FIGURE 8-2 RULE GOVERNING THE MOTION FOR A NEW TRIAL

The court on motion of the defendant may grant a new trial to that defendant if required in the interest of justice. If trial was by the court without a jury the court on motion of the defendant for a new trial may vacate the judgment if entered, take additional testimony and direct the entry of a new judgment. A motion for a new trial based on the ground of newly discovered evidence may be made only before or within two years after final judgment, but if an appeal is pending the court may grant the motion only on remand of the case. A motion for a new trial on any other grounds shall be made within 7 days after verdict or finding of guilty or within such further time as the court may fix during the 7 day period.

FED. R. CRIM. P. 33

As in the case of a motion for judgment n.o.v., the time within which a motion for a new trial may be requested is limited. Paralegals must be familiar with all rules concerning the request for such relief. The federal rule cited in Figure 8-2 provides that the motion for a new trial must be made within seven days of the verdict, unless it is based on newly discovered evidence.

A new trial may be requested up to two years after the verdict if it is based on new evidence. If new exculpating evidence is discovered after two years, another remedy is available to the defendant. We will discuss that remedy below when we consider the writ of *habeas corpus*.

The court may allow argument and presentation of evidence at a hearing on the motion for a new trial. The paralegal must be prepared to support allegations giving rise to the motion. For example, if the motion is based on newly discovered evidence, the court may require that the moving party demonstrate that the evidence is genuine and that it was not discoverable with due diligence at an earlier date.

As with the motion for a judgment n.o.v., the motion for a new trial can only be raised by the defense. The language of the rule makes it clear that the court may grant a new trial "on a motion of the defendant."

Our discussion of a judgment n.o.v. and the motion for a new trial has centered around the federal procedure. These two devices are also available in all state jurisdictions. The paralegal who must prepare requests for either remedy in state court must therefore examine local rules and statutes for guidance.

THE PRESENTENCE

If all defense maneuvers fail and the guilty verdict returned by the jury is not reversed, the defendant must be brought before the court for sentencing. The time between the return of the verdict and the sentencing is an important interval for all involved with the case. It is especially important for the defense team.

Following a felony conviction, the norm for courts in all jurisdictions is to withhold sentencing of a defendant until a presentence report can be prepared by the appropriate agency. In the federal system, a **presentence investigation (P.S.I.)** is performed by the U.S. Probation Office. Corresponding services exist in all state jurisdictions. It is an investigation into the personal background and criminal history of a defendant awaiting sentence. The results of the investigation are usually formulated into a presentence report, which includes sentencing recommendations and an analysis of sentencing guidelines.

The federal standard, once again, provides an insight into presentencing practice as it prevails in most courts. The "guidelines" mentioned in Rule 32 (see Figure 8-3) refer to federal presentencing guidelines. We will have more to say about these guidelines later.

The Presentence Role of the Paralegal

A great deal of background material must be presented to the investigating agency for preparation of the presentence report. It is not unusual for the paralegal to be given the assignment of working with the defendant to gather and present the needed information.

In addition to gathering information regarding the defendant's family history, social and educational background, financial condition, and marital, military, and other data, the person who is assisting in the presentence phase must be prepared to help the defendant explain his or her role in the offense.

The presentence investigation provides the final opportunity to present the defendant in the best possible light before the judgment of the court (i.e., the sentence) is pronounced.

FIGURE 8-3 FEDERAL PRESENTENCING GUIDELINES

The report of the presentence investigation shall contain:

(A) information about the history and characteristics of the defendant, including his prior criminal record, if any, his financial condition, and any circumstances affecting his behavior that may be helpful in imposing sentence or in the correctional treatment of the defendant;

(B) the classification of the offense and of the defendant, under the categories established by the Sentencing Commission pursuant to section 994(a) of title 28, that the probation officer believes to be applicable to the defendant's case; the kinds of sentence and sentencing range suggested for such category of offense committed by such a category of defendant as set forth by the guidelines issued by the Sentencing Commission pursuant to 28 U.S.C. 994(a)(1) and an explanation by the probation officer of any factors that may indicate that a sentence of a different kind from one within the applicable guideline would be more appropriate under all the circumstances;

(C) any pertinent policy statement issued by the Sentencing Commission pursuant to 28 U.S.C. 994(a)(2);

(D) verified information stated in nonargumentative style containing an assessment of the financial, social, psychological and medical impact upon, and cost to, any individual against whom the offense has been committed;

(E) unless the court orders otherwise, information concerning the nature and extent of nonprison programs and resources available for the defendant; and

(F) such other information as may be required by the court.

Fed. R. Crim. P. 32(c)(2)

Objections to the Presentence Report

When the report has been completed, the defendant and the defense team are given the opportunity to make objections to the contents of the report. The paralegal may be assigned to prepare objections to the report that necessitate careful study of the document and discussion of its contents with the defendant. Any problems discovered in the report's account of the background or history of the defendant must be brought to the attention of the attorney so that a proper and timely objection may be lodged.

The prosecution ordinarily has an equal opportunity to object to errors in the report of the presentence investigation. The paralegal working with the prosecution may also be given the task of studying and evaluating the report.

Sentencing Hearing

The judge will allow the defense to make a presentation in court regarding the alleged factual inaccuracies in the presentence report. (See Figure 8-4.)

FIGURE 8-4   THE RIGHT TO OBJECT TO ALLEGED INACCURACIES IN THE PRESENTENCING REPORT

The court shall afford the defendant and the defendant's counsel an opportunity to comment on the report and, in the discretion of the court, to introduce testimony or other information relating to any alleged factual inaccuracy contained in it.

FED. R. CRIM. P. 32(c)(3)(A)

At the sentencing hearing, the court shall consider and rule upon the comments and objections of the defendant to the presentence report. If the objections are well founded, the court may alter the sentence. If no basis for the objections is found, the court may note its findings and append them to the report, in accordance with Rule 32(c)(3)(D) of the Federal Rules of Criminal Procedure.

IMPOSITION OF SENTENCE

After the hearing of objections, the court imposes the sentence. Usually the sentence is handed down on the day of the sentencing hearing. Occasionally, a special hearing date for objections is set prior to the date for imposition of sentence.

At the sentencing, the defendant is given the opportunity to address the court. The paralegal working with the defense may be given the assignment of preparing the defendant for his or her statement, called the **allocution**, which is delivered to the judge at the time of sentencing prior to the sentence being imposed.

The right to make a statement is not a perfunctory right. It may not be treated as a meaningless formality. If a defendant is sentenced without having the right to address the court, at the very least, the district court may be forced to resentence the defendant. See *United States v. Jackson*, 807 F.2d 1185 (5th Cir. 1986).

SENTENCING GUIDELINES

A relatively recent development in the criminal justice process is the use of **sentencing guidelines**, a schedule employed by the courts to ensure uniformity of sentence among persons convicted of similar offenses. Our treatment of criminal law cannot offer an exhaustive analysis of the guidelines employed in federal and state jurisdictions. The objective here is to alert the student to the significance and extent of the guideline system and to encourage further study by those who intend to pursue a career in criminal law.

The federal sentencing guidelines serve as an excellent model for learning the basics of standardized sentencing schemes. In 1987 federal courts implemented the guideline system for sentencing persons convicted of crimes against the United States. The sentencing formulae were produced by the U.S. Sentencing Commission and were issued pursuant to the Sentencing Reform Act of 1984.

The guidelines are extensive and pervasive. They refer to offenses specifically and apply to all crimes other than minor misdemeanors. The guidelines also classify defendants into groups according to criminal history. The penalty range for an offense increases as the defendant's criminal history worsens.

Typically the guidelines specify a base offense level for a crime. For example, the federal crime of robbery has a base offense level of **20**. To that base level points may be added or subtracted for various factors. Thus, if during the course of the robbery, property of a financial institution or post office was taken, the base level is increased by **2** steps. If a firearm was used, another upward adjustment of **6** levels would be made. If bodily harm resulted, there could be an increase of **3** to **6** levels, depending on the seriousness of the injury. Finally, the level of the offense may be raised if the loss occasioned by the robbery exceeded ten thousand dollars. The increase could range up to **7** levels if the loss was greater than five million dollars.

Similarly, the base level may be decreased because of the existence of other factors. For example, if the defendant suffers from a reduced capacity to know and appreciate the severity of an offense, the offense level may be lowered. Also, if the defendant, after a guilty plea or conviction, fully accepts responsibility for the offense, gives indications of recognizing the wrong, and displays contrition, the base level may be further reduced, usually by **2** or **3** levels.

In our example, if the crime of robbery was committed without a firearm, no injuries attached, and the amount stolen was less than ten thousand dollars, the offense level would be **20**. If the defendant demonstrated acceptance of responsibility, that level would be reduced to **17**.

After the offense level is determined, the defendant's prior criminal history comes into play. Different categories of sentence ranges exist for persons with past criminal convictions. A person with no prior convictions is a Category I offender. A person with thirteen or more prior convictions is a Category VI offender. The potential severity of the sentence increases as the category number increases.

In our example, for a Category I offender, the sentence would range from twenty–seven to thirty-three months. If the defendant had fourteen prior convictions, he or she would be a Category VI offender and the sentence range would be fifty-seven to seventy-one months. A copy of the federal sentencing table is reproduced as Figure 8-5.

As seen earlier, the presentence report of the probation officer contains an analysis of the applicable guidelines. The findings and the calculation of guideline standards by the probation officer are revealed to the defendant, who is given the opportunity to object, as discussed above.

FIGURE 8-5   SENTENCING TABLE (IN MONTHS OF IMPRISONMENT)

	Criminal History Category (Criminal History Points)					
Offense Level	I (0 or 1)	II (2 or 3)	III (4,5,6)	IV (7,8,9)	V (10,11,12)	VI (13 or more)
1	0–6	0–6	0–6	0–6	0–6	0–6
2	0–6	0–6	0–6	0–6	0–6	1–7
3	0–6	0–6	0–6	0–6	2–8	3–9
4	0–6	0–6	0–6	2–8	4–10	6–12
5	0–6	0–6	1–7	4–10	6–12	9–15
6	0–6	1–7	2–8	6–12	9–15	12–18
7	1–7	2–8	4–10	8–14	12–18	15–21
8	2–8	4–10	6–12	10–16	15–21	18–24
9	4–10	6–12	8–14	12–18	18–24	21–27
10	6–12	8–14	10–16	15–21	21–27	24–30
11	8–14	10–16	12–18	18–24	24–30	27–33
12	10–16	12–18	15–21	21–27	27–33	30–37
13	12–18	15–21	18–24	24–30	30–37	33–41
14	15–21	18–24	21–27	27–33	33–41	37–46
15	18–24	21–27	24–30	30–37	37–46	41–51
16	21–27	24–30	27–33	33–41	41–51	46–57
17	24–30	27–33	30–37	37–46	46–57	51–63
18	27–33	30–37	33–41	41–51	51–63	57–71
19	30–37	33–41	37–46	46–57	57–71	63–78
20	33–41	37–46	41–51	51–63	63–78	70–87
21	37–46	41–51	46–57	57–71	70–87	77–96
22	41–51	46–57	51–63	63–78	77–96	84–105
23	46–57	51–63	57–71	70–87	84–105	92–115
24	51–63	57–71	63–78	77–96	92–115	100–125
25	57–71	63–78	70–87	84–105	100–125	110–137
26	63–78	70–87	78–97	92–115	110–137	120–150
27	70–87	78–97	87–108	100–125	120–150	130–162
28	78–97	87–108	97–121	110–137	130–162	140–175
29	87–108	97–121	108–135	121–151	140–175	151–188
30	97–121	108–135	121–151	135–168	151–188	168–210
31	108–135	121–151	135–168	151–188	168–210	188–235
32	121–151	135–168	151–188	168–210	188–235	210–262
33	135–168	151–188	168–210	188–235	210–262	235–293
34	151–188	168–210	188–235	210–262	235–293	262–327
35	168–210	188–235	210–262	235–293	262–327	292–365
36	188–235	210–262	235–293	262–327	292–365	324–405
37	210–262	235–293	262–327	292–365	324–405	360–life
38	235–293	262–327	292–365	324–405	360–life	360–life
39	262–327	292–365	324–405	360–life	360–life	360–life
40	292–365	324–405	360–life	360–life	360–life	360–life
41	324–405	360–life	360–life	360–life	360–life	360–life
42	360–life	360–life	360–life	360–life	360–life	360–life
43	life	life	life	life	life	life

Levels 1–6 bracketed as A; 7–10 as B; 7–12 as C.

KEY
A—Probation available (see § 5B1.1(a)(1))
B—Probation with conditions of confinement available (see § 5B1.1(a)(2))
C—New "split sentence" available (see §§ 5C1.1(c)(3), (d)(2))

The Role of the Paralegal in the Sentencing Process

It should be evident that the paralegal who assists in the presentation to the presentence investigator has a very serious assignment. What happens during the sentencing investigation will have a great impact on the sentence that is ultimately imposed.

Historically, judges have been given wide discretion when imposing sentence. In the federal system, as in all state jurisdictions, the information available to the sentencing judge for use and consideration in formulating a sentence is virtually unrestricted.

A judge may consider information that is inadmissible in trial. He or she may consider the fact of other convictions, even those that have been overturned for technical reasons. The judge may use practically any source to develop information regarding the defendant. As a practical matter, the court usually relies on its presentence investigators for the information it uses; however, it is not restricted to that source, as seen in Figure 8-6.

FIGURE 8-6   THE COURT PLACES NO RESTRICTIONS ON SOURCES USED TO IMPOSE SENTENCE

No limitation shall be placed on the information concerning the background, character, and conduct of a person convicted of an offense which a court of the United States may receive and consider for the purpose of imposing an appropriate sentence.

18 U.S.C. § 3661

The court may consider factors that were not part of the trial evidence in setting sentence. For example, the defendant's past conduct that did not result in criminal convictions may be used for sentencing purposes. Also, if the defendant displays a defiant and unremorseful attitude, the court may use that fact to increase a sentence.

The sentencing court may not rely on false information when sentencing the defendant. The appellate court may order a resentencing if the defendant can demonstrate that information used by the sentencing judge was inaccurate.

It is very important that the person working on preparing the defendant for sentencing be aware of the factors that can and do affect a sentence. The defendant should be informed and educated as to those factors. For example, it is much better for the defendant to remain silent than to attempt to influence the judge by speaking falsely. The judge may not use the fact of the defendant's silence as a reason for an increased sentence. However, the sentence will almost certainly be more severe if the court feels that the defendant is lying.

The duty to thoroughly research the defendant's background and accurately present all mitigating material to the court is an important facet of the defense because the court is able to consider all such material in fashioning a sentence. Likewise, the prosecution is generally given the opportunity by the presentence investigator to present information for the judge's consideration even though the material may not have been used as evidence at the defendant's trial.

Sentencing guidelines have the effect of curtailing the judge's sentencing discretion. In those jurisdictions that do not employ guidelines for imposition of a sentence, the duty to fully inform the court of aggravating or mitigating circumstances becomes even more important.

Departure from the Guidelines

Though the guidelines are meant to cover all situations, obviously instances occur when they do not seem appropropriate. The court may depart from the prescribed guidelines by imposing a lesser or greater sentence than the one provided by the sentencing table (See Figure 8-5). However, the authority to depart is limited to instances in which the court finds that aggravating or mitigating circumstances were not contemplated by the sentencing commission. Judges who elect to depart from the guideline standards must give reasons for their departure. A sentence may be changed by the appellate court if it finds that the sentencing judge failed to give proper reasons for departure.

*   *   *

We shall consider the guidelines again when we discuss the process of plea bargaining later in the course.

THE APPEAL

After a sentence has been imposed, the defendant has a right to appeal. Through the process of appeal, the defendant who feels that a grievous error was made during the trial—an error so serious that it constitutes sufficient reason for a reversal of a conviction—can ask the appellate court to examine the issue. If a reversible error has been committed, the appellate court can set aside the conviction. If other irregularities not serious enough for reversal are identified, the appellate court may order a new trial. If no error or only minor error (harmless error) is found, the appellate court will affirm the conviction and deny relief. On appeal a defendant may raise issues relating to the verdict and to the sentence.

The right to appeal, as we have noted, is not guaranteed by the Bill of Rights or elsewhere in the Constitution, but it is provided to every defendant in all state jurisdictions and in the federal system.

An Overview of the Appeal Process

In all court systems, the usual procedure for beginning an appeal is to notify the district court of the intent to appeal and to lodge the case in an appellate court. The ordinary appeal venue from the district level is the circuit court of appeals. The appellate circuit court generally comprises several lower court districts. In some larger urban districts, the circuit court hears cases from only one district court.

In the appellate court, no jury is seated for the review process. The appeal panel is comprised of several judges, usually three, who study the case presented to them from the trial court, review the issues and briefs of counsel, and decide the issue with or without oral argument from the parties.

The appellate process is a scholarly one. The case that was tried in all of its detail at the district level is reduced to only those issues of contention raised by the appellant. **Appellant** is the title given to the party who asks for a review, thus initiating an appeal. **Appellee** is the party who responds to the appellant's request. The appellant, in all instances, seeks modification or reversal of the lower court's decision. Usually the appellee merely seeks to have the trial court's judgment affirmed, that is, upheld by the appellate judges. Instances occur, almost all of them in civil cases, when the appellee also seeks some sort of modification of the judgment.

Usually very strict time limitations are imposed on the parties who must file notice of an appeal and *perfect* the appeal to the reviewing court. The paralegal who works on an appeal must be thoroughly familiar with the rules of the appellate court and with all of the time restrictions that apply. It is not possible to cover all the rules for all jurisdictions. We will take a look at the federal process, which should acquaint us with the type of rules that apply to appeals.

POINTER: *Perfect* is a term commonly used in the appeal process. It means to complete the task. Thus, an appeal is *perfected* when all the components necessary to place the matter before the appellate judges have been assembled and delivered to the appellate court. We will learn more about the components of the appellate record later in this chapter.

Appeal by the Defendant

As we noted earlier, in a criminal case, it is usually the defendant who takes a case to the appellate court. This is true for two reasons. First, because most criminal trials end in conviction, it is most frequently the defendant who wants the judgment reviewed and reversed. Second, in those instances when the prosecution loses, there are very limited circumstances under which it may appeal. (See Figure 8-7.)

Under ordinary circumstances, the notice of appeal must be filed by a defendant within ten days of the entry of judgment. In a criminal case, the judgment is the sentence. Thus, a defendant wishing to appeal the finding of guilt and the sentence of the court must give notice of appeal within ten days of the imposition of sentence. In those instances when it is allowed to appeal, the government must file its notice within thirty days. See Figure 8-8, which illustrates the pertinent rule from the Federal Rules of Appellate Procedure (FED. R. APP. P.).

FIGURE 8-7   THE RIGHT TO APPEAL

After imposing sentence in a case which has gone to trial on a plea of not guilty, the court shall advise the defendant of the defendant's right to appeal, including the right of a person who is unable to pay the cost of an appeal to apply for leave to appeal in *forma pauperis*. There shall be no duty on the court to advise the defendant of any right of appeal after sentence is imposed following a plea of guilty or nolo contendere, except that the court shall advise the defendant of any right to appeal his sentence. If the defendant so requests, the clerk of the court shall prepare and file forthwith a notice of appeal on behalf of the defendant.

FED. R. CRIM. P. 32(a)(2)

FIGURE 8-8   NOTICE OF APPEAL

In a criminal case the notice of appeal by a defendant shall be filed in the district court within 10 days after the entry of (i) the judgment or order appealed from or (ii) a notice of appeal by the Government. A notice of appeal filed after the announcement of a decision, sentence or order but before entry of the judgment or order shall be treated as filed after such entry and on the day thereof. If a timely motion in arrest of judgment or for a new trial on any ground other than newly discovered evidence has been made, an appeal from a judgment of conviction may be taken within 10 days after the entry of an order denying the motion. A motion for a new trial based on the ground of newly discovered evidence will similarly extend the time for appeal from a judgment of conviction if the motion is made before or within 10 days after entry of the judgment. When an appeal by the government is authorized by statute, the notice of appeal shall be filed in the district court within 30 days after the entry of (i) the judgment or order appealed from or (ii) a notice of appeal by any defendant. A judgment or order is entered within the meaning of this subdivision when it is entered in the criminal docket. Upon a showing of excusable neglect the district court may, before or after the time has expired, with or without motion and notice, extend the time for filing a notice of appeal for a period not to exceed 30 days from the expiration of the time otherwise prescribed by this subdivision.

FED. R. APP. P. 4(b)

Appeal by the Prosecution

In discussing the appeal process in a criminal case, most attorneys will tell you that the prosecution has no right to appeal. Technically, that statement may be inaccurate, but from a practical point of view, it properly describes the situation. The prosecution has a right to appeal but only in very limited instances.

The law in the federal system is that the government may appeal in only three situations:

1. From an order dismissing an indictment or information or granting a new trial after a jury verdict of guilty
2. From a decision suppressing or excluding evidence, if the ruling is made before trial
3. From an order releasing a defendant charged or convicted of an offense.

These three grounds for an appeal by the prosecution are spelled out in detail at 18 U.S.C. § 3731.

Rules governing appeals in state jurisdictions are similar in most respects to those controlling appeals in the federal system. Time limitations may vary from jurisdiction to jurisdiction; thus, it is very important to be familiar with local regulations.

Filing of the notice of appeal is just the beginning of the process. The entire appeal procedure is one in which the paralegal has the opportunity to play a significant role.

POINTER: As pointed out above, the notice of appeal is filed in the district court, not in the appellate court. It is the trial court that must prepare the case record for transmittal. Thus, to get the appeal started, the district court must be notified to begin the process.

Release of the Defendant on Appeal

If the defendant is free on bond prior to conviction, there is no assurance that he or she will be continued on bond during the appeal process. In fact, in the federal system and in most state jurisdictions, present rules call for execution of the sentence to begin while the verdict is being appealed.

The law cited in Figure 8-9 may be summarized as follows: even if the defendant poses no flight risk or danger, he or she shall be jailed during appeal unless the district court feels that a substantial possibility for a reversal exists or that a new trial will be ordered by the appeal court. If the district court does not release the defendant during appeal, the defense team may ask the appellate court to order the release.

An application for release made to the appellate court is based on documents, affidavits, and portions of the record specified by both parties, as seen in Figure 8-10.

As set forth in the rule illustrated in Figure 8-10, the criteria for granting release in the court of appeals are identical to those for granting the release in the lower court. It is most unlikely that the appellate court will release a defendant whose detention has been ordered by the district judge. All requests are handled expeditiously.

It is important to understand that there is usually no bail hearing at the appellate level, though a judge can set a hearing if he or she desires. Understanding that there will be no hearing underscores the importance of being thorough and comprehensive in the original written application.

FIGURE 8-9   THE STATUTE SURROUNDING IMPRISONMENT DURING APPEAL

The judicial officer shall order that a person who has been found guilty of an offense and sentenced to a term of imprisonment, and who has filed an appeal or a petition for a writ of certiorari, be detained, unless the judicial officer finds—

(1) by clear and convincing evidence that the person is not likely to flee or pose a danger to the safety of any other person or the community if released under section 3142(b) or (c) of this title;

AND

(2) that the appeal is not for the purpose of delay and raises a substantial question of law or fact likely to result in—

(A) reversal,
(B) an order for a new trial,
(C) a sentence that does not include a term of imprisonment,
(D) a reduced sentence to a term of imprisonment less than the total of the time already served plus the expected duration of the appeal process.

If the judicial officer makes such findings, such judicial officer shall order the release of the person . . .

18 U.S.C. § 3143(b)

FIGURE 8-10   CRITERIA FOR GRANTING RELEASE ON APPEAL

(b) Application for release after a judgment of conviction shall be made in the first instance in the district court. If the district court refuses release pending appeal, or imposes conditions of release, the court shall state in writing the reason for the action taken. Thereafter, if an appeal is pending, a motion for release, or for modification of the conditions of release may be made to the court of appeal or to a judge thereof. The motion shall be determined promptly upon such papers, affidavits and portions of the record as the parties shall present and after reasonable notice to the appellee. The court of appeals or a judge thereof may order the release of the appellant pending disposition of the motion.

(c) The decision as to release pending appeal shall be made in accordance with Title 18 U.S.C. 3143. The burden of establishing that the defendant will not flee or pose a danger to any other person or to the community and that the appeal is not for purpose of delay and raises a substantial question of law or fact likely to result in a reversal or in an order for a new trial rests with the defendant.

FED. R. APP. P. 9

The Record on Appeal

It is the duty of the appellant, usually the defendant, to order the transcript from the court reporter. The transcript, or such portions thereof as may be designated by the parties as pertinent to the issues to be raised before the appellate court, along with the original papers (such as pleadings, motions, responses, orders and judgments, and exhibits) and copies of all docket entries, constitute the **record on appeal**. If the appellant decides to order no transcript, that fact must be certified in writing to the appellate court.

Should the appellee, ordinarily the prosecution, desire that parts of the transcript other than those designated by the appellant be included in the record, the appellee may make such designation. It is then the appellant's duty to order the needed transcripts from the court reporter.

FIGURE 8-11   COMPOSITION OF THE RECORD ON APPEAL

(a) Composition of the Record on Appeal. The original papers and exhibits filed in the district court, the transcript of proceedings, if any, and a certified copy of the docket entries prepared by the clerk shall constitute the record on appeal in all cases.

(b)(1) Within 10 days after filing the notice of appeal, the appellant shall order from the reporter a transcript of such parts of the proceedings not already on file as the appellant deems necessary, subject to local rules of the courts of appeals. . . . If no such parts of the proceedings are to be ordered, within the same period the appellant shall file a certificate to that effect.

(b)(3) Unless the entire transcript is to be included, the appellant shall, within the 10 days time provided in (b)(1) . . . file a statement of the issues the appellant intends to present on the appeal and shall serve on the appellee a copy of the order or certificate and of the statement. If the appellee deems a transcript or other parts of the proceedings to be necessary, the appellee shall, within 10 days after the service . . . file and serve on the appellant a designation of additional parts to be included.

(b)(4) [A]t the time of ordering, a party must make satisfactory arrangements with the reporter for payment of the cost of the transcript.

FED. R. APP. P. 10(a), 10(b)(1), (b)(3), (b)(4)

Preparing the Appellate Brief

After the record on appeal has been properly designated by the parties, the transcript prepared by the reporter, and the record compiled and docketed in the appellate court by the clerk, the appellant must prepare the brief on the issues comprising the appeal.

Rules of the appellate court are usually very specific regarding the content and format of the appellate briefs that must be filed by the parties. (See Figure 8-12.) The appellee's brief must be in the same format as that of the appellant. However, the appellee does not have to list issues unless there is a disagreement with those stated by the appellant. See Rule 28(b) of the Federal Rules of Appellate Procedure.

FIGURE 8-12 RULES GOVERNING THE CONTENT AND FORMAT OF AN APPELLATE BRIEF

(a) Brief by the Appellant. The brief of the appellant shall contain under appropriate headings and in the order here indicated:

(1) A table of contents, with page references, and a table of cases (alphabetically arranged), statutes and other authorities cited, with references to the pages of the brief where they are cited.

(2) A statement of the issues presented for review.

(3) A statement of the case. The statement shall first indicate briefly the nature of the case, the course of proceedings, and its disposition in the court below. There shall follow a statement of the facts relevant to the issues presented for review, with appropriate references to the record (see subdivision (e)).

(4) An argument. The argument may be preceded by a summary. The argument shall contain the contentions of the appellant with respect to the issues presented, and the reasons therefor, with citations to the authorities, statutes and parts of the record relied on.

(5) A short conclusion stating the precise relief sought.

FED. R. APP. P. 28(a)

There is also provision in the rules for the filing of a reply brief by the appellant after appellee's submission. See Rule 28(c) of the Federal Rules of Appellate Procedure.

 POINTER: Remember that we are using federal procedures as an instructive tool. State jurisdictions may employ a slightly different process. Always consult the rules of the specific courts involved. The appeal process is "rule intensive." That means that the process is highly regulated. Never rely solely on memory in preparing an appeal. Consult the rules in each case to be sure all requirements are met.

Local Rules regarding Appeals

While we are considering the subject of appeals, it is worth noting that the local rules for appellate courts generally contain important instructions and requirements concerning the appeal process.

Local rules can and often do govern every step in the appeal process. The local rules may relate to all matters, from the manner in which the transcript is ordered and the record is perfected through the argument and request for a rehearing in an appeals court. One very important consideration concerns time restrictions applicable in the circuit; another concerns the length of briefs and the printing requirements for the documents.

An interesting example of printing and binding requirements is contained in the local rules of the U.S. Court of Appeals for the Fifth Circuit. Among other dictates, one local rule declares that briefs shall be bound in such a manner "so as to permit them to lie flat when open, and they must do so if the cover is plastic or any material not easily folded."

The local rules may seem tedious and picayunish, but they are extremely important to the judges who will review the case. In some instances, an attorney's or paralegal's failure to heed the rules may have a disastrous effect on the cause of the client.

 POINTER: Some circuits have a policy of assisting in the proper preparation of briefs. In the U.S. Court of Appeals for the Fifth Circuit, there is an internal operating procedure requiring the clerk of courts to supply to attorneys and their assistants sample briefs and appendices that exemplify proper form and content. Anyone preparing a presentation for the appeals court who does not take advantage of such help may be asking for trouble.

Oral Argument

After the briefs and record are accepted by the appellate court, the case is assigned to a panel of three judges for disposition. The case need not be orally argued to the panel. The three judges to whom the case has been assigned may feel as though argument is unnecessary, in which instance, the case may be decided without an appearance by the attorneys.

When oral argument is allowed, seldom is it necessary for the defendant/appellant to be present. Usually the hearing is attended only by the attorneys who are to argue the case. Paralegals may be present, but they will be given no opportunity to participate in the hearing. The federal rule surrounding the presentation of oral arguments to an appellate court is given in Figure 8-13.

Even though the rule is phrased in the affirmative, "Oral argument shall be allowed in all cases . . . ," it is becoming commonplace for appellate courts to eliminate attorneys' arguments before the court and decide cases solely on written presentations. The growing tendency toward elimination of oral presentations highlights the importance of the written presentation, an area in which the paralegal assistant has an opportunity to excel.

The Petition for Rehearing

Statistically, the most probable result of an appeal is that the judgment of the lower court will be affirmed. When this occurs, the appellant has the opportunity to request a rehearing in the appellate court. In the event that the appellate court reverses the judgment of the lower court, the appellee may petition for rehearing. The rehearing is frequently requested but seldom granted. When the petition for a rehearing is filed, it is not necessary that the adverse party lodge a response unless the appellate court requests that one be filed.

FIGURE 8-13   AN ORAL ARGUMENT IS NOT ALWAYS PERMITTED

Oral argument shall be allowed in all cases unless pursuant to local rule a panel of three judges, after examination of the briefs and record, shall be unanimously of the opinion that oral argument is not needed. Any such local rule shall provide any party with an opportunity to file a statement setting forth the reasons why oral argument should be heard. A general statement of the criteria employed in the administration of such rule shall be published in or with the rule and such criteria shall conform substantially to the following minimum standard:

Oral argument will be allowed unless

(1) the appeal is frivolous; or

(2) the dispositive issue or set of issues has been recently authoritatively decided; or

(3) the facts and legal arguments are adequately presented in the briefs and record and the decisional process would not be significantly aided by oral argument.

Fed. R. App. P. 34(a)

If a rehearing is requested, the petition must be very specific as to the reasons for the suggested rehearing. No oral argument is allowed on the issue of granting a rehearing. If the court decides to rehear the case, oral argument may be permitted. Ordinarily, however, no rehearing will be granted without the court first requesting a response from the adverse party. See Rule 40 of the Federal Rules of Appellate Procedure.

THE WRIT OF *CERTIORARI*

Most criminal cases do not go beyond the first appeal level. As we learned at the beginning of the course, usually there is no right to appeal a decision in a criminal case to the Supreme Court. Cases usually get to the high court via the process of *certiorari*.

An application for writ of *certiorari* is, for all practical purposes, a last resort. Rule 17 of the Rules of the Supreme Court of the United States (Sup. Ct. R.) explains how the Supreme Court regards applications for *certiorari*.

From the tenor and content of the rule illustrated in Figure 8-14, it should be apparent that applications for review by the highest court are rarely granted. However, on occasion, the case warrants or the client demands that an application be filed. When that time comes, it is important that the paralegal working on the application be aware of content requirements. They are found in the Rules of the Supreme Court governing applications for *certiorari*.

It would serve little purpose to review the entire process in detail or cite the rules extensively. The instances in which the process is used are not

FIGURE 8-14   THE SUPREME COURT HAS DISCRETION TO GRANT WRITS OF *CERTIORARI*

1. A review on writ of certiorari is not a matter of right, but of judicial discretion, and will be granted only when there are special and important reasons therefor. The following, while neither controlling nor fully measuring the court's discretion, indicate the character of reasons that will be considered.

(a) When a federal court of appeals has rendered a decision in conflict with the decision of another federal court of appeals on the same matter; or has decided a federal question in a way in conflict with a state court of last resort; or has so far departed from the accepted and usual course of judicial proceedings; or so far sanctioned such a departure by a lower court as to call for an exercise of this Court's power of supervision.

(b) When a state court of last resort has decided a federal question in a way in conflict with the decision of another state court of last resort or of a federal court of appeals.

(c) When a state court or a federal court of appeals has decided an important question of federal law which has not been but should be, settled by this Court, or has decided a federal question in a way in conflict with applicable decisions of this Court.

Sup. Ct. R. 17(1)

numerous. However, in order to impart some understanding of the process, we will summarize some of the important considerations that must be addressed when a writ is sought.

Time Limitations

The petition for a writ of *certiorari* from the judgment of a state court of last resort or from a federal court of appeals shall be filed within sixty days of the entry of the judgment [Sup. Ct. R. 20(1)].

Format and Content of the Application

The requirements for content and form are set out by the rules of the Supreme Court. Generally, the content is similar to that required by the lower appellate court. However, it should be noted that the rule requires reference to the appropriate section of Rule 17 (Figure 8-14), which sets out the criterion upon which review is sought (Sup. Ct. R. 21).

Form for the Brief

Should the writ be granted, further briefing will be required. The form for the brief, appendices, and other documents filed with the Court must be followed conscientiously (Sup. Ct. R. 33).

Time Limitations for Filing the Brief

Usually the appellant must file the brief forty-five days after the Court grants the petition of *certiorari*. The brief of the appellee must follow within thirty days. Forty copies are usually required (Sup. Ct. R. 35).

Oral Argument

"The Court is also reluctant to accept the submission of briefs, without oral argument [in cases in which] certiorari has been granted. . . . The court looks with disfavor on any oral argument that is read from a prepared text" (Sup. Ct. R. 38).

THE WRIT OF *HABEAS CORPUS*

To this point we have considered the processes of appeal and *certiorari*. We now take a look at the **writ of** *habeas corpus* as a means of securing postconfinement relief for aggrieved persons. The writ of *habeas corpus*—some call it the great writ—is a procedural device, distinct from an appeal or a writ of *certiorari*, designed to prevent injustice in those cases that may have slipped through the trial and appeal processes and that may have resulted in the illegal imprisonment of a person.

Whether the incarceration comes as a result of the action of federal courts or from the state court system, a person who is being illegally held or who is about to be taken into custody contrary to the guarantees of the Constitution, may petition for relief in the federal court system.

Theoretically, the writ of *habeas corpus* is not part of the criminal justice system. It is a civil action brought into the courts through procedures set out in Title 28 of the *United States Code*. (See Figure 8-15.) The power to grant such relief is given to all federal judges and the justices of the Supreme Court.

FIGURE 8-15   PROCEDURE FOR BRINGING FORTH A WRIT OF *HABEAS CORPUS*

(a) Writs of habeas corpus may be granted by the Supreme Court, any justice thereof, the district courts and any circuit judge within their respective jurisdictions . . .

28 U.S.C. § 2241(a)

(b) The Supreme Court, any justice thereof, and any circuit judge may decline to entertain an application for a writ of habeas corpus and may transfer the application for hearing and determination to the district court having jurisdiction to entertain it.

28 U.S.C. § 2241(c)

Earlier we noted that the federal system and the state court systems are parallel. The federal courts retain no authority over the administration of criminal justice in the states. This concept is a valid one, but it must be understood in context with the inherent authority of the federal courts to enforce the Constitution of the United States. That authority extends beyond the criminal jurisdiction of U.S. courts. What this means is that federal courts are not in the appeal path of state defendants. However, if any process, federal or state, works to deprive a person of a guaranteed right, the federal courts may be used to correct the situation. (See Figure 8-16.)

FIGURE 8-16   REASONS FOR GRANTING A WRIT OF *HABEAS CORPUS*

The writ of habeas corpus shall not extend to a prisoner unless—

(1) He is in custody under or by color of the authority of the United States or is committed for trial before some court thereof; or

(2) He is in custody for an act done or omitted in pursuance of an Act of Congress, or an order, process, judgment or decree of a court or judge of the United States; or

(3) He is in custody in violation of the Constitution or laws or treaties of the United States; or

(4) He, being a citizen of a foreign state and domiciled therein, is in custody for an act done or omitted under any alleged right, title, authority, privilege, protection, or exemption claimed under the commission, order or sanction of any foreign state, or under color thereof, the validity of which depends upon the law of nations; or

(5) It is necessary to bring him into court to testify or for trial.

28 U.S.C. § 2241(c)

28 U.S.C. §§ 2254 and 2255

Two statutes are commonly used to bring the application for a writ of *habeas corpus*. One applies to state detainees; the other applies to federal prisoners. Both are found in Title 28 of the *United States Code*.

Section 2254 is used whenever a person is being held pursuant to a judgment of a state court. In order for the Supreme Court to entertain an application from a state prisoner, the applicant must show that he or she has exhausted all state court remedies. (See Figure 8-17.)

Section 2255 is used whenever the allegedly illegal custody is the result of federal action. The right to apply for relief under 28 U.S.C. § 2255 requires that the defendant first seek relief in the district court where the illegal sentence was imposed. If relief is denied at that level, the defendant may apply for a writ of *habeas corpus* to the court of appeals.

FIGURE 8-17   WRIT OF *HABEAS CORPUS* AS IT APPLIES TO STATE DETAINEES

(a) The Supreme Court, a Justice thereof, a circuit judge, or a district court shall entertain an application for a writ of habeas corpus in behalf of a person in custody pursuant to the judgment of a state court only on the ground that he is in custody in violation of the Constitution of the United States.

28 U.S.C. § 2254(a)

(c) An application for a writ of habeas corpus in behalf of a person in custody pursuant to the judgment of a state court shall not be granted unless it appears that the applicant has exhausted the remedies available in the courts of the State . . .

28 U.S.C. § 2254(c)

FIGURE 8-18   WRIT OF *HABEAS CORPUS* AS IT APPLIES TO FEDERAL PRISONERS

An application for a writ of habeas corpus in behalf of a prisoner who is authorized to apply for relief by motion pursuant to this section, shall not be entertained if it appears that the applicant has failed to apply for relief, by motion, to the court which sentenced him, or that such court has denied him relief, unless it also appears that the remedy by motion is inadequate or ineffective to test the legality of his detention.

28 U.S.C. § 2255

Form of Application for *Habeas Corpus*

Of significant note to the paralegal who may be directed to assist in the preparation of a writ of *habeas corpus* is the model form used in such applications. The Appendix of Forms to 28 U.S.C. contains two model forms for use in *habeas* applications: one for applications by state prisoners; the other for use by federal prisoners. Acquaintance with these practice aids will benefit any paralegal. They are not reproduced in this text because of space constraints.

Response to the *Habeas* Application

The *habeas* application must be served upon the appropriate state official prior to the conduct of a hearing on the application. See 28 U.S.C. § 2252. In such an instance, the state official is charged with the responsibility to appear and defend the detention. In the case of a person seeking relief from federal detention, it is the U.S. attorney who has the duty to defend against the action.

9 JUVENILE JUSTICE SYSTEM

AN OVERVIEW

Thus far in our survey we have dealt with the justice system as it pertains to the adult offender. We have seen that the differences and peculiarities of systems among various states are slight, almost to the point of being insignificant.

The federal criminal justice organization is a constant in each state, and it provides a certain uniformity to our justice system. A degree of continuity is brought to the process by the fact that the attorneys who work in the federal courts are the same attorneys who function in the state courts. Customs, habits, and methods of procedure are somewhat standardized by the overlap between federal and state bars.

Unfortunately, for our understanding of the juvenile justice system, no unifying element exists among the systems employed by the states. Nor is there the conforming presence of a pervasive structure, such as a federal juvenile justice program. As a consequence, the juvenile courts spread throughout the nation present a hodgepodge of entities, each bearing little resemblance to the systems of other states, with a jumble of procedures, practices, and theories.

No definition can be universally applied to the term *juvenile court.* In some states, the juvenile court may be part of the larger general district court. In such states, a judge who sits on juvenile matters may be the same judge who presides over criminal cases involving adult offenders. Other states have courts that handle juvenile matters exclusively; that is, they have no authority or jurisdiction over other types of cases or defendants.

The types of cases heard by juvenile courts vary as widely as the types of courts set up to handle those cases. Some states utilize the juvenile courts to hear all manner of problems involving minors. In those states, the juvenile court may have jurisdiction over child custody matters, child support cases, nonsupport cases in which an adult is the actual defendant, adoption proceedings, noncriminal misbehavior, delinquency, and even traffic cases.

It would be impractical to attempt a comprehensive treatment of the juvenile court system in each state. Since many of the functions of juvenile courts are not involved with delinquency problems, we must be careful not to confuse our treatment of juvenile crime with a broad analysis of the juvenile court system. We cannot concern ourselves with the numerous responsibilities of the juvenile or family court that are not crime related. Our purpose is to learn what we can of the system as it pertains to juvenile offenders. The other functions of the juvenile or family court may be proper material for other studies.

In this chapter, we will look to the *Louisiana Children's Code* (LA. CHILD. CODE) for examples of current trends to illustrate our lessons on juvenile justice. Louisiana completely revised its former laws into a new children's code while this text was being prepared. As such, it is representative of the current thinking on such matters.

Purpose and Philosophy

Various state statutes that create juvenile courts wax eloquent with high-sounding language regarding the benevolent purposes and goals for the institutions they empower. The Louisiana statute is an apt example. (See Figure 9-1.)

FIGURE 9-1   THE PURPOSE OF THE JUVENILE JUSTICE SYSTEM, AS DEFINED BY STATUTE

The provisions of this Code shall be liberally construed to the end that each child and parent coming within the jurisdiction of the court shall be accorded due process and that each child shall receive, preferably in his own home, the care, guidance, and control that will be conducive to his welfare. In those instances when he is removed from the control of his parents, the court shall secure for him care as nearly as possible equivalent to that which the parents should have given him . . .

LA. CHILD. CODE, art. 102 (1992)

The stated purposes and philosophies of the court are seldom recognizable in daily operations. In actual practice, the juvenile courts have become virtually indistinguishable from criminal courts. The only conspicuous difference is the absence of a jury. The Supreme Court has held that a jury is not required in juvenile proceedings. See *McKeiver v. Pennsylvania*, 403 U.S. 528 (1971). However, it has consistently ruled that the other rights guaranteed to criminal defendants are applicable in delinquency proceedings.

The underlying precept of children's courts, when they came into being in the previous century, was that the child should be sheltered from the harsh, often retributive processes of the legal system. In some instances, juvenile institutions were not even called courts. Names such as Children's Bureau or Child Welfare Board reflect the thinking that minors should be taken out of the legal system. It was just such thinking that moved Father Flanagan, the founder of Boy's Town, to declare: "There is no such thing as a bad boy." Such reasoning permeated the systems that were put in place by the states to afford proper guidance to the wayward child.

The second half of this century has marked a noticeable departure from earlier philosophies. Juvenile courts still pay lip service to the language of the past, but the child-sheltering objectives of the system are fading fast. State laws still refrain from labeling a youthful offender *criminal*, opting instead for the euphemistic *delinquent*. **Delinquent** is the designation given to a minor who has been adjudicated a law violator. For all practical purposes, the penalties meted out to delinquents are indistinguishable from those imposed upon adults.

Although many institutions and group homes emphasize treatment and counseling for youthful offenders, many juvenile confinement centers are very similar to adult penal institutions. In some instances, juvenile institutions are virtually identical to adult prisons. If anyone were so naive as to suggest to a juvenile court judge or to anyone else familiar with the system that there is no such thing as a bad boy or girl, that person would do so at the risk of being declared *non compos mentis* (not of sound mind).

Crime statistics reflect the reasons for the evolution to a harsher system. Fully two-thirds of all violent crimes in the year 1990 were committed by persons under the age of twenty-five years. A substantial portion of these offenders were juveniles, persons who had not reached their eighteenth birthdays.

Juvenile courts have become, and are yet becoming, more than social welfare centers: they are courts of law. As we shall see, procedures employed in juvenile courts, when they are convened for a delinquency hearing, are very similar to procedures employed at the trial of a criminal case. Minors who are brought to a delinquency hearing are entitled to all the guarantees of the Constitution. The Supreme Court noted, in *Breed v. Jones*, 421 U.S. 519 (1975), that the realities of the juvenile justice system make it necessary to apply constitutional guarantees to juvenile proceedings.

For the paralegal working on an assignment in juvenile court, the process of preparing for a hearing is the same as the process of preparing for trial in an adult criminal matter. As noted earlier, there will be no jury for which to prepare, but few other procedural differences exist.

Jurisdiction

The term *jurisdiction* has multiple meanings in the juvenile justice system. There are at least three significant translations for the term.

The first meaning concerns the court's geographical setting. Frequently, when the court's jurisdiction is mentioned, the reference is to the physical area within which the court exercises authority. The geographic boundaries are often those of a city or county. However, it is not uncommon for a court's territorial boundaries to correspond to those of the district court of general authority. We have seen that a judicial district often ranges over a multicounty area.

Another variation of meaning for jurisdiction as it pertains to juvenile matters concerns the finding that the court makes regarding the status of a minor. If a child is adjudged to be a delinquent (or given some other status such as abused or abandoned), the court may be said to have jurisdiction over the minor or the situation.

A third meaning has to do with subject matter. A court may be authorized to act in particular situations. For example, if a minor is accused of an act of delinquency occurring within the territorial boundaries of the forum, the court is said to have jurisdiction over the person.

Thus, when jurisdiction is mentioned, the context of its use often determines its meaning. As alluded to in the preceding paragraphs, the court may have other jurisdictional parameters that have not been considered in our discussion, such as matters involving nonsupport or child custody cases. The juvenile court may even exercise jurisdiction over adults in cases involving failure to support, for example.

Problems Involving Venue

Venue refers to the proper location for a legal action. Frequently situations in the law occur when more than one proper venue for a court action exists. For example, in a tort action involving an automobile accident, there could be at least two proper venues where a lawsuit could be instituted. Often the laws of a state allow a case to be filed in the court of the county where the accident happened. A second possibility for venue might be the county where the defendant resides, if it is different from the county where the accident occurred. The courts of either county may provide a proper venue for the lawsuit.

In juvenile proceedings, proper venue is a matter of local control. As in so many aspects of the juvenile justice system, there is no way to generalize our discussion regarding proper venue.

The laws of a state may provide that all delinquency hearings take place in the court of the county where the delinquent act is alleged to have been committed. The law of the state of New York provides that proper venue is the county of the offense's commission. Other states, such as Missouri, provide that a delinquency hearing may be conducted in either the county where the juvenile resides or in the county where the offense occurs.

The variances in venue designations may reflect philosophical differences between locales. In the first instance, providing that the hearing must be held where the offense was committed may manifest a concern by the legislature for the safety of the community. On the other hand, providing that the hearing take place in the county where the accused minor resides may evince a concern for the rehabilitation of the juvenile. Both points of view are legitimate concerns; they simply emphasize different aspects of the juvenile justice system.

Perhaps the law of Texas handles the problem as effectively as possible. According to Texas law, the hearing to determine delinquency is held in the county where the offensive conduct occurred. After an adjudication of delinquency, the case may be transferred to the county wherein the minor is domiciled for supervision and further action. Texas is not the only state to provide for transfer of cases. Such laws form an example of yet another approach to the venue problem.

THE AGE FACTOR—WHO IS A JUVENILE?

When we considered the factors that negate intent (Chapter 2), we noted that one of the factors was immaturity. You will recall that, at common law, a youth became fully accountable for his or her actions at the age of fourteen years. The common law attached no criminal responsibility whatsoever to a child for actions committed prior to the seventh birthday.

Minimum Age

Most state laws do not set a minimum age limit below which a child is exempt from juvenile court authority. In the usual situation, the law sets out the juvenile court's jurisdiction in terms of the maximum age of the offender (e.g., a minor within the meaning of a state's juvenile code may be defined as any person who has not reached his or her eighteenth birthday). In the example, the maximum age of the child is spelled out, but no mention is made of a minimum age at which the court's authority would attach. This is the norm throughout the country.

Some states do employ a minimum age factor in setting the jurisdiction of juvenile courts. In some instances, the law codifies the common law standard (i.e., seven years). At least one state, Texas, has raised the minimum age to ten years. In North Carolina, the statutory age at which juvenile court authority attaches has been set at six years.

Maximum Age

All states employing a juvenile court system set a maximum age limitation upon the jurisdiction of such courts. In some instances, it is the fourteen-year rule recognized in common law. The most frequent age mentioned is eighteen; however, some courts use fifteen years, sixteen years, or seventeen years.

Of some interest is the point at which the offender's age comes into play. Is it at the date of the lodging of charges? Is it the date of the commission of the offense? Is it the date of the hearing or the date of adjudication? It is not unusual to find that the statutes that define *juvenile* or that set out the authority of the court do not establish the point at which the offender's age establishes jurisdiction. Some of the more recent statutes do fix jurisdiction by the offender's age at the date of the commission of the act.

The point at which age determines jurisdiction may seem to be a somewhat technical consideration, but it could have significant ramifications. If a person is apprehended at age twenty-two for an act that he or she committed as a juvenile, which court would possess jurisdiction? Would the juvenile court try the adult for delinquency? There are no answers to age questions that are acceptable in all jurisdictions. Seemingly, however, there is an upper limit to the jurisdiction of the juvenile court. In *Application of Johnson*, 178 F. Supp. 155 (1957), a 1957 decision of the federal district court from New Jersey cited in the Federal Supplement, it was determined that a twenty-seven-year-old adult could not be subjected to the authority of the New Jersey juvenile court.

Unfortunately for our studies, little generalization is possible regarding answers to the questions we have raised. Because the answers are not certain in all instances, the paralegal who is confronted with such a situation must closely examine the law of his or her jurisdiction, including the state's constitution, for answers. The good news is that questions of this nature only rarely occur.

DEFINING DELINQUENCY

In Chapter 1, when we set out to define crime, we were able to reach a definition without a great deal of difficulty. Defining delinquency is not so simple. We must avoid the great temptation of oversimplifying the term by translating delinquency as a criminal act committed by a minor.

Such a generalization may hold some value, but it would not be totally accurate. The problem is not that the definition would be too broad; rather, it is quite the opposite. Defining delinquency as the violation of a criminal law by a minor is too narrow a definition. It does not take into consideration offenses applicable only to children, such as curfew violations or truancy.

Some jurisdictions have created a special category of offending minors who exhibit antisocial behavior that falls short of criminal law violations. Such persons are not judged to be delinquent, but they are sometimes called status offenders. A **status offender**, or a **child in need of supervision (CHINS)** as some states label such persons, is a minor who is not yet considered a delinquent but who has been found to need some behavior modification by a juvenile court. A status offender is in something of a limbo. In fact, the status offender label reflects the confusion surrounding his or her status. Its meaning is so nonapparent as to be vague.

What this discussion leads to is this conclusion: it is not possible to offer a universally accepted definition of delinquency because the definition varies from state to state. In order to be certain of its precise meaning, the statutes of specific locales must be consulted. For our purposes, however, we will define **delinquency** in these general terms: conduct by a juvenile that is beyond parental control and is thus subject to legal action; a violation of the law committed by a juvenile.

The notion of delinquency is further complicated by another factor. Conduct that might form the basis for delinquency in one state may not be sufficient grounds in another state. The breadth of a state's definition of delinquency can reflect its philosophy regarding the purpose of the juvenile justice system. There is still wide acceptance, or apparent acceptance, for the principle that the juvenile justice system is more than a penal process for minors. Such philosophical leanings are demonstrated by the lengths to which some states go to extend jurisdiction over wayward minors.

It is axiomatic in criminal cases that a state's authority to prosecute stops at that state's boundaries. If an adult commits a crime in state **A**, he or she cannot be prosecuted for that offense in state **B**. Not so in juvenile delinquency matters, at least not in all states.

We have already looked at the philosophy that forms the basis for the juvenile system of Louisiana (Figure 9-1). In support of its stated belief that a child coming within the jurisdiction of the juvenile court "shall receive . . . the care, guidance, and control that will be conducive to his welfare, Louisiana has broadened the range of its courts' authority.

In Louisiana and in Iowa and in other states that espouse a similar philosophy, a minor may be adjudicated a delinquent based on conduct that occurred anywhere within the state in contravention of its laws and ordinances or even based on conduct that occurred *outside* the state. Louisiana also allows a finding of delinquency based on violation of federal law.

Some states hold the traditional view that their business, even the juvenile justice business, should be confined to their own territory. In Massachusetts, for example, the authority of the juvenile courts extends only to minors, sixteen years of age and younger, who violate the criminal laws, local ordinances, or bylaws of any town located within the state.

It should be noted that among various state systems, juvenile jurisdiction laws, such as those of Massachusetts, are among the most restrictive. Yet even in those jurisdictions, the juvenile courts are given authority that is extremely broad by criminal law standards.

In a criminal prosecution, one of the elements that must be proved is that the crime occurred within the *territorial* jurisdiction of the court in which the case is pending. Even under the restrictive Massachusetts law, the juvenile court of county **A** can find a minor delinquent because of an act that occurred in contravention of a town ordinance in county **Z**.

WAIVING JUVENILE JURISDICTION

Almost every state gives its juvenile authorities a right to transfer certain cases from the jurisdiction of the juvenile court to the adult justice system to be handled as criminal cases. In a juvenile proceeding, **waiver** is a determination that a minor who has committed an offense should be subjected to an adult criminal prosecution. The waiver process is sometimes referred to as "certifying" a juvenile to stand trial as an adult.

The Supreme Court decision in *Kent v. United States*, 383 U.S. 541 (1966) is usually cited as the case controlling waiver, or certification, procedures. In *Kent* the Court held that the waiver of jurisdiction by the juvenile court is so significant that it may not be accomplished without affording the minor a right to a hearing on the issue. The minor has a right to counsel at the hearing, and the court must assign reasons for sending the case to the criminal justice system.

Usually waiver is only considered for offenders who are close to the age at which they may be charged criminally. Also, the underlying offense is usually a very serious matter. Typically, waiver would be used in the case of a fifteen- or sixteen-year-old offender who has committed a heinous act, such as murder or rape, or who has repeatedly been brought before the juvenile courts.

Most states have criteria for certification set in statutory form. Usually the statutes are very broad and use language such as "best interest of the minor" or "the public interest." Whatever the language, the practice seems to favor public protection over the interest of the minor. It is hard to imagine the child's interest being furthered by conviction of a felony and confinement in an adult prison.

Some of the traditional considerations for waiving juvenile court jurisdiction are

■ Whether the alleged offense is particulary violent or indicative of a violent personality
■ Whether the public is adequately protected by confining the minor to a juvenile facility
■ Whether juvenile facilities have adequate rehabilitative capabilities for the minor
■ The age of the minor and his or her previous record

Some states limit the age at which a minor's case may be transferred to the adult system. In some instances, the age limits are astonishingly low, sometimes being as low as thirteen or fourteen years of age.

The waiver hearing cannot be the same as the adjudication hearing. A separate hearing on the issue of waiver must be held, and it must precede the adjudication hearing. In *Breed v. Jones, supra,* the Court held that it would be double jeopardy, and thus unconstitutional, to subject a minor to waiver, that is, to criminal prosecution, after an adjudication hearing. Usually the minor who has had his or her case transferred may appeal the court's decision to waive juvenile jurisdiction. Of course, the state may *not* usually appeal a decision denying transfer.

One other important note: in *Kent* the Supreme Court held that the decision of the juvenile court to waive jurisdiction must be accompanied by "a statement of the reasons or considerations therefor." Should a case be transferred to the adult system, as previously mentioned, it is handled in accordance with the procedures applicable to all other criminal cases. In this chapter, though, we are primarily concerned with the conduct of proceedings in juvenile court.

PROCEDURE IN JUVENILE COURT

We have already alluded to the fact that the processes leading to an adjudication of juvenile delinquency are very similar to the trial and sentencing phases of criminal cases. Now we will look at some of the similarities between the two processes and some of the variances that distinguish the juvenile system from the criminal justice system.

Intake

In Chapter 3, we discussed the screening process employed by the district attorney who must decide whether or not to proceed with the prosecution of a case referred by criminal investigators. The juvenile process of **intake**, the case evaluation process, resembles the criminal screening process to a point.

In the juvenile system, a decision must be made regarding the reports and investigations of juvenile officers. Actually, the task of the juvenile intake officers, as they are usually called, may be more onerous than that of their screening counterparts in the adult system. The intake official must sift through much more material than the screener in a criminal case. The sources of reports and complaints involving juveniles are not limited to police and officers of the juvenile bureau. Many cases originate from citizen complaints and reports of school officials. Minors are subjected to scrutiny by a wide range of adults, and the reports and complaints finding their way into juvenile halls reflect that fact.

In the juvenile system, the traditional approach has been to explore for reasons not to bring minors into the court system. A strong current of belief in the theory that the experience of being exposed to the authority of the court has a deleterious effect upon the child underpins this approach. Hence, if at all possible, the intake officer isolates or screens the minor from formal proceedings. Persons reviewing reports in criminal cases are seldom so protective of offenders. They are more inclined to take in than they are to screen out.

During intake, it is routine for the person making the decision to confer with complainants, police, parents, teachers, and the minor in order to arrive at a decision regarding the case. A parent and the child may be represented by counsel at the meeting, though court officials will declare that such representation is unnecessary.

Historically, such representation has *not* been necessary. The goal of most intake officials has never been viewed as contrary to the interest of the minor. In cases where it is obvious that the child must be brought before the court, the meeting is frequently eliminated and action is initiated as quickly as possible.

Informal Adjustment

The intake officer has an alternative to think about when weighing case reports. It is not always necessary to recommend a child for handling as a delinquent. The recommendation may involve an attempt at an informal adjustment procedure for the minor.

Informal adjustment has a specific meaning in juvenile cases. It is an agreement between juvenile authorities, the minor, the family of the minor, and the court regarding the conduct that kindled the interest of the authorities in the first place. It provides for voluntary behavior modification practices by the minor and some form of supervision or monitoring by juvenile authorities. It is usually agreed to in lieu of filing a formal petition against the minor. Informal adjustment is similar to deferred prosecution, or diversion, in criminal cases, which we considered in Chapter 4.

The goal of adjustment is to establish some form of supervision over the minor without the necessity of a formal hearing. Ordinarily, the adjustment agreement must be reduced to writing and must specify the terms and conditions agreed to by all parties as a solution to the problems exhibited by the juvenile.

At the adjustment stage of the proceedings, it is advisable for the minor and his or her family to be represented by an attorney. The adjustment may have onerous conditions with which the minor must comply.

It is usual for the adjustment agreement to contain a probation period that requires the agreement of the juvenile probation service. Thus, the probation service is usually a party to the informal adjustment. Some jurisdictions require the approval of the court to all adjustments. Some require approval only in situations in which the adjustment lasts more than a minimal period, such as six months.

In some jurisdictions, the court may authorize an informal adjustment even after the filing of a formal petition against the juvenile. In such a situation, the adjustment has the effect of suspending formal proceedings. However, there are jurisdictions where the adjustment will not prevent the filing of a formal petition. Paralegals assigned to work on a case where informal adjustment has been suggested must become thoroughly acquainted with the laws of the jurisdiction where the case is pending.

The Formal Petition

Formal proceedings to obtain an adjudication of delinquency or to have a minor declared a CHINS begin with the filing of a petition by the proper authority. A **formal petition** for adjudication is a statement of complaint against a minor. It is tantamount to an indictment or a bill of information in a criminal case.

Adjudication is another term that has special meaning in the juvenile system. It is analogous to the term *conviction* in criminal law. It is the official finding of delinquency or need of supervision.

The proper authority who may file for an adjudication varies from jurisdiction to jurisdiction. In many states, the district attorney retains the authority to petition to have a minor declared delinquent. In other jurisdictions, only a representative of a special juvenile authority may so petition.

Special juvenile authorities have various titles among the states. A common title for the office is the Bureau of Children's Services or the Department of Social Services. Whatever its title, the agency usually possesses the authority to petition the court for an adjudication of delinquency or to declare a need of supervision. Some states give such authority jointly to the district attorney and to the child welfare agency.

Form and Content of the Petition. The petition for an adjudication is usually titled in such a way as to distinguish it from criminal cases. A caption such as State ex rel. John Doe is common. Some states do not identify the minor in the title of the case as shown in the following example:

Possible case caption: In the Interest of the Minor Ronald K.

In all jurisdictions, the petition is required to set out the facts that demonstrate that the child is a delinquent or is in need of supervision. Most states require not only identification of the minor by name in the petition but other particulars such as date of birth, place of birth, gender, race, address, and present location of the child if different from the permanent address. The petition may also require facts such as the name and addresses of the minor's parents or the nearest relative if the parents cannot be located.

If violation of a law or ordinance is the basis for the petition, that statute must be identified specifically in the petition. The Supreme Court has declared that due process requires identification of the law allegedly violated that serves as the basis for the requested adjudication. See *In re Gault*, 387 U.S. 1 (1967).

Notice and Summons. *In re Gault* is must reading for anyone who intends to work in the area of juvenile justice. It is probably the Supreme Court's most extensive pronouncement on due process in juvenile proceedings. One of its most important holdings concerns who must be notified of the pendency of a petition for adjudication of delinquency. In *Gault* the Supreme Court declared that notice to parents is a requirement of due process. All states now have statutes that govern such matters. Generally speaking, the minors and the parents or guardian must be notified in writing as soon as practicable after a petition has been filed.

Taking the lead from *Gault*, some states have enacted notice provisions that are wide and far-reaching. For example, if the parents of the minor are divorced or separated, some states require notice not only to the custodial parent but to the noncustodial parent as well. (See Figure 9-2.)

FIGURE 9-2   NOTICE PROVISION

A copy of the petition and the notice of the nature of the hearing and the rights of the parent, as provided for in Article 639, shall be served upon every parent of the child.

LA. CHILD. CODE, *art. 638*

The Answer. In a juvenile proceeding, the **answer** is the response of the minor to a petition filed by authorities. It is equivalent to the plea made by a defendant at an arraignment in a criminal case. The summons served upon the minor will contain a notice of a required appearance to answer the petition. In almost every state, along with the summons, the minor is also notified of the right to be represented by counsel at the hearing and at subsequent proceedings.

At the hearing, the minor may admit the allegations of the petition or deny the allegations. This hearing is, for all intents and purposes, identical to an arraignment in a criminal case. In juvenile proceedings, however, no plea of guilty or not guilty is made. The minor merely makes an admission or a denial of the petition's allegations.

The procedures followed in most courts require that an admission, if there is one, be made by the minor personally; that is, the child must acknowledge the accuracy of the contents of the petition. The admission cannot be made by a parent or by an attorney on behalf of the juvenile. If there is an admission, the proceedings move to an adjudication by the judge. If there is a denial of the petition, the next formal step is the adjudication hearing, the equivalent of the trial in a criminal case.

If minor chooses to plead special factors, such as insanity, the answer should include such a defense. Earlier when we discussed the factors that can negate intent, we looked at the common law concept of infancy or, as we know it, immaturity. We noted at that time that some states, such as California, provide that immaturity may negate the intent required even in juvenile proceedings. If the immaturity issue is to be raised, it should be included in the answer of the minor.

The Right to Counsel

In the *Gault* case, the Supreme Court held that the right to counsel in juvenile proceedings is a due process requirement. Since the right to counsel is mandated by the Constitution, counsel for those minors who are unable to afford representation must be appointed.

The minor's right to counsel raises an interesting question. What must a judge do in a situation where the parents of the minor refuse to use the services of an attorney because they are convinced that the court will act in the best interest of the child? Though it is difficult to find reported decisions on this question, it would appear that the child's *right* to be represented can be served only if the court appoints counsel to advise the minor even if the parents want no attorney.

The Supreme Court decision in *Gault* involved a delinquency case in which the delinquent minor was ordered confined in a state "training school." There is no such definitive decision regarding the necessity of an attorney in a CHINS, or status offender, case.

Many states now have laws that deal with the question of appointing attorneys in CHINS cases. It is difficult to generalize beyond this statement. Some states require the appointment of an attorney; others do not. It appears that the majority of jurisdictions presently require appointment. If the question arises, the issue must be researched in the law of the state that is involved.

The Adjudication Hearing

The adjudication hearing equates to the trial phase in criminal court. The two are indistinguishable, except for the absence of a jury. The similarity has been recognized by the country's highest court. (See Figure 9-3.)

FIGURE 9-3   THE ADJUDICATION HEARING IS ALMOST INDISTINGUISHABLE FROM THE TRIAL PHASE IN A CRIMINAL PROCEEDING

[T]here is little to distinguish an adjudicatory hearing such as was held in this case from a traditional criminal prosecution.

Chief Justice Warren Burger in Breed v. Jones, *421 U.S. 519 (1975)*

More and more the juvenile courts are moving—perhaps it would be more accurate to say they are being moved—to conduct adjudication hearings in a formal, legalistic manner. The reason for this movement is not all that difficult to perceive.

Uninformed persons may still picture the delinquency hearing as though it were painted by Norman Rockwell—a youngster, with a sling shot extending from his back pocket, stands contrite before a grandfatherly judge who is trying to look stern. The scene in a juvenile court in no way resembles this image. If it were ever accurate, it belongs to a bygone era.

In today's courts, the minor has probably had all pockets searched and weapons removed, contrition is less likely than contempt, and the judge is not grandfatherly. Predictably, the judge is a young man or woman who does not have to force a serious face.

The description of the court's function may still be described in terms of the best interest of the minor, but its objective is as much to protect society as it is to provide for the child's welfare. Justice Burger noted that fact in the *Breed* decision cited above: "[The delinquency hearing] is designed to vindicate [the] very vital interest in enforcement of criminal laws." Consequently, the procedure at a delinquency hearing is almost identical to that employed at trial. Opening statements are usually given, with the "prosecutor" speaking first. Then the state presents its evidence. The minor has a right to confront and cross-examine witnesses. The "defense" may then present its evidence. Since no jury is involved, closing arguments are usually very limited. Some courts make it a practice to eliminate such arguments entirely.

We have stressed that juries are not required in juvenile hearings by the Constitution. Of course, there is no constitutional prohibition against a jury trial. In some states, such as Texas, the laws may provide for a jury. See *Texas Family Code*, § 54.03(c).

Evidence.   There is a great temptation to state that all evidence rules applicable in criminal trials apply to juvenile hearings. As a general rule, this statement is a fair summary. In most states, it is also completely accurate. However, some small differences occur among the states. In the state of Georgia, for example, illegally seized evidence may be used at a delinquency hearing.

A case in which this situation arose involved evidence obtained from an illegal search of a school locker by school officials. The Georgia Supreme Court allowed use of the evidence at the hearing, noting that each situation must be examined in order to determine if the benefits of admitting the evidence outweigh the unfavorable effects of excluding the material. See *State v. Young*, 234 Ga. 488, 216 S.E.2d 586 (1975), which can be found in the Georgia Reports and in the South Eastern Reporter, second series. However, the rule prevailing in most states is exemplified by a statement contained in the *Louisiana Children's Code*. (See Figure 9-4.)

FIGURE 9-4   RIGHTS IN JUVENILE COURT PROCEEDINGS

All rights guaranteed to criminal defendants by the Constitution of the United States or the Constitution of Louisiana, except the right to jury trial, shall be applicable in juvenile court proceedings brought under this Title.

LA. CHILD. CODE, art. 808

Burden of Proof. In a delinquency hearing, the burden of proof, of course, is borne by the state. The Supreme Court has ruled that when the delinquency is based on violation of a criminal statute, the state must prove every element of the crime *beyond a reasonable doubt.*

In its ruling, the Supreme Court dealt specifically with the question of delinquency based on violation of criminal law. It did not deal with other possible grounds for delinquency, nor did it rule on the proof requirements in a CHINS situation. In fact, the decision, which emanated from a New York case, specifically declared that the Court was making no ruling on the New York law governing "need of supervision." See *In re Winship*, 397 U.S. 358 (1970).

Thus, there is no constitutional rule pronounced by the Court regarding the quality of proof required in CHINS cases. In delinquency hearings, if the allegations supporting delinquency are based on violation of criminal law, the proof must be beyond a reasonable doubt. State laws that spell out the type of proof required are valid as long as they comply with *Winship*.

Adjudication

At the formal adjudication hearing, the judge makes a finding regarding the request for adjudication contained in the state's petition. This phase of the juvenile proceeding is equivalent to the return of a verdict by the jury or by the judge in a criminal trial. The court may find that the requested adjudication is warranted by the facts proved at the hearing, in which case it will find the minor delinquent or a child in need of supervision. If the evidence does not support the requested adjudication, the court will dismiss the petition.

Most state laws provide for a responsive verdict in juvenile cases. The term *responsive verdict* is technically inappropriate since there is no verdict in a juvenile case. However, in a situation where the petition asks for a finding of delinquency, the court instead may find the minor in need of supervision. The decision that the minor is in need of supervision is very similar to finding that the accused is guilty of a lesser included offense in a criminal case.

The judge may find that the juvenile is not delinquent or in need of supervision but that he or she is a child in need of care. This type of finding can be expected if the minor's mental capacity is an issue.

The Predisposition Report

In criminal cases, the sentencing judge usually requires an investigation into the background of the defendant with the results reported prior to imposition of sentence. In juvenile cases, the equivalent procedure is called a **predisposition report**.

The predisposition investigation (P.D.I.) is at least as comprehensive as the presentence investigation (P.S.I.) done prior to sentencing an adult. In many instances, the predisposition investigation is even more extensive. Of course, the report of the predisposition investigation must be made available to the minors and their counsel prior to the disposition hearing.

One major difference between the P.S.I. and the P.D.I. is that, in juvenile proceedings, the court may order a physical or mental examination of the minor in connection with the investigation. Many jurisdictions have statutory requirements covering the contents of P.D.I. reports. Paralegals must study the laws of the state to determine if such requirements exist. (See Figure 9-5.)

FIGURE 9-5 PREDISPOSITION INVESTIGATION AND REPORT

> Following adjudication, the court may order a predisposition investigation. The investigation *shall* include the circumstances, needs, and social history of the child and his family, and also the circumstances surrounding the factual allegations of the petition. A written report of the investigation and findings *shall* be submitted to the court prior to the disposition hearing. (Emphasis added)
>
> LA. CHILD. CODE, art. 878

Disposition Must Follow Adjudication—The Bifurcated Process

Among state systems, it is dogma that the disposition hearing be separate and distinct from the adjudication hearing. The whole case cannot be considered and disposed of at one sitting. This two-stage proceeding is called a bifurcated process. **Disposition**, in a juvenile court proceeding against a minor, is the action of the court equivalent to the sentence in a criminal case.

The reason for separating the disposition hearing from the fact-finding hearing is easy to understand. What is not at all clear is why the procedure has been given such prominence in state codes. Perhaps it is to ensure that the court's full and complete attention will be directed to the most significant question of the child's status during the fact-finding stage. No matter the reason, it is a tenet of faith within the juvenile justice establishment that the adjudication hearing and the disposition hearing may not be combined.

At the disposition hearing, the court is vested with very wide authority and almost unlimited latitude regarding the disposition. The alternatives available to the court at disposition include the following:

- Mere reprimand and release to the custody of the parents, unconditionally or on terms deemed to be in the best interest of the child
- Reprimand and release to some person other than a parent, unconditionally or on terms deemed to be in the best interest of the child
- Probation on terms and conditions deemed to be in the best interest of the child
- Custody in a private or public institution or agency
- Commitment to a juvenile correctional institution

The choices outlined above are illustrative. They do not exhaust the alternatives available to the court. Also, probationary conditions may include onerous conditions and may severely regulate conduct, thus limiting the liberty of the minor.

In order to be certain of the parameters of the court's authority in a particular jurisdiction, paralegals must consult local statutes. It is sufficient for our purposes to understand that the court's authority is generally very broad.

Maximum Confinement

Historically, the juvenile courts have used indeterminate commitment orders; that is, the commitment may extend for an indefinite period *not to exceed the minority of the delinquent.* Thus, a delinquent cannot be confined beyond his or her twenty-first birthday.

Some states limit commitment by the class or type of crime that formed the basis of delinquency. If the crime carries a maximum sentence of two years imprisonment, an adjudicated delinquent cannot be committed for a period longer than the maximum criminal penalty.

In other jurisdictions, the sentence for the underlying crime has no bearing on the confinement of the minor. It is not only possible but it has happened regularly that a delinquent's commitment exceeds the term that could be served by an adult. The Supreme Court has not ruled on this subject; however, state courts have allowed this anomaly on the theory that the juvenile is not being punished but protected and "trained" through confinement. The most recent statutes concerning commitment tend to set maximum limits upon the commitment corresponding to the underlying criminal statute, as seen in Figure 9-6.

FIGURE 9-6   MAXIMUM LIMITS CONCERNING JUVENILE COMMITMENT

No judgment of disposition shall remain in force for a person exceeding the maximum term of imprisonment for a felony forming the basis for the adjudication.

LA. CHILD. CODE, art. 898(4)

The Appeal

As we learned in Chapter 8, there is no constitutionally guaranteed right to appeal a criminal case; however, this issue diminishes in significance because an appeal process is provided for defendants in every state. The same can be said about juvenile appeals. Every state provides an appeal process for juveniles.

In most instances, the procedure is equivalent to the appeal process in a criminal case. State laws ordinarily restrict appeals to final dispositions.

This is similar to a criminal appeal, which is taken after the imposition of sentence. Generally speaking, the state has no right to appeal when the petition for adjudication has been dismissed.

EXPUNGEMENT

Many states provide that a juvenile's record may be expunged of references to the conduct that resulted in an adjudication of delinquency. **Expungement** is the eradication of official records pertaining to a conviction of a crime or to an adjudication of delinquency. The idea behind expungement is that a person ought not be plagued for life by indiscretion committed as a minor. Expungement, however, is far from automatic and is not always easy to obtain.

Some states place a minimum waiting period on petitions to wipe clean the record. For example, the *Louisiana Children's Code* provides that a person over the age of twenty-one may petition for expungement of an adjudication of delinquency *but only after the passage of five years* from the date that the disposition was satisfied. Also, some adjudications may not be expungeable. If the underlying criminal offense was murder, manslaughter, rape, robbery with a dangerous weapon, or a similar offense, the law may forbid a cleanup of the delinquent's record.

In some states, expungement is unnecessary because proceedings in juvenile court are closed. In Missouri, for example, even law enforcement personnel (excluding juvenile authorities) do not have access to juvenile records.

POLICE ACTION AND DETENTION

The action of the police in stopping, questioning, arresting, holding, and releasing juveniles is an important aspect of the juvenile justice scheme. However, police action in response to juveniles is not sufficiently distinctive from police actions relative to adults to cause us to treat the subject specially. Generally speaking, all constitutional protections we have considered and will consider apply equally to adults and juveniles.

It is important to note that many local and state police authorities have special departmental guidelines for handling of minor arrestees by their officers. In order to become aware of the procedures used by any particular department, it is necessary to check with local officials and with others familiar with those rules. In some instances, the rules are codified in the juvenile code of the state. Researching those statutes is a must for paralegals working in the area of juvenile justice.

Most communities provide special facilities to house minors who are arrested or detained. Such facilities are separate from those used to hold adult offenders. Also, all states provide for the release of arrested juveniles to their parents or guardians in lieu of detention at a juvenile facility. The criteria for release vary among jurisdictions.

What should be understood is that there are rules that can come into play regarding where and under what circumstances a child may be held by authorities prior to an adjudication. If ever those issues become important in a case, local procedures must be researched.

Time constraints upon the arresting and holding authorities are also important in juvenile cases. The police and the juvenile authorities must act expeditiously whenever a minor is detained and not released to his or her family. It is important that the regulations of the local jurisdiction be thoroughly examined by anyone working on a case involving the detention of a minor.

10 THE PLEA BARGAIN

THE BETTER PART OF VALOR

We have learned a great deal about the processes of criminal law. We started our discussion of criminal law with the Constitution and discovered that it is the cornerstone of our entire system. The essentials of due process and the other rights guaranteed by that document form the fundamental elements for our concept of justice.

The procedures we have studied have been put into place to ensure the efficient and fair administration of the system through trial, sentencing, and appeal. In fact, it should be apparent that the entire process is directed toward a correct resolution of the issues presented at a formal trial.

The trial is the focal point of the plan. All preliminary procedures have been designed to ensure that it is orderly and that only properly obtained, competent evidence is placed before the trier of fact. After a conviction, the appeals court examines the trial and the judgment from the near-perfect perspective of hindsight.

It would appear to the uninformed observer, from all the preparation directed at providing a fair trial and all the appellate scrutiny focused on what took place at trial, that most criminal matters must be disposed of by the trial process. Although it might appear that way, such is not the case.

Most criminal cases never make it to the trial stage. The majority of cases in which persons are formally charged are resolved by guilty pleas. Some persons may be shocked to learn that fact, but they should not be surprised.

In practice our system can provide trials for only a small percentage of the thousands of persons arrested each day. In every large city, the system would be hopelessly overtaxed if even half its felony cases made it to trial. Of

175

course, we know that the system must handle not only felony offenses but misdemeanors and petty offense violations as well. Logistically speaking, there is simply no way to provide a trial in every case.

Think of the system as a funnel. The police and other enforcement agencies operate at the wide end. In any sizeable urban area, thousands of such officers and agents investigate crime and make arrests. As the funnel tapers to the middle, in an area much smaller than the mouth, we find the prosecutors. A large district attorney force could number a hundred or so prosecutors.

Toward the smaller end of the funnel, we find the felony trial courts, perhaps twenty or twenty-five divisions in a large urban area. When we get to the smallest end of the funnel, we find the appeals court, usually just one, which reviews all cases from the multiple divisions of the trial court.

Of course, if we want to carry our image even further, consider that each state has only one supreme court to sit in review of all circuit appeals courts. And, for those cases that get there, the U.S. Supreme Court is a single institution serving as the final arbiter of constitutional questions arising in criminal cases from all state and federal courts.

It takes very little imagination to picture the congestion as the legal funnel tapers to its end. Thousands of officers and agents making arrests, hundreds of prosecutors processing cases, but only tens of judges holding trials. If every defendant demanded a trial, the system would be blocked in a few weeks. You might wonder what prevents blockage and keeps cases flowing. The answer is our topic for this chapter, the plea bargain.

When we discuss plea bargains, we are speaking of the defendant tendering a plea of guilty, thus eliminating the necessity for a trial, in return for a concession from the prosecutor.

Of course, the defendant would have no reason to plead guilty if the sentence would be the same as the one handed down after trial and conviction. That is the purpose of the negotiations, in a plea bargain: the prosecutor gains by eliminating a trial and the possibility of an acquittal; the defendant gains by getting a reduced penalty.

At trial, one side wins it all and the other loses everything. Perhaps this winner-take-all scenario is why the plea bargain is so prevalent. No one wants to risk losing it all. Discretion would indicate that a compromise is a good way to ensure at least a partial victory. After all, discretion is the better part of valor.

An Even Playing Field

A reasonable first impression of the plea bargaining process might be that the defendant is dealing from a strong position since the plea bargain is a virtual necessity for the prosecution and the courts. In reality, neither side has a built-in advantage. Whereas the prosecution's incentive to bargain is provided by the pressures of a heavy caseload, defendants derive great incentive from the fact that it is they who face the consequences of conviction.

The strengths and weaknesses of opposing positions are determined by the facts of a particular case. If the evidence is very strong for the prosecution, a defendant is not very likely to command much consideration in negotiating with the state. On the other hand, if the case is weak and the likelihood of acquittal is strong, the defendant may be able to obtain meaningful concessions from the prosecution.

Home Field Advantage for the Prosecution

As we have noted earlier, the state begins a case with a decided advantage. In the first instance, the prosecutor decides whether or not a case will be pursued. This initial decision is usually made during the screening process. Under most circumstances, the state's attorney has no interest in initiating prosecution if a case is of questionable merit. Consequently, because the prosecutor gets to choose the issues over which the battle will be fought, it is unlikely that he or she will choose a loser.

Of course, instances occur when the prosecutor is obligated to bring a charge even though the evidence is not as strong as it should be. Under circumstances involving sensational crimes or in situations where the suspect is very prominent, societal considerations may militate an acceptance of an otherwise refusable case. On the whole, however, even though the district attorney has a big stake in getting a defendant to "cop out," he or she usually does not have to give away the store in order to persuade the defendant to negotiate. Because the government's case is probably quite strong, the defendant is usually eager to talk deal.

Who Blinks First?

We all know the scene: two adversaries lock eyes and try to stare down each other. Neither will divert his eyes; neither will even blink. Blinking is a sign of weakness, and it is dangerous to show your opponent a sign of weakness. To the inexperienced practitioner, it may seem that the blinking rule would apply in criminal cases, but generally, it does not. If the parties possess even a modest amount of experience, they know from the outset that eventually discussion will focus on disposing of the case without a trial. No weakness is betrayed by being the first to broach the subject.

It Is Never Too Early to Talk

The exact point at which talks begin between prosecutor and defense depends in large measure on when defense counsel enters the case. As a rule, it is never too early to discuss a negotiated settlement.

We are aware that a criminal case can come into being in two ways. We briefly discussed this idea earlier. A common occurrence is that a crime is committed, the police make an immediate arrest, and a report is given to the district attorney. The investigation begins and ends at the scene. No defense attorney is present at the time of the arrest. Everything is in place for a decision to be made by the prosecutor before the defendant even speaks to an attorney.

A second situation occurs when an ongoing investigation is instituted prior to arrest or formal charges. Under these circumstances, the suspect is probably aware that he or she is under investigation; therefore, it is very likely that a defense attorney will enter the picture before the arrest or indictment is made.

As soon as defense counsel has had an opportunity to evaluate a case, discussions may begin between the two sides. It is not at all unusual to find that a plea bargain is made even before formal charges have been filed. In fact, agreements between prosecution and defense often control the contents of a formal charge. Distinct advantages can be realized by striking a bargain as early in the case as possible.

We will learn more about the objectives of plea bargaining negotiations in the following sections. At this juncture, it is important to understand several major points:

- The operation of the criminal justice system is facilitated by the plea bargain process.
- The plea bargain is a valuable tool for both the prosecution and the defendant.
- It is not a sign of weakness for either party to make first contact regarding a discussion of a negotiated settlement.
- Some advantages can be attained by beginning bargaining sessions early in the case.

OBJECTIVES OF THE PLEA BARGAIN

In general terms it is easy to describe the bargaining objectives of the two sides. They each begin by trying to deliver the total package. For the prosecution, the entire package includes having the defendant plead guilty without having to modify the charges or grant concessions regarding the sentence. For the defendant, the ultimate is having the prosecutor drop the charges without entering a guilty plea to any charge, even to a reduced one. Practical considerations usually alter the objectives of both sides.

The Prosecutor's Point of View

No prosecutor likes to *nol pross*, that is, dismiss a charge after the indictment has been returned or a bill of information has been filed. If a prosecutor is inclined to reject a case, he or she is most apt to do so prior to the acceptance of charges.

The fact of the matter is that courts and prosecutors keep records. A dismissed case forms part of the record. In most jurisdictions, the district attorney is an elected official. It simply is not good politics for the prosecutor's performance record to reflect a multitude of *nol prossed* cases.

Reducing the district attorney's decision to dismiss a case to a matter of politics may seem cynical. Of course, many factors other than political considerations make up the decision to keep or dismiss a case. The point to be understood here is that the prosecutor has a very strong mind set against *nolle prosequi.*

The Prosecutor's Incentives to Negotiate

There are several reasons why a prosecutor may consider refusing, dismissing, or reducing the charge against a defendant. We already know that the caseload in most prosecutors' offices makes bargaining a necessity. We now want to look at some of the factors considered by the prosecutor in deciding which cases are suitable for negotiation. What follows is not an exhaustive list of the prosecutor's motives, but it addresses the considerations most often used to explain reductions. The order of presentation is not designed to indicate the popularity of each reason.

To Ensure Conviction. One important consideration for the district attorney concerns the belief that the defendant may be able to "beat the rap" although he or she is guilty as sin, owing to the lack of admissible, competent evidence to prove the case. Under such circumstances, the government's attorney might be very receptive to a negotiated resolution because it can be sure that the defendant does not walk away from the case with an acquittal.

To Obtain Cooperation. Another of the prosecution's incentives to negotiate with an accused may involve securing that defendant's assistance. In a multiple-defendant case, the prosecution may need evidence from one of the possible defendants to strengthen the case against others involved in the crime.

In such a situation, the district attorney will be quite receptive to dealing on a *quid pro quo* basis. By *quid pro quo* we mean an exchange of consideration. If a suspect or a defendant can provide assistance to the government's case, the prosecutor will reciprocate by reducing (or maybe even dismissing) charges against him or her.

For a defendant or a possible defendant, assisting the prosecution most frequently takes the form of testimony. As we know, a person may not be forced to testify at his or her own trial. By striking a bargain with a potential defendant, the prosecutor can obviate the need for a trial in the case of that party. Then at the trial of the codefendants, the prosecutor may use the bargaining party as a witness. Of course, the testimony of a potential defendant must be voluntary, but the bargain between the prosecution and the witness will have provided for that eventuality.

Sometimes the government wants more than testimony from an individual seeking to bargain. More than testimony frequently means surreptitious involvement as an agent of the prosecution. Surreptitious involvement can take several forms. It may mean that the cooperating individual will allow investigators to tape-record conversations with other defendants or suspects, or it may involve more dynamic participation, such as taking an active role in undercover operations.

To Express Sympathy for the Defendant. A third consideration for making concessions to a defendant or potential defendant revolves around the sympathetic nature of some of those persons. Prosecuting attorneys are not without human feelings. One of the factors that can play an important role in the decision to negotiate with a defendant are the circumstances of the person's involvement in the crime. In a case where there are extenuating circumstances, a prosecutor may be genuinely sympathetic to the cause of a defendant.

A key to understanding the sympathetic frame of mind displayed by prosecutors involves recognizing what prosecutors face on a daily basis. In practically every case handled by a state's attorney, defendants are aggressive, blameworthy individuals. When the attorney encounters a potential defendant who does not fit the mold of the usual subject, the prosecutor recognizes that fact and may be moved to treat the accused with greater understanding.

The Defendant's Incentives to Negotiate

In the case of the defendant, the motivation to plea bargain is readily apparent. It is always undertaken with a view to minimizing the penalty. Of course, as we noted previously, the initial thrust of the defendant is often directed not at reducing its effect but at having the entire charge dropped. In many instances, dropping charges is an unrealistic objective and not a serious goal of the negotiations.

The defendant or the potential defendant who understands that the case against him or her is strong and that the prosecutor is not going to roll over usually approaches the discussions with a more tenable plan than merely hoping that charges will be dismissed. It almost always involves an offer embodying some sort of guilty plea.

The factors that may move a prosecutor to reduce are well known to defense attorneys and to many defendants who have had previous experience with the system. A defendant usually formulates his or her approach to plea bargaining negotiations to embrace one of the motivating factors discussed in the previous segment: to ensure conviction, to obtain cooperation, to capture sympathy.

Whenever the case against a client is weak, the defense attorney is certain to let the prosecutor know that he or she is aware of the case's weaknesses. If the defendant has information that is valuable to the prosecution, the defense team may proffer that evidence to the government's counsel to see what kind of return it may bring by way of lessening the consequences for the defendant. Of course, if the defendant is a particularly sympathetic individual, that factor will also be worked into the discussion.

What is significant about the approach of the defense team is that it almost never relies entirely on the court's overcrowded docket to supply the impetus for a bargain. Despite what we know of the system's overload and the high number of cases that must be disposed of by prosecutors and judges, there is always a place on the court calendar for one more trial. A defendant who gives the prosecutor no reason to negotiate may well find himself or herself sitting before a jury.

OTHER CONSIDERATIONS

Many considerations other than those already mentioned go into the decision to bargain. What follows is a look at some of the major considerations that confront the prosecution, the defense, and the court.

The Avoidance of Greater Harm

Some may believe that no one would ever consider pleading guilty to a crime that he or she did not commit. To those persons it may come as a great shock to learn that such situations do occur and that the Court sanctions the acceptance of a guilty plea from a defendant who refuses to admit wrongdoing.

It is a troubling complication when a defendant adamantly maintains his or her innocence but wants to plead guilty in order to avoid the full wrath of the law. This situation arose in the case of *North Carolina v. Alford*, 400 U.S. 25 (1970). The facts of the case are quite interesting. Alford was charged with first-degree murder. On advice of counsel, he decided to plead guilty to second-degree murder to avoid the death penalty.

Alford, who was sentenced to life in prison, adamantly declared his innocence of any crime. However, he made it clear that he wanted to plead guilty in order to avoid, in his own words, "being gassed." The Supreme Court allowed the plea to stand, holding that it was an intelligent waiver made by a defendant who weighed the consequences and chose to avoid the greater harm. The term *Alford* **plea** is used today to designate plea bargains wherein the defendant is allowed to maintain his or her innocence but has decided to plead guilty to avoid potentially more severe consequences. (See Figure 10-1.)

FIGURE 10-1   THE *ALFORD* PLEA

An individual accused of crime may voluntarily, knowingly and understandingly consent to the imposition of sentence even if he is unable or unwilling to admit his participation in the acts constituting the crime.

Justice White in North Carolina v. Alford, *400 U.S. 25 (1970)*

Before the *Alford* decision, many judges, prosecutors, and defense attorneys were troubled by circumstances such as those that arose in *Alford*. In an effort to alleviate their misgivings, the federal rules were altered in 1966 to add a requirement that no judgment of guilt may be entered on a plea of guilty unless the court is satisfied that there is a factual basis for the plea. (See Figure 10-2.) In other words, unless there is some reasonable basis, other than the defendant's plea, to believe that the defendant is guilty, the court will not enter a judgment of conviction. No guidance is given regarding the establishment of a reasonable basis.

FIGURE 10-2   A FACTUAL BASIS FOR A GUILTY PLEA MUST BE ESTABLISHED BEFORE A COURT WILL ENTER A JUDGMENT OF CONVICTION

> Notwithstanding the acceptance of a plea of guilty, the court should not enter a judgment upon such plea without making such inquiry as shall satisfy it that there is a factual basis for the plea.
>
> FED. R. CRIM. P. 11(f)

The rule also requires that the judge address a defendant personally to make certain that the defendant is aware of the nature of the charge, his or her right to an attorney, and his or her right to plead not guilty; that the guilty plea eliminates a trial; and that the plea is voluntary. We considered this process when we discussed Boykinization procedures in Chapter 4. The duty to address the defendant personally is provided in Rule 11(c) of the Federal Rules of Criminal Procedure and its subparts.

It must be noted here, and all defense attorneys are aware of this fact: the decision to plead guilty or to go to trial must remain exclusively with the defendant. The defense team would be remiss not to explore for advantages or to fail to counsel the client on the possible and probable outcomes of such a decision. However, there is such a thing as pushing too hard. The client must know what the possibilities are, and he or she must know what offers have been tendered by the prosecution. The ultimate decision, however, belongs to the client.

The Conditional Plea

In certain situations, the defendant and the prosecution may be unable to reach agreement regarding a negotiated plea because of a particular defense or objection to certain evidence. For example, if a defendant is confronted with almost certain conviction, based on evidence of questionable admissibility, that person may be reluctant to enter into any type of plea arrangement. Pleading guilty would cancel his or her right to have an appeals court examine the question of admissibility. Under these circumstances, the parties may become polarized and the court forced to use valuable trial time to hear a case that could have been negotiated away but for the existence of one issue.

In 1983 the Federal Rules of Criminal Procedure were amended to make it easier to resolve this difficult problem. The solution made available by the rules involves a *conditional* plea of guilty. (See Figure 10-3.) A **conditional plea** is a plea of guilty entered by a defendant who reserves the right to appeal a judgment of conviction on a specific issue or issues. By written agreement, the parties consent to set aside a guilty plea if the issue is decided in favor of the defendant on appeal.

FIGURE 10-3 THE CONDITIONAL PLEA

> With the approval of the court and consent of the government, a defendant may enter a conditional plea of guilty or nolo contendere, reserving in writing the right, on appeal from the judgment, to a review of the adverse determination of any specified pretrial motion. A defendant who prevails on appeal shall be allowed to withdraw the plea.
>
> *FED. R. CRIM. P. 11(a)(2)*

It should be apparent that the provision for a conditional plea can go a long way toward eliminating single-issue trials.

The rule cited in Figure 10-3 makes one interesting point very obvious. Though the court likes to stay out of plea arrangements, when it comes to conserving the court's time, the rules make it possible for judges to approve bargains that eliminate the necessity of a trial. Though some judges may take a disdainful view toward sullying themselves by association with a plea bargain, they are very interested in seeing that the bargaining gets done. Conservation of court time is very much in the forefront of judicial thinking.

The conditional plea is a tool available only in a minority of state jurisdictions. The major objection to the plea seems to be the argument that it foists on the appellate courts an abundance of partially tried cases. That is, the facts are not fully developed in the trial process and therefore the appeals courts have to rule on issues instead of being able to rely on the harmless error rule. **Harmless error** is any error, defect, irregularity, or variance in procedure or the trial process that does not affect the substantial rights of the defendant. Harmless errors will be overlooked by appellate courts and will not form the basis for a reversal of a conviction. It is defined in the Federal Rules of Criminal Procedure. (See Figure 10-4.)

FIGURE 10-4 HARMLESS ERROR, DEFINED

> **Harmless Error.** Any error, defect, irregularity or variance which does not affect substantial rights shall be disregarded.
>
> *FED. R. CRIM. P. 52(a)*

In actual practice, the appeals courts have not been inundated by cases stemming from conditional guilty pleas. Most observers feel that the use of the conditional plea will grow in popularity among the states.

By reducing the case to its essential elements, it is sometimes possible to work out a plea bargain by using the conditional plea. A beneficial effect of the conditional plea is that it gives the defendant his or her day in court, which he or she understandably may desire. At the same time, it allows some room for the parties to work out an arrangement for disposing the case without a full-blown trial.

Deferred Prosecution, or Diversion

One of the concepts we discussed when we considered the responsibilities of the prosecutor was the use of diversion, or deferred prosecution. You will recall that deferred prosecution refers to an arrangement between the parties, the prosecutor and the defendant, whereby formal charges are withheld in return for the defendant submitting to some form of probationary overseeing. The idea behind deferred prosecution against a defendant is that the charges will be dismissed if he or she successfully demonstrates a willingness to alter the lifestyle that brought him or her under the scrutiny of the law. As a condition for diversion, the defendant frequently agrees to some sort of community service as payment of his or her debt to society. If the defendant falters during the diversion period, charges can be resurrected.

The process of diversion has gained popularity in some jurisdictions and has fallen into disuse in others. However, nearly all states and the federal system provide for deferred prosecution under some circumstances.

It is not difficult to see how helpful such an alternative can be during negotiations between prosecution and defense. Earlier we mentioned the human side of the defendant and noted that the prosecuting attorney is sometimes moved by sympathy for a defendant who does not fit the mold of the hardened criminal. Under these circumstances, the diversion alternative to formal prosecution may serve the interests of both parties.

An interesting question sometimes arises regarding the appropriate time to consider the diversion process. We have considered the advantages of beginning negotiations early in the case. We need to give some thought to the question of how long negotiations should continue. The National Association of Pretrial Services Agencies (NAPSA) has taken the position that some of the benefits of diversion are lost if the process is introduced too early in the case. (See Figure 10-5.)

The commentary illustrated in Figure 10-5 demonstrates that the bargaining between prosecution and defense can continue even after the lodging of formal charges. To answer the question regarding how long negotiations should continue, one should understand that the process can carry on up to sentencing. As a practical matter, the bargaining usually stops when the trial begins. However, it is not unheard of that an agreement between prosecution and defense is reached after trial has begun.

FIGURE 10-5   NAPSA STANDARDS SURROUNDING DIVERSION

While these standards recognize that pretrial diversion is offered as a cost saving, time saving, non-duplicative process and therefore should occur as soon as possible after arrest, nevertheless, pretrial diversion enrollment prior to formal filing of charges is viewed as premature and generally inconsistent with the requirements for voluntariness contained in this Standard. The post-charging state in the proceedings has been purposely selected as the earliest recommended point for diversion eligibility determination because it is only at this point that the government has documents indicating its intention to prosecute. The requirement that formal charges be filed prior to an eligibility determination minimizes the likelihood that individuals whose cases lack sufficient merit to support the filing of a simple information by the prosecutor will be diverted. It is axiomatic that if non-meritorious cases should not be prosecuted, they also should not be funnelled into the diversion process.

Commentary to Standard 1.1
NAPSA

FORM AND CONTENT OF PLEA AGREEMENTS

The content of an actual agreement varies as the situation and circumstances vary. Generally, *no secret agreements* are permitted.

Tacit Agreement

We used the word *generally* because situations can occur in which the parties come to an understanding without reducing the agreement to formal terms. Such understandings are usually tacit; that is, they are nonspecific, yet understood, although not spelled out by either party. An example may help illustrate our point:

> Authorities execute a search warrant at the home of Mr. and Mrs. Doe. The search uncovers two closets filled with stolen merchandise. Mr. Doe is the suspected burglar, who acquired the merchandise through the unlocked back doors of the community. Although Mr. Doe is the only person known to have burglarized, Mrs. Doe probably had knowledge of his activities and certainly had constructive possession of the loot.

Under the circumstances discussed above, a **tacit agreement** (i.e., an unwritten, nonspecified understanding between the prosecution and the defense) might be reached to exclude Mrs. Doe from the case if Mr. Doe confesses to the burglaries and gives up his accomplice. The prosecution may make known to defense counsel its assumption: We know Doe had a partner. We have to assume it was his wife. Doe's subsequent agreement to cooperate and disclose the identity of the actual accomplice would probably not include any reference to his wife's involvement. If Doe follows through, the case against his wife will be refused or forgotten.

The Doe case is an example of a tacit agreement because the understanding regarding Mrs. Doe was implied; it was never reduced to writing or even specified. Such understandings are frequently reached between prosecutor and defendant. The paralegal who analyzes a case for the prosecution or the defense must be aware of the potential usefulness of tacit agreements.

Explicit and Written Agreements

Though tacit agreements are possible and occur with some regularity, the vast majority of plea agreements are written and very explicit. In the federal rules (see Figure 10-6) and in the rules by which most state courts operate, plea agreements are required to be disclosed in the record of the case.

FIGURE 10-6   PLEA AGREEMENTS MUST BE DISCLOSED

If a plea agreement has been reached by the parties, the court shall, on the record, require the disclosure of the agreement in open court, or, on a showing of good cause, in camera . . .

FED. R. CRIM. P. 11(e)(2)

For the sake of clarity and to avoid any misunderstanding, the entire plea agreement should be reduced to writing. Since the agreement is to be made a part of the court record, there is hardly a reason not to put the agreement in black and white.

The Authority of the Prosecution to Negotiate

The defendant is generally without restriction in the bargaining process. However, the government's attorney must operate within certain limits. In the federal rules, these constraints are spelled out specifically. The limitations employed by individual states may vary in detail from state to state and from the federal standards; in practice, however, most state prosecutors exercise comparable authority. The federal rule gives us a fairly accurate picture of the authority possessed by most prosecutors to negotiate. (See Figure 10-7.)

In most systems, including the federal system, the court retains authority to accept or reject plea bargains. If an agreement is rejected by the court, the defendant must be given the opportunity to withdraw a guilty plea, according to Rule 11(e)(4) of the Federal Rules of Criminal Procedure. As a practical consideration, the court does not seriously entertain the notion of a rejection of a plea. If the parties agree, the court almost always goes along. However, it is important that the parties know the judge so that their agreement can be couched in terms that the court will approve.

FIGURE 10-7 THE PROSECUTOR'S AUTHORITY TO NEGOTIATE

The attorney for the government and the attorney for the defendant or the defendant when acting pro se may engage in discussions with a view toward reaching an agreement that, upon entering a plea of guilty or nolo contendere to a charged offense or a lesser or related offense, the attorney for the government will do any of the following:

(A) move for dismissal of other charges; or

(B) make a recommendation or agree not to oppose the defendant's request, for a particular sentence, with the understanding that such recommendation or request shall not be binding upon the court, or;

(C) agree that a specific sentence is the appropriate disposition of the case.

The court shall not participate in any such discussions.

FED. R. CRIM. P. 11(e)(1)(A)(B)(C)

Negotiating under Sentencing Guidelines

The introduction of the guideline system into the sentencing process has somewhat altered the historical positions of the parties. This is certainly true in the federal system, and it may become more of a factor in other jurisdictions as the guideline concept spreads through the states. Every indication is that the states are moving in the direction of sentencing guidelines.

The scheme currently being used by the federal courts allows the prosecuting authority to make sentencing recommendations based on the cooperation of the defendant. The authority of the prosecution to suggest a downward departure is significant to our subject. The prerogative of the prosecutor to suggest leniency, as contained in the guidelines, is relegated to the form of a motion. That is to say, the U.S. attorney cannot guarantee that the court will sentence the defendant below the level recommended by the guidelines, it can only *move* that the judge do so. It is important that the limitation of the prosecutor's authority be understood.

Substantial Assistance

In the rule appearing in Figure 10-8, the term *substantial assistance* is mentioned. Section 5K1.1 of the U.S. Sentencing Guidelines (U.S.S.G.) does not define substantial assistance; however, it does give the court the authority to review the prosecution's evaluation of the defendant's cooperation. In short, the rule reduces the commitments of the prosecutor to the point where they are merely recommendations Thus, any plea bargain containing an agreement regarding a sentence is necessarily nonbinding. **Substantial assistance**, therefore, is a means of allowing a sentencing judge to depart downward from a sentencing guideline in consideration for meaningful cooperation by the defendant with law enforcement officials.

FIGURE 10-8 SUBSTANTIAL ASSISTANCE RULE

> Upon motion of the government stating that the defendant has provided substantial assistance in the investigation or prosecution of another person who has committed an offense, the court may depart from the guidelines.
>
> (a) The appropriate reduction shall be determined by the court for reasons stated that may include, but are not limited to, consideration of the following:
>
> (1) the court's evaluation of the significance and usefulness of the defendant's assistance, taking into consideration the government's evaluation of the assistance rendered;
>
> (2) the truthfulness, completeness, and reliability of any information or testimony provided by the defendant;
>
> (3) the nature and extent of the defendant's assistance;
>
> (4) any injury suffered, or any danger or risk of injury to the defendant or his family resulting from his assistance;
>
> (5) the timeliness of the defendant's assistance.
>
> *U.S.S.G. § 5K1.1*

Even though sentence agreements contained in a plea bargain are non-binding, the government is not prevented from making recommendations for a specific sentence. In the event that such a recommendation is made as part of a negotiated agreement between the prosecution and the defendant, the court may accept the plea agreement. The criteria for acceptance of the agreement by the court is twofold:

1. Is the recommended sentence within the guidelines?
2. Is there justifiable reason for departure from the guidelines?

In other words, the court may approve a specific sentence recommended by the prosecutor if there is good reason for the recommendation. See § 6B1.2(c) of the U.S. Sentencing Guidelines.

In the event that the plea agreement is rejected by the court, the defendant is given the opportunity to withdraw the plea of guilty. See § 6B1.3 of the U.S. Sentencing Guidelines.

THE PARALEGAL'S ROLE IN THE NEGOTIATION PROCESS

It is impossible to make many general statements regarding the role of the paralegal in the bargaining phase of a case because the assignment of the paralegal depends on too many variables. However, it is possible to examine some of the factors that are important to the process with an understanding that the paralegal will probably be assigned to handle one or more of those elements. Several tasks become urgent when the possibility of a plea is being considered.

The Potential Sentence

First, the paralegal must be or become familiar with the range of sentences likely to be imposed. In states that use sentencing guidelines and in the federal system, which relies exclusively on sentence guidelines, the paralegal's job may be more easily focused. Having a chart of sentence ranges to consult is a big help in briefing the attorney and the client about possible sentences, in the case of the defense.

If the paralegal is working in a jurisdiction that does not employ guidelines for sentences, the tasks are somewhat more exacting. Determining a judge's propensities is an inexact science at best. Whether or not guidelines are available to aid in this task, the paralegal might consider discussing the facts with a probation officer who is familiar with sentencing procedures. The client has a right to an educated estimate of the exposure that will be incurred by a plea of guilty or a conviction.

The Defendant's Background

Next, the background of the defendant is very important in planning a bargain hunt. Of course, we have seen that the background of the defendant is important even if the case is to be tried. What is important to understand is that knowledge of the background and criminal record of the defendant is essential while negotiating a case. Uncovering that background is not a task that can be delayed.

Alternatives to the Charged Offense

Another aspect of the case that the paralegal must consider concerns alternative charges that a prosecutor might use. For example, if the defendant is charged with murder, it is unlikely that the prosecution will consider an alternative such as possession of stolen property. If a reduction in the charge is desirable, the suggested reduced offense must correspond to the facts of the case. If the charge proposed by the prosecution is murder, an alternative proposal such as manslaughter would make more sense.

In actual practice, the problem of finding a suitable alternative charge may not be as apparently simple as it may seem from our example. Sometimes finding a suitable alternative requires ingenuity and research. Consider the case of a group of people engaged in the distribution of illegal narcotics. If one of the defendants is only peripherally involved, it may be that his or her inclusion in the proposed conspiracy charge can be reduced to a charge of misprison in return for assistance to the prosecution's efforts against the ring leaders.

Of course, if the paralegal is not aware of the elements of the crime of misprison or that the sentencing guidelines (*in this case the federal guidelines*) classify misprison nine levels lower than the principal offense, then, under these circumstances, the paralegal would not be able to suggest misprison as an alternative to the proposed charge. The point we are making here is that it may be necessary for the paralegal to hit the books from time to time in order to make a contribution.

A final task that might have a relation to the bargaining process involves the development of evidence. If paralegals are performing investigative functions, they may have some input regarding evaluation of the evidence. If evidence is particularly strong or convincing, the defense may be very interested in working out an agreement. If evidence is lacking or is weak, the prosecution may have added incentive to consider bargaining.

For the job assignments mentioned above, it makes little difference whether the paralegal works with the defense or with the prosecution. We have considered the paralegal's role in the negotiation process primarily in the defense context; however, it has equal applicability on the other side of the case.

Finding a suitable substitute charge is as likely an assignment for the paralegal who works for the prosecution as it is for the paralegal working for the defense. Often it is the prosecutor who suggests to a defendant that some relief may be gained through cooperation with the authorities. The impetus to negotiate does not always stem from the defense side. It is sometimes up to the government to dangle an attractive proposition before the defendant—as in our example of a reduction from conspiracy to misprison—in order to induce cooperation.

A FINAL NOTE

Hard and fast rules regarding when to recommend a bargain and when to recommend a trial are impossible to formulate. The variables are limitless. We have seen that plea bargaining is a common process. In practice, it enables the justice system to operate. Without the plea bargain, the process would not work.

However, the decision to try a case is in every case a fresh one. No prosecutor intentionally accepts a case that is unprovable. No defendant voluntarily gives up his or her liberty without careful thought. The factors that compel a prosecutor to step back from a winnable case and the factors that move a defendant to accept conviction, without proof at trial, are never predictable. Every case requires close scrutiny by each party and by all representatives of each party. Even as they are preparing a case for trial, paralegals who work for the prosecution and the defense must be alert for factors that make bargaining desirable.

One caveat must be stressed for paralegals working with the defense: *the decision to plead guilty or to go to trial must remain exclusively with the defendant!* The defense team would be remiss not to explore for advantages, and it must also counsel and advise clients regarding their decisions, but the ultimate decision belongs to the client.

The defense team must be certain that its client is not coerced into a plea of guilty. We have discussed plea bargains and have noted that the prosecution and the court can reward a defendant for cooperation. It must be understood that the reverse is not true: *a defendant may not be penalized for refusing to cooperate or for demanding his or her right to trial.* (See Figure 10-9.)

FIGURE 10-9   A DEFENDANT CANNOT BE PENALIZED FOR REFUSING TO COOPERATE

A defendant's refusal to assist authorities in the investigation of other persons may not be considered as an aggravating sentencing factor.

U.S.S.G. § 5K1.2

11 SEARCH, SEIZURE, AND EVIDENCE

EVIDENCE—INFORMATION THAT SUPPORTS A CONCLUSION

We have discussed motions, trials, and the bargaining that takes place between parties. A common thread runs through all these subjects. In some fashion, all are concerned with evidence and the question of its legality and admissibility.

When we discussed pretrial motions in Chapter 5, we noted that one of the maneuvers engaged in prior to trial is the motion to suppress. The suppression motion is designed to test the admissibility of evidence. It may be directed at any evidence that the defendant believes to be improper.

In Chapter 6, we looked at developing a theory of the case and at effectively using evidence that supports that theory. When we examined the bargaining process in the preceding chapter, we saw that lack of admissible evidence may alter the negotiating positions of the parties.

We have learned that evidence has no special meaning in law. It means just what it means in every other context: information upon which a conclusion or a judgment may be based. However, in the law, to be admissible (i.e., usable), evidence must be both competent and lawfully obtained. In this chapter we will look more closely at the factors that determine the competency and admissibility of evidence.

COMPETENCE

When we speak of the competence of evidence, we are speaking of an inher-

193

ent quality of the information's source. The definition of competent evidence may be made more apparent through an example:

> Assume that during a trial an issue arises involving the defendant's mode of dress. A blind person would not be able to offer *competent* evidence regarding the color of the defendant's clothing because a sightless person would not be able to determine color through his or her faculties.

Frequently, the issue of competence occurs when experts are employed as witnesses. If a person has particular training or experience through which he or she has acquired special knowledge, that person is allowed to testify at trial as an expert and to advance opinions within his or her area of expertise. A fire marshal would be able to give competent opinions regarding the origin of a fire. An architect would not have a competent opinion on that issue. Thus, the competence of evidence is a factor of the evidence's source. Formally defined, **competent evidence** is plausible evidence from a source worthy of consideration.

Rules of Evidence

The Federal Rules of Evidence are designed to deal with all facets of evidence, including questions related to competence. All states have rules or codes governing the reception of evidence in their legal proceedings. Most state rules are very similar to the federal rules. For the most part, rules of evidence are codifications of common sense norms; therefore, there is little need for variation between the states and very few differences exist.

As seen in Figure 11-1, the federal rule on the question of competence is typical. This rule codifies the reason for excluding the testimony of the sightless person in our example involving the issue of color. There is no way to prove that a blind witness could have personal knowledge of the defendant's clothing.

FIGURE 11-1   THE COMPETENCE OF EVIDENCE, ACCORDING TO FEDERAL RULES

A witness may not testify to a matter unless evidence is introduced sufficient to support a finding that the witness has personal knowledge of the matter. Evidence to prove personal knowledge may, but need not, consist of the witness' own testimony. This rule is subject to the provisions of Rule 703 relating to opinion testimony by expert witnesses.

FED. R. EVID. 602

General Rules Regarding Competence

When we consider the personal knowledge of the witness, we must understand that the court usually presumes that the witness is competent unless incompetence becomes an issue. See Rule 601 of the Federal Rules of Evidence.

What this means is that a witness is allowed to testify regarding the color of clothing unless it becomes apparent that the testimony is baseless. If the witness is able to see well enough to walk into the courtroom, find the witness stand, and not stumble or bump into objects, the reliability of the witness's vision is presumed. However, if the witness carries a white cane and is led into the courtroom by a dog, competence would not be presumed.

If we are looking for general rules regarding competence, we might consider the following:

- The witness must possess the ability to perceive the facts about which he or she testifies.
- The witness must have personally perceived the facts.
- The witness must be able to recall the facts.
- The witness must understand the obligation to tell the truth.

Specific Competency Questions

The courts have considered many issues involving competency. It may be helpful to note some of the areas about which rulings have been made.

Minors. There is no automatic exclusion of testimony because the witness is a minor. See *United States v. Schoefield*, 465 F.2d 560 (D.C. Cir. 1972).

The court will explore certain factors if the child is very young. For example, Rule 603 requires the witness to declare that his or her testimony will be truthful. A judge certainly would want to be satisfied that a youngster who is a potential witness understands the obligation to tell the truth.

Witness with Mental Illness. The mere existence of a mental defect does not automatically disqualify a person as a witness. See *United States v. Roach*, 590 F.2d 181 (5th Cir. 1979). Of course, the court has great discretion regarding matters of mental capacity, and no judge would allow a raving lunatic to offer testimony. An interesting situation involving the sanity of a witness arose in the same circuit that handed down the *Roach* opinion. The U.S. Court of Appeals for the Fifth Circuit pronounced, as *dictum*, that a judge is not required to receive expert testimony on the mental competency of a witness. The trial court's finding on the issue of witness competency will be reversed only where there is a clear abuse of discretion. See *Shuler v. Wainwright*, 491 F.2d 1213 (5th Cir. 1974).

In *United States v. Lightly*, 677 F.2d 1027 (4th Cir. 1982), it was decided that a person who is incompetent to stand trial as a defendant may nonetheless testify as a witness at the trial of an accomplice. Apparently competence to testify is not the same as the competence required to assist counsel or to understand the nature of the charges.

An interesting question arises when the *sole* witness against a defendant is retarded. The prosecution would probably not pursue such a case; however, factual circumstances might constrain the prosecution to go forward. Consider the decision in *Ruocco v. Logiocco*, 104 Conn. 583 (1926), a case cited from the Connecticut Reporter. In this case, the defendant's conviction was reversed because the sole witness was a mentally deficient minor.

Witness on Drugs. A complication that seems to occur more frequently today than ever before involves the testimony of a witness who is an admitted drug user. As a rule, the witness may testify. The jury can give less credibility to the testimony because of the condition of the witness, but the testimony is competent.

A provocative situation occurred in the case of *United States v. Meerbeke*, 548 F.2d 1141 (2d Cir 1976). At the trial in the district court, the witness took drugs while testifying. The court allowed the testimony to go to the jury because the witness was apparently coherent and the jury could decide how much weight to give the witness's evidence.

The reasoning in the *Meerbeke* case was followed by the U.S. Court of Appeals for the Sixth Circuit in the case of *United States v. Ramirez*, 871 F.2d 582 (6th Cir. 1989). The holding in *Ramirez* is that drug addiction affects only credibility, not competence. Displaying an unusually wry outlook, the court noted that as a rule only judges and jurors can never give testimony at a trial. Drug addicts, on the other hand, are frequently regarded as competent.

Hypnotized Witness. Our section heading is deliberately worded to catch your attention. No reported cases address the issue of a witness testifying while under hypnosis. However, there is a precedent for the admissibility of testimony from a witness who, prior to trial, underwent recollection enhancement through hypnosis.

In one case, the witness was a defendant who claimed not to recall the details of shooting her husband until she was hypnotized. The court allowed her testimony to go to the jury because it felt that a defendant's right to testify in her own defense could not be abridged by a state rule that excluded hypnotically refreshed testimony. See *Rock v. Arkansas*, 479 U.S. 947 (1987).

Following *Rock*, the U.S. Court of Appeals for the Eleventh Circuit allowed testimony from a witness other than the defendant during a murder trial even though the witness had previously undergone hypnosis to aid his recollection. The defendant argued that he (defendant) was denied his right to confront the witness, as required by the Sixth Amendment. The appeals court saw it otherwise. It held that the effect of the hypnosis could be measured by the jury. Regarding the defendant's claim that he was precluded from confronting the witness, the court found that the defendant could cross-examine the witness as well as the hypnotist and even produce expert testimony regarding the issue of recollection under hypnosis. According to the court, the witness was competent. The issue in this case was one of credibility, not competence. See *Bundy v. Dugger*, 850 F.2d 1402 (11th Cir. 1988).

Witnesses Who Cannot Speak English. Of course, a witness must be able to understand the proceedings and the questions and be able to articulate his or her answers. In the event that a witness does not speak or understand English, Rule 604 of the Federal Rules of Evidence provides for the use of an interpreter.

The interpreter must be sworn to translate accurately and possess sufficient expertise to do so continuously. See *United States ex rel. Negron v. New York*, 434 F.2d 386 (2d Cir. 1970). The court is given wide latitude in deciding on the qualifications of an interpreter. In one celebrated case, *United States v. Addonizio*, 451 F.2d 49 (3d Cir. 1971), the court even allowed the defendant's wife to serve as an interpreter.

Opinion Testimony by Nonexperts

On several occasions we have mentioned that an expert may give an opinion regarding a situation falling within his or her area of expertise. From what we have already learned, it may seem as though opinion testimony may be elicited only from an expert. Although this statement may be generally true, it is not always the case. A lay witness may give an opinion regarding common experiences, according to the Federal Rules. (See Figure 11-2.)

FIGURE 11-2   OPINIONS BY NONEXPERTS, OR LAY WITNESSES, ARE PERMITTED AT TRIAL

If the witness is not testifying as an expert, the witness' testimony in the form of opinions or inferences is limited to those opinions or inferences which are (a) rationally based on the perception of the witness and (b) helpful to a clear understanding of the witness' testimony or the determination of a fact in issue.

FED. R. EVID. 701

Situations in Which Lay Opinion Is Allowed. It may be helpful to examine some of the areas in which the courts have allowed opinion evidence from nonexpert witnesses. The discussion that follows is not intended to be an all-inclusive listing, but some common situations for which lay opinions may be offered are given.

It is a matter of discretion for the judge presiding over a trial to determine when a lay witness may give opinion testimony. See *United States v. Burnette*, 698 F.2d 1038 (9th Cir. 1983). Judges exercising their discretion have allowed opinion testimony from laypersons in many different factual situations. Whether a particular situation warrants the admission of a lay opinion can only be determined on a case-by-case basis.

Identifying Photographs In *United States v. Allen*, 787 F.2d 933 (4th Cir. 1986), the trial judge allowed a witness to identify the defendant in a photograph made from bank surveillance film. There was every reason to believe that the witness was competent to make the identification since the witness and defendant had known each other prior to the photograph being taken.

In an earlier case, *United States v. Ingram*, 600 F.2d 260 (10th Cir. 1979), a lay witness was allowed to give an opinion regarding the identity of a defendant in a bank robbery photograph even though the actual photograph was viewed by the jury and may have been inconclusive regarding the identity of the robber. The theory in *Ingram* was that the witness was more familiar with the defendant and could more easily identify him in the photograph than could jury members.

Identifying a Voice The court allowed a layperson to give an opinion regarding the identity of the speaker from voice recognition. The witness had to assure the court that he had no doubt as to the speaker because he was familiar with the voice having heard it prior to the recording. See *United States v. Rizzo*, 492 F.2d 443 (2d Cir. 1974).

The *Rizzo* case is very interesting because it concerned the voice identification made by detectives who had worked the case against the defendant. Their previous exposure to the defendant's voice had been minimal. This case points to the great discretion given the trial judge in deciding to allow the introduction of nonexpert opinion.

Identifying Handwriting Ordinarily we think of handwriting identification as an area of expertise. After all, many experts in the private sector and many government agents specialize in the identification of handwriting. However, a precedent has been set for allowing a lay witness to state an opinion regarding the author of a signature because of previous exposure to the writing of the suspect. See *Schaefer v. United States*, 265 F.2d 750 (8th Cir. 1959).

Identifying Insanity Another area in which nonexpert opinion testimony has been allowed concerns the issue of sanity. As is true in the case of handwriting identification, experts abound in the field of psychiatry and psychology. Nonetheless, courts have ruled that laypersons may be competent to testify relative to the sanity of a person with whom they are acquainted. See *United States v. Pickett*, 470 F.2d 1255 (D.C. Cir. 1972).

The Standard for Nonexpert Opinion. The key to understanding the court's allowing a nonexpert to draw a conclusion from the evidence, as a witness in the *Schaefer* case and in the *Pickett* case was permitted to do, is the recognition that the court requires that a lay witness's conclusion be based on personal observation and recollection. This criterion is quite different from the standard applied to an expert. An expert may testify as to opinion and draw conclusions on purely theoretical and hypothetical grounds based on facts not personally observed.

Not only must a lay witness have personally observed the facts and circumstances upon which his or her opinion is based, but those facts must be admitted into evidence. The courts have recognized that the jury must know the facts in order to know what weight to accord the testimony of the witness. This specific issue arose in a robbery case when the brother of the accused testified that the defendant was insane. The court allowed the conclusionary testimony to be properly admitted but noted that the underlying factual basis for the testimony must also be disclosed. See *United States v. Minor*, 459 F.2d 103 (5th Cir. 1972).

The *Minor* case dealt specifically with the issue of insanity; however, it is apparent that the requirements for admissibility may easily be extended to any situation in which a lay witness expresses an opinion. The reason for this standard is that the trier of fact has a right to evaluate the witness's observations in order to determine what weight should be accorded the opinion of that witness.

Thus, a party relying on the conclusions and opinions of a lay witness must be prepared to establish the facts upon which the testimony is based. Further, the witness must be prepared to relate those facts in open court. At this stage in the evolution of our system, it is not so much a question of whether a layperson's opinion will be admitted into evidence; rather, it is a question of how much reliance can be placed on that opinion. The only way that the trier of fact can resolve this issue is by knowing the facts that the witness observed and upon which the conclusion was based.

Evidence from Experts

Our consideration of the competence of evidence must include another mention of the testimony of experts. The federal rules provide for such testimony in Rule 702. (See Figure 11-3.)

FIGURE 11-3   THE TESTIMONY OF EXPERTS, AS PERMITTED BY THE FEDERAL RULES

If scientific, technical, or other specialized knowledge will assist the trier of fact to understand the evidence or to determine a fact in issue, a witness qualified as an expert by knowledge, skill, experience, training, or education, may testify thereto in the form of an opinion or otherwise.

FED. R. EVID. 702

Having noted the wide discretion of the court for allowing use of nonexpert opinion at trial, there would seem to be nothing more to say regarding expert testimony. Certainly, if a court can allow a nonexpert to give an opinion, it can allow an expert to do so. In the main, this condition is true; however, a few points must be made regarding this type of testimony.

When Are Experts Allowed? First, the court is under no obligation to allow an expert to testify. Nothing in the rules makes it mandatory for a judge to admit expert testimony. The rule makes it clear that an expert may be used if specialized knowledge will "assist the trier of fact to understand the evidence or to determine a fact in issue." Not every fact or bit of evidence needs expert explanation in order to be understood.

In actual practice, the court practically never disallows expert testimony on relevant issues. Much of the credit for that fact may belong to the bar. Lawyers are not often interested in producing experts who have nothing to add to a proceeding. For one thing, experts are expensive; for another, the unnecessary squandering of a jury's time is apt to bring unhappy results.

The key word in determining when an expert may be used is *assist*. Even in situations where the jury may thoroughly understand the evidence, a judge may nonetheless allow an expert to give an opinion because it can *assist* jurors in reaching a decision.

Who Are the Experts? An old courthouse saying defines an expert as "someone from out of town." This mildly humorous definition may not be far from the truth. Most persons think of experts in the traditional sense—as scientists, physicians (who are specialists), or engineers (whose business attire has special pockets for calculators). Today we recognize experts in practically every field—real estate, accounting, law, business or trade, and coded language used by narcotics traffickers. See *United States v. Simmons*, 923 F.2d 934 (2d Cir. 1991). Of course, this list merely exemplifies, it does not exhaust the possibilities.

In short, an expert can be anyone with a special skill or special knowledge that may be helpful to the trier of fact. The decision as to whether a witness's expertise will be helpful is left to the judge.

One interesting observation on the use of expert testimony and the qualification of experts occurred in a civil case: *In re Air Crash Disaster at New Orleans*, 795 F.2d 1230 (5th Cir. 1986). It may provide some insight to the thinking of appeals courts on the subject. In that case, the appeals court let it be known that the trial judge should indeed exercise some discretion in admitting expert testimony. It signaled the lower court to avoid a let-it-all-in attitude. Further, the circuit judges noted that they would examine the qualifications of experts with a sharp eye.

Invading the Province of the Jury. Historically, the most significant limitation on the use of expert testimony concerned a common law prohibition against witnesses expressing opinions about the ultimate issue. This objection has been eliminated by Rule 704. (See Figure 11-4.)

FIGURE 11-4 OPINIONS THAT EMBRACE THE ULTIMATE ISSUE MAY BE ADMISSIBLE

(a) Except as provided in subdivision (b), testimony in the form of an opinion or inference otherwise admissible is not objectionable because it embraces the ultimate issue to be decided by the trier of fact.

(b) No expert witness testifying with respect to the mental state or condition of a defendant in a criminal case may state an opinion or inference as to whether the defendant did or did not have the mental state or condition constituting an element of the crime charged or of a defense thereto. Such ultimate issues are matters for the trier of fact alone.

Fed. R. Evid. 704

Of course, the rule does not usurp the discretion of the court. The requirement that an opinion must *assist the jury* provides ample leeway for the judge to restrict the use of testimony that is of no evidentiary value. If, in the opinion of the judge, the jury needs no assistance in understanding the evidence, an expert's opinion may be unnecessary and not admitted by the judge because it is superfluous.

Subsection (b) disallows the use of expert testimony to address the issue of *mens rea*. Of course, we remember that *mens rea* is the mental element of a crime. The rule also prohibits the use of expert testimony to express an opinion on a defense based on a lack of subjective intent.

Disclosure of an Underlying Factual Basis for an Opinion. Earlier, we noted that an expert is not under an obligation to relate all of the factual data used to formulate an opinion. In this regard, the use of expert opinion differs from that of the nonexpert. The court, in its discretion, however, may require that the factual basis be disclosed. Further, the opposing counsel may cross-examine the expert on the basis for the opinion expressed.

From the perspective of detailing the factual basis for an opinion, there would seem to be little practical difference between the requirements placed on experts and those governing nonexperts who are allowed to give opinion testimony. In the case of an expert, the offering party is sometimes relieved of the onus for setting a proper factual foundation for the introduction of the opinion testimony. However, the party desiring to place such evidence before the jury is hardly ever well served by concealing factual basis. If the jury is to accord any weight to an opinion, it would expect to know the reasons for the expert's testimony. In any event, if the reasons are unsound, the court or the opposing side may explore that weakness.

Hearsay Testimony

Strictly speaking, the question of the admissibility of hearsay evidence may not be a matter of competence. **Hearsay testimony** is testimony by a witness repeating what was overheard from another party. Nevertheless, the objection to the use of hearsay evidence is so well known that it deserves some mention in our study.

The Federal Rules of Evidence (see Figure 11-5) are totally on point with state rules regarding the use of such evidence. The rules define the subject of hearsay evidence and give exceptions to the doctrine of nonadmissibility. Our treatment of the subject will necessarily be cursory. We simply do not have the space in this treatise to delve into the details and nuances of the subject. Perhaps a course on evidence would be a more fitting format for a broader treatment. What we are able to do in this course is to direct attention to this important aspect of the use of evidence.

FIGURE 11-5   THE USE OF HEARSAY EVIDENCE IS GENERALLY NOT ADMISSIBLE

> Hearsay is not admissible except as provided by these rules or by other rules prescribed by the Supreme Court pursuant to statutory authority or by act of Congress.
>
> FED. R. EVID. 802

What Is Hearsay? Some attorneys and paralegals, even those who have practiced their profession for many years, misunderstand the definition of hearsay. Rule 801 of the Federal Rules of Evidence clarifies the meaning of the term. (See Figure 11-6.)

FIGURE 11-6   HEARSAY, AS DEFINED BY THE FEDERAL RULES

> The following definitions apply under this article:
>
> (a) Statement—A "statement" is (1) an oral or written assertion or (2) nonverbal conduct of a person, if it is intended by the person as an assertion.
>
> (b) Declarant—A "declarant" is a person who makes a statement.
>
> (c) Hearsay—"Hearsay" is a statement, other than one made by the declarant while testifying at the trial or hearing, *offered in evidence to prove the truth of the matter asserted.* (Emphasis added)
>
> FED. R. EVID. 801

In the illustrated rule (Rule 801), emphasis is added to the portion of the standard that is most frequently overlooked. The prohibition covers statements that are offered to prove the truth of the matter asserted. An example may be helpful.

A testifies that **B** said "The automobile is red." The statement is inadmissible hearsay if the purpose of **A's** testimony is to prove that the color of the automobile is red. However, if the purpose of the testimony is merely to establish that *B* saw the automobile, it is admissible.

Reason for Excluding Hearsay. The primary reason for the exclusion of hearsay evidence is that it prevents confrontation of the witness. In our example, **B** cannot be cross-examined regarding the accuracy of the observation. **B** is not present. The aggrieved party is denied the right to confront the observer. Under such circumstances, the right to challenge the evidence would be lost.

Exceptions to the Hearsay Rule. Rule 803 of the Federal Rules of Evidence lists twenty-three specific exceptions and one catchall exception to the hearsay exclusion rule. The catchall uses this time-honored criterion as a reason for admitting hearsay testimony: if the interests of justice will best be served.

As indicated at the beginning of our discussion on hearsay testimony, there is no way to fully cover this subject in a general-purpose treatise such as ours. We have mentioned the most prominent features of the rule, but the details are myriad and beyond the scope of this course. Even reproducing Rule 803 in full would require more space than permitted by the scope of this text. If the subject is of particular interest, many fine sources are available for detailed research.

SEARCH AND SEIZURE

The second significant aspect of evidence that we want to explore concerns its admissibility as determined by how the material is obtained. Even competent evidence may be inadmissible if improperly gathered. The search for and seizure of evidence is our topic for this segment.

The Exclusionary Rule

In Chapter 1, we learned that the protection against unreasonable searches is a fundamental right guaranteed by the Fourth Amendment to the Constitution. (See Figure 11-7.)

FIGURE 11-7 FOURTH AMENDMENT RIGHT TO BE FREE FROM UNREASONABLE SEARCHES AND SEIZURES

The right of the people to be secure in their persons, houses, papers, and effects, against unreasonable searches and seizures, shall not be violated, and no Warrants shall issue, but upon probable cause, supported by Oath or affirmation, and particularly describing the place to be searched, and the persons or things to be seized.

U.S. CONST. amend. IV

Early in this century, the Supreme Court decided that strong measures were needed to adequately safeguard against unreasonable searches and seizures. The remedy struck upon was to exclude the use of evidence obtained in an unreasonable search. Since 1914 the operative procedural rule has been that unlawfully seized evidence cannot be used in federal prosecutions. This principle was announced by the Supreme Court in *Weeks v. United States*, 232 U.S. 383 (1914).

We already know that the Fourteenth Amendment extends certain safeguards of the Bill of Rights to persons prosecuted for crimes in state courts. In 1961 the Supreme Court decided *Mapp v. Ohio, supra* (Chapter 5), which brought the *Weeks* rule to bear upon state prosecutions. Justice Clark, writing for the majority in *Mapp*, declared that all evidence obtained through an unconstitutional search and seizure must be excluded from use in state prosecutions.

Thus, the state of the law today is that illegally obtained evidence is not admissible in either federal or state prosecutions. This procedural standard—the practice of not admitting evidence at trial that was illegally obtained—is commonly and widely referred to as the **exclusionary rule.**

In the remainder of this chapter, we will mainly concern ourselves with this rule and with how it affects the presentation of evidence in criminal prosecutions.

Rationale for Exclusion. The chief reason for excluding illegally obtained evidence from use at trial in a criminal case is for deterrent effect. The Supreme Court has called this deterrent effect the ''prime purpose'' for exclusion.

Interestingly, the characterization of deterrence as the rule's prime purpose came out of a decision in a civil lawsuit, *United States v. Janis*, 428 U.S. 433 (1976). In this case, the Court refused to extend the exclusionary rule to a situation involving evidence illegally obtained by state officials in a civil action against the federal government. It declared that extension of the rule to cover such matters was unnecessary. The Court went on to say that the rule's primary purpose is to deter unlawful police activity in *criminal* investigations.

Controversy over the Exclusionary Rule. The rule barring use of illegal evidence has been criticized from its very inception in the *Weeks* case. A respected jurist, Justice Benjamin Cardozo, has condemned the practice observing that it ''frees the criminal because the constable blundered.'' The criticism voiced by Justice Cardozo is the most commonly heard argument against excluding evidence under *Weeks* and *Mapp*; however, it is not the only one.

In 1976 Justice Byron White wrote a strong dissenting opinion in the case of *Stone v. Powell*, 428 U.S. 465 (1976). The specific holding of the Court in *Stone* disallowed a collateral attack upon a state conviction, via a *habeas corpus* petition, based on violation of the exclusionary rule. Justice White wanted to go further and "substantially modify" the exclusionary rule to allow use of evidence when agents act in "good faith."

The attack on the exclusionary rule by Justice White has not been the only assault on the exclusion of evidence. When the *Mapp* decision was handed down, the Court listed several reasons for its ruling. As we have already noted, one of those reasons was the deterrent effect of disallowing use of the fruits of improper police activity. Today deterrence is the only reason still viable. All other justifications for the rule have been eliminated by subsequent rulings of the Court.

It would be desirable to examine each of the rulings that have brought us to our current place in the evolution of the exclusionary rule. Unfortunately, as previously noted, space considerations in a broad-ranging survey such as ours do not allow for detailed history. What is important to understand is that dissatisfaction with the rule of *Mapp* and *Weeks* has not abated. If anything, it has grown more intense. As we shall see shortly, some modifications to the exclusionary rule have already been made.

LAWFUL SEARCH

What constitutes a reasonable search is a subject worthy of an entire course. Determination of reasonableness is necessary because the Constitution forbids only *unreasonable* searches. An **unreasonable search** is a warrantless search not covered by a recognized exception to the requirement that a warrant be obtained prior to conducting a search. Most law school curricula include a specific course on evidence wherein the concept of lawful search is explored in great depth. What we cover here will necessarily be condensed and, in some instances, generalized. However, we should leave our discussion of lawful searches with a sufficient understanding of the subject. Research is the way to solve the problems concerning unlawful searches once they are recognized.

Fourth Amendment

To begin at the logical starting point, we are once again forced back to the basics, in this instance, to the Fourth Amendment. The amendment declares "The right of the people to be secure . . . against *unreasonable* searches and seizures, shall not be violated, and no Warrants shall issue, but upon *probable cause*, supported by Oath or affirmation, and particularly describing the place to be searched, and the persons or things to be seized."

The declaration cited above has come to mean that no search shall take place and no evidence may be taken without a warrant, except incident to a lawful arrest, or with the consent of the person searched, or under limited emergency circumstances. Further, no warrant shall be granted unless the issuing authority is satisfied that the facts, sworn to by the person seeking the warrant, constitute good reason (i.e., probable cause).

The average person might think that the language of the amendment is clear enough to eliminate serious interpretive problems. That assumption is anything but accurate. There has been, and there still is, a great deal of controversy over the meaning of the amendment.

Probable Cause. The Fourth Amendment forbids only unreasonable searches. As it is used in the context of searches and seizures, the existence of probable cause is tantamount to reasonableness. See *Draper v. United States*, 358 U.S. 307 (1959). Of course, this does not mean that a search is lawful in all instances where sufficient probable cause supports the issuance of a warrant. If probable cause exists, the general rule is that a warrant must be obtained. See *Coolidge v. New Hampshire*, 403 U.S. 443 (1971).

We are familiar with the definition of probable cause that is derived from the *Brinegar* case (Chapter 3). Probable cause is more than suspicion and less than proof required at trial. The problem presented by such a definition is obvious. It is not precise. It requires some form of factual interpretation in every instance where it is invoked.

In dealing with warrants and arrests, probable cause is of the utmost importance. We have looked at the same requirement in connection with the return of an indictment and from the perspective of the preliminary hearing. We also mentioned, in Chapter 3, that an arrest warrant will issue on a showing of probable cause. A complicating factor is that probable cause varies as the circumstances vary, with the implication that each situation must be examined on its own merits.

The *Leon* and *Krull* Decisions. Further complicating the situation is the procedural maneuver of reexamining the facts underlying the issuance of a warrant after the warrant has been executed. The purpose of the procedure is relatively clear. Prior to the execution of a warrant, the aggrieved party has had no opportunity to contest the facts or to examine their sufficiency. Traditionally, the postexecution challenge to a search warrant was accorded the same significance as if it had been raised prior to the search. That is, if the warrant was found to be improperly issued or if the facts relied on for probable cause were shown to be inaccurate, the evidence obtained would be suppressed.

The Supreme Court altered that remedy by its decision in the celebrated case of *United States v. Leon*, 468 U.S. 397 (1984). Justice White wrote the majority opinion and used the opportunity to implement some of the changes he espoused in *Stone v. Powell, supra.* The *Leon* rule has amended the exclusionary rule to include the good faith factor of police officers.

What the *Leon* decision means is that an officer, in good faith, may rely on a warrant that has been issued to authorize a search. Further, evidence obtained during that search will be admissible for all purposes even if the warrant is "ultimately found to be unsupported by probable cause." (See Figure 11-8.)

In *Illinois v. Krull,* 480 U.S. 340 (1987), the Court recognized that good faith reliance on a statute should be accorded the same treatment as reliance on a warrant. As a consequence, even if the relied-upon statute is ultimately declared invalid, evidence seized, in good faith, based on the statute, will be usable at trial.

FIGURE 11-8   A SUMMARY OF THE IMPLICATIONS OF GOOD FAITH RELIANCE, ACCORDING TO THE *LEON* AND *KRULL* DECISIONS

The state of the law today may be summarized as follows: To be reasonable a search must be based on probable cause. Probable cause is a determination made on a case by case basis. Whenever possible, a warrant *must* be obtained from a judge or magistrate prior to the initiation of a search. To obtain a warrant, an officer or agent must submit a sworn statement containing the facts constituting probable cause.

If a warrant is issued and an officer, in good faith, conducts a search in reliance thereon, whatever evidence is obtained may be used in all formal proceedings. The same rule applies to good faith reliance on a statute or regulation.

Exceptions to the Requirement of a Search Warrant

Now that we have become acquainted with the general rule, we must look at its exceptions. In *Coolidge, supra,* the Court noted that all warrantless searches are unreasonable unless they come within one of the recognized exceptions to the rule requiring a valid warrant.

Whenever a search is conducted without a warrant and the authorities seek to use evidence thus obtained, *it is the duty of the prosecution* to demonstrate that the search falls within one of the exceptions to the requirement of a warrant. What follows is an examination of some of the major exceptions.

Search by Consent. A person may *voluntarily* consent to a search and thereby obviate the need to obtain a warrant. The test commonly used to determine voluntariness is the *totality of circumstances* standard. Some of the circumstances historically considered have been actual or threatened physical abuse; allowing the suspect to consult with an attorney; the suspect's background and education; the mental state of the suspect. In essence, the totality of circumstances test requires an examination of each case to ascertain all of the factors surrounding the search to determine whether or not it is voluntary.

In *Schneckloth v. Bustamonte,* 412 U.S. 218 (1973), the Court found that there is no need to show that a person was advised of the right not to allow the search. However, the knowledge of the person granting consent is one of the factors in the overall totality of circumstances that will be considered in determining if consent is voluntary. Whenever a question arises regarding the circumstances affecting the voluntary nature of a search, *Schneckloth* is a good place to begin research.

The totality of circumstances standard is considerably different from the *Miranda* warning required by the Fifth Amendment. For example, under *Miranda*, if a defendant waives the assistance of counsel, it must be shown that he or she was clearly advised of that right before a waiver is recognized. Under the totality test, such a warning is only one of the factors considered.

It is clear that a consent to search induced by fraud does not justify a warrantless search. In the case of *Bumper v. North Carolina*, 391 U.S. 541 (1968), the officer pretended to have a warrant in order to secure permission to search. The fraud vitiated the consent, and the evidence so obtained was excluded from use.

Search Incident to a Lawful Arrest. A second exception to the requirement that a search warrant be obtained before conducting a search involves a **search incident to a lawful arrest**. For affirmation of this precept, see *Draper v. United States, supra,* and *Ker v. California*, 374 U.S. 23 (1963). The arrest that precipitates a search may be made with or without a warrant. In either case, a search conducted contemporaneously with an arrest is quite apt to be valid.

Notice the language of the previous sentence: "the search is *apt* to be valid." The search, even incident to an arrest, must be within acceptable bounds in order to produce admissible evidence.

Extent of a Search In *Chimel v. California*, 395 U.S. 752 (1969), the Court spelled out the most important limitation upon a warrantless search incident to an arrest. The search must be confined to the arrestee and the area immediately accessible to the person arrested.

According to the *Chimel* holding, there are two reasons to allow a search at the time of arrest:

1. To remove weapons that the arrestee might use to harm the officers or to effect an escape;
2. To protect evidence that might be concealed or destroyed by the arrested party.

Therefore, a search without a warrant and justified only because it accompanies an arrest must be limited to the person of the arrestee and the area immediately surrounding that person.

For example, it would be inappropriate for the arresting agents to search a house, without a warrant, simply because an arrest was effected outside the premises. See *Shipley v. California*, 395 U.S. 818 (1969).

The *Chimel* rule has been stretched to some extent when an automobile is involved. In *New York v. Belton*, 454 U.S. 454 (1981), the Court found that a search of the entire passenger section of an automobile was justified incident to a lawful arrest. Further, the search could extend to all containers found in the passenger section, whether opened or closed.

In *Belton*, the police stopped the automobile for a speeding violation. The officers explained that the vehicle reeked of marijuana and that they saw an envelope of the type frequently used to package marijuana in plain view inside the auto. Those facts, said the Court, were sufficient reason to search the entire passenger compartment. See also *Michigan v. Long*, 463 U.S. 1032 (1983) in which the Court allowed an automobile search prior to an arrest on the theory that the safety of the officers required the search.

Effect of an Illegal Arrest It is well established that a search cannot be validated by what it produces nor an arrest justified by the fruit of an illegal search. See *Byars v. United States*, 273 U.S. 28 (1927). An illegal arrest, that is, one effected without probable cause, cannot justify a warrantless search. See *Henry v. United States*, 361 U.S. 98 (1959). Interestingly, however, a good faith arrest of the wrong person may result in a valid search. See *Hill v. California*, 401 U.S. 797 (1971).

When an Arrest Follows a Search One final point must be made regarding the exception based on arrest. The Court has allowed use of evidence obtained in a warrantless search of persons preceding an arrest. However, it must be noted that even though an arrest follows a search, good cause for the arrest must exist prior to the search and the arrest must follow immediately thereafter. See *Rawlings v. Kentucky*, 448 U.S. 98 (1980).

Stop and Frisk. A third acceptable reason for searching without a warrant involves the traditional right (could it be called a duty?) of the police to confront suspicious persons or persons engaged in suspicious activity. Police officers may, at times, happen upon suspicious situations without prior knowledge and, of course, without a search warrant or an opportunity to obtain a warrant. If, under these circumstances, an officer encounters a situation that seems suspicious, what can be done?

The Court has stated that warrantless stop and frisk practices, historically and traditionally engaged in by police officers, may be reasonable under circumstances that a person of "ordinary caution" might deem appropriate. See *Terry v. Ohio*, 392 U.S. 1 (1968). **Stop and frisk** is a type of search conducted without a warrant by police officers who are exercising their right to momentarily detain suspicious persons. It is an exception to the requirement that a warrant must be obtained before conducting a search.

The Court has also noted that the totality of circumstances must be considered when determining if an officer's detaining of a person is justified. Included in the consideration is the training of the officer. Thus, the *totality* test for a legal *stop and frisk* may be more subjective than indicated by *Terry*. The circumstances surrounding the stop must be viewed from the perspective of the officer, who is "versed in law enforcement." See *United States v. Cortez*, 449 U.S. 441 (1981).

Hot Pursuit. The Court coined a memorable phrase in deciding the case of *Warden v. Hayden*, 387 U.S. 294 (1967). Since then the term *hot pursuit* has taken on great popularity. Perhaps it just sounds funny. No matter its sound, it has a very serious meaning. **Hot pursuit**, the close, continuous pursuit of a fleeing suspect, constitutes another exception to the requirement of a search warrant.

The standing rule is that the police may not intrude into the home of a person, *without a warrant*, to make an arrest. See *Payton v. New York*, 445 U.S. 560 (1980). The hot pursuit concept is an exception to that rule. In *Payton*, the police were told that a robbery suspect they were chasing had hidden in a house. The Court allowed the evidence seized from the house to be used as evidence. The theory used by the Court to permit admissibility was that the police were in hot pursuit and thus were justified in entering the house and in searching every place where the suspect might have hidden or have hidden a weapon.

Inventory Searches. Another exception to be considered involves routine police searches for reasons other than the discovery of evidence. In *Illinois v. Lafayette*, 462 U.S. 604 (1983), the police inventoried the carrying bag of a person who had been lawfully arrested. The bag had not been searched at the time of arrest, and the inventory was carried out at the booking station. Even though other less intrusive means were available for securing the possessions of the arrestee, the Court allowed the search to stand and ruled that the evidence thus obtained could be used at trial.

An **inventory search** is a search of a person's belongings for the purpose of listing their contents. This exception to the requirement that a warrant be obtained prior to a search most frequently comes into play in cases involving impounded automobiles. A vehicle may be towed for improper parking, which would ordinarily give the police no authority to search. However, if the authorities are to maintain custody of the vehicle for any length of time, an inventory of its contents is justifiable. See *South Dakota v. Opperman*, 428 U.S. 364 (1976).

Plain View. The final exception that we must consider is the one most frequently referred to as the plain view rule. Simply stated, **plain view** means that the police do not have to close their eyes to evidence of a crime that inadvertently comes into their view.

If an officer is lawfully in a position to observe evidence of a crime, that evidence may be seized and used in a prosecution. The key here is *inadvertent* discovery. If there is any advance knowledge or suspicion that the evidence exists, a warrant should be obtained. See *Coolidge, supra.*

CONFESSIONS AND SELF-INCRIMINATION

Another important area to consider in any discussion of evidence is a confession made to enforcement officers by an arrestee. The Court's definitive statement on a person's right against self-incrimination was handed down in *Miranda v. Arizona*, 384 U.S. 436 (1966).

We have already mentioned the *Miranda* opinion (Chapter 5). It is a featured segment of every police movie, and most persons can recite its litany of warnings as well as any officer. In 1968 Congress enacted the Crime Control and Safe Streets Act. It is codified at 18 U.S.C. 3501. (See Figure 11-9.) Its purpose is to redefine the guidelines for admission of confessions, that is, to modify *Miranda*. It has applicability only in federal prosecutions.

FIGURE 11-9   ADMISSIBILITY OF CONFESSIONS, AS REDEFINED BY THE CRIME CONTROL AND SAFE STREETS ACT

> In any criminal prosecution brought by the United States or by the District of Columbia, a confession as defined in subsection (e) hereof, shall be admissible in evidence if it is voluntarily given. Before such confession is received in evidence, the trial judge shall, out of the presence of the jury, determine any issue as to voluntariness.
>
> *18 U.S.C. § 3501(a)*

The statute changes *Miranda* by making the only test for admissibility one of voluntariness. It does away with all of the warnings as *absolute* requirements. The *absolute* requirements of *Miranda* are discussed in the succeeding paragraphs.

Current Standing of *Miranda*

Miranda still controls the admissibility of all confessions in state prosecutions. As a practical matter, it is still the operative rule in federal prosecutions as well. In determining the voluntariness of a confession, federal judges almost always look to the *Miranda* dictates for guidance and control.

The following is a summary of the *Miranda* rules:

- The rules apply only while the subject is in custody or deprived of liberty "in a significant way."
- *Miranda* does not apply in "on-the-scene" questioning or in the "fact-finding process."
- Under all circumstances, a person in custody must be advised "in clear and unequivocal terms" of the right to remain silent.
- The warning regarding silence must be "accompanied by an explanation that anything said can and will be used against the individual in court."
- In all circumstances, the individual must be advised of the right to be represented by counsel during questioning.
- In all circumstances, the individual must be advised that an attorney will be appointed if he or she cannot afford to hire one.
- Questioning must cease whenever an individual indicates that he or she wants to stop answering questions or at the time that the individual expresses a desire for an attorney.

The Right to Remain Silent

As should be perfectly clear by now, the election of a defendant to say nothing is a Constitutional right. This right has been reaffirmed in *Miranda* and in subsequent decisions. As a *right*, a defendant's silence is unassailable. This fact has led to an important adjunct to the *Miranda* rule: the defendant's decision to rely on the right of silence cannot be used against him or her at trial. To allow such use after a *Miranda* warning would be "fundamentally unfair," according to the Court. See *Doyle v. Ohio*, 426 U.S. 610 (1976).

There are two important exceptions to *Miranda* and *Doyle* regarding the use of a defendant's silence or a prior contradictory statement. In *Anderson v. Charles*, 447 U.S. 231 (1980), the Court found that use of a prior inconsistent statement to impeach a defendant/witness—during cross-examination—was permissible. The decision distinguishes inconsistency from silence.

The second exception is found in *Jenkins v. Anderson*, 447 U.S. 231 (1980). There the court found that silence of the defendant before he was arrested could be used to impeach his testimony regarding self-defense. In *Jenkins* the Court noted that, since the silence was not induced by a *Miranda* warning, its use did not violate "fundamental fairness."

THE RIGHT TO COUNSEL

The fundamental right to counsel (Sixth Amendment) is important to our consideration of evidence. Of course, the right to be represented by an attorney is most frequently thought of in terms of the trial itself (*Gideon v. Wainwright, supra*, Chapter 4). Here we are more concerned with the right during preliminary stages of the trial process. It is important to be aware that there are times, prior to trial, when the denial of an attorney can render certain evidence inadmissible.

At a lineup or other identification procedures, the suspect has a right to have an attorney present to safeguard his or her interests in having the process conducted fairly. See *United States v. Wade*, 388 U.S. 218 (1967).

Further, we have been told by the Court that the right to counsel does not depend on a specific request by the defendant. See *Kitchens v. Smith*, 401 U.S. 847 (1971). We already know that a waiver of counsel must be intelligently and knowingly made and cannot be inferred from silence. See *Boykin v. Alabama, supra* (Chapter 4).

FRUIT OF THE POISONOUS TREE

The significance of the right to counsel becomes clear when we consider the final subject in our discussion of evidence. The subject is *derivative evidence*. Many lawyers refer to this type of evidence as "poison fruit."

The quaint expression derives from the language used by the Court in the case of *Silverthorne v. United States*, 251 U.S. 385 (1920). In *Silverthorne*, the government issued a subpoena for evidence and testimony based on information turned up in an illegal search. The Court held that information from the search could not be used as the basis for subpoenae or to further the government's case in any way. Because the original search was illegal, all leads derived from that search were tainted as "the fruit of the poisonous tree."

We can now understand the Court's reasoning in *Wade*. There the identification of the defendant at an illegal lineup tainted a subsequent identification made in court. The second identification was inadmissible because it derived from the poison tree.

The point to be understood with respect to the **poisonous tree doctrine** is that the evidence derived from an illegal search, arrest, confession, or other similar process, is itself inadmissible. The effects of this doctrine, thus, can be far-reaching. Once the poison is introduced, it may spread throughout the body of evidence.

A FINAL NOTE

It is with great reluctance that we leave the subject of searches, seizures, and evidence at this point. The topic of evidence is very interesting and broad. No matter where we conclude, one more topic could have been covered, and one more case might have been cited.

What we have seen is the big picture. The details are left for further discovery. There are many important treatises on the subject of evidence. Whenever new problems regarding evidence arise, it is important to consult such references.

At this point, we know enough to get started. In the final analysis, getting started is what has to be done anew in each case. In many ways, a career in law is a never-ending search. We have seen only the peaks of the tallest mountains. Much is to be discovered in the valleys.

12 PARALEGAL REGULATION AND ETHICS

Our treatise would not be complete without discussing the regulation of paralegal conduct and some ethical situations of relevance to paralegals who work in the field of criminal law. The general principles we will examine relate to the regulation of lawyers and paralegals. The ethical topics we will consider are conflicts of interest, the counseling of clients, and the requirement of confidentiality.

We are not disposed to present a complete review of the subject of ethics. Our decision is no reflection upon the significance of the subject nor upon the need for paralegals to incorporate the highest ethical standards into their everyday work. In fact, our assumption is that ethics is so worthy a subject that it will be accorded in-depth consideration elsewhere in your studies.[1]

ETHICAL STANDARDS

Although you have probably learned the sources of ethical standards in other courses, a quick review of those sources will fashion the context for our discussion of the standards most directly applicable to paralegals.

The American Bar Association (ABA) has promulgated a **Model Code of Professional Responsibility** and **Model Rules of Professional Conduct**. Although this *Model Code* and these *Model Rules* are disseminated by the American Bar Association, it does not enforce their standards. Enforcement is left to the states. Most state regulations closely resemble the bar association's *Model Code* or the *Model Rules*. In some instances, the models have been adopted by the states verbatim. The guidelines contained in these publications provide information concerning the conduct of legal professionals and rules to guide the discipline of persons whose conduct falls below standard.

An Attorney's Obligation to Supervise

The attorney bears the responsibility of supervising the conduct of nonlawyer employees. In guiding and directing paralegals, attorneys must realize that the standards that govern their conduct apply equally to nonlawyer assistants whom they employ.

Regulation of the practice of law and of attorneys are matters controlled by the states. An attorney may be reprimanded, suspended from practice, or disbarred for violation of ethical standards. The general rule is that a lawyer may also be disciplined for ethical infractions of a paralegal under his or her supervision. Bar associations seldom take direct action against paraprofessionals.

The model rule dealing with the supervision of nonlawyer personnel is cited in Figure 12-1. This standard, or one substantially similar to it, is the rule in all states.

FIGURE 12-1   THE SUPERVISION OF NONLAWYERS IS CODIFIED IN THE *MODEL RULES*

With respect to a nonlawyer employed or retained by or associated with a lawyer:

(a) a partner in a law firm shall make reasonable efforts to ensure that the firm has in effect measures giving reasonable assurance that the person's conduct is compatible with the professional obligations of the lawyer;

(b) a lawyer having direct supervisory authority over the nonlawyer shall make reasonable efforts to ensure that the person's conduct is compatible with the professional obligations of the lawyer; and

(c) *a lawyer shall be responsible for conduct of such person that would be a violation of the Rules of Professional Conduct if engaged in by a lawyer if:*

(1) the lawyer orders or, with the knowledge of the specific conduct, ratifies the conduct involved; or

(2) the lawyer is a partner in the law firm in which the person is employed, or has direct supervisory authority over the person, and knows of the conduct at the time when its consequences can be avoided or mitigated but fails to take reasonable remedial action. (Emphasis added)

MODEL RULES OF PROFESSIONAL CONDUCT Rule 5.3

Model Rules of Professional Conduct and Code of Judicial Conduct. Copyright © 1989 by the American Bar Association. All rights reserved. Reprinted by permission of the American Bar Association.[2]

Communication between Paralegal and Attorney

Most ethical pitfalls faced by the paralegal can be avoided if communication between the paralegal and the supervising attorney is frequent and clear.

The attorney must be kept abreast of the work of the paralegal and of the discussions between the paralegal and any clients. Client requests and inquiries must be relayed quickly to the attorney, and responses to those inquiries should be quickly delivered to the client. Of course, it is very important that the client understand that the responses come from the lawyer. We will have more to say later about techniques for handling client questions.

Guidance of Paralegals

As emphasized in Rule 5.3, the burden of guiding and instructing paralegals in ethics is an obligation of the employing attorney. An attorney who fails to properly supervise a paralegal may be sanctioned by the bar association for such neglect. (See Figure 12-2.)

FIGURE 12-2   A LAWYER'S DUTY TO INSTRUCT AND SUPERVISE PARALEGALS

Lawyers generally employ assistants in their practice, including secretaries, investigators, law student interns, and paraprofessionals. Such assistants, whether employees or independent contractors, act for the lawyer in rendition of the lawyer's professional services. *A lawyer should give such assistants appropriate instruction and supervision concerning the ethical aspects of their employment*, particularly regarding the obligation not to disclose information relating to representation of the client, and should be responsible for their work product. The measures employed in supervising nonlawyers should take account of the fact that they do not have legal training and are not subject to professional discipline. (Emphasis added)

MODEL RULES OF PROFESSIONAL CONDUCT Rule 5.3 cmt.

Model Rules of Professional Conduct and Code of Judicial Conduct. Copyright © 1989 by the American Bar Association. All rights reserved. Reprinted by permission of the American Bar Association.[3]

Since attorneys are ultimately responsible for the work of the assistants whom they employ, if problems arise concerning the work or ethics of a paralegal, the supervising attorney may be held to answer for such failings.

UNAUTHORIZED PRACTICE OF LAW

Because paralegals are not authorized to practice law, it is very important to know just what is meant by the term *practice of law*. Generally, bar associations, courts, and legislatures do not regulate or control the activities of paralegals; however, they do regulate and control the practice of law. To the extent that laws and statutes define the practice of law, they bear upon the tasks that can be performed by nonlawyers.

It is expected that attorneys licensed to practice law will police their own profession. To that end, ethics regulations place responsibility upon the lawyer to assist in suppressing the unlawful practice of law. This means that an attorney must guard against allowing an assistant to overstep the bounds for paralegals as established in his or her state. The **unauthorized practice of law** is generally defined as counseling, advising on legal matters, offering legal opinions, or representing persons before a court or other official forum with or without compensation by any person not licensed to do so. The specific definition of this term varies from state to state.

Defining the Practice of Law

Defining the *practice of law* is left to the states. For paralegals, familiarity with the definition is of monumental significance. Generalizing a definition for practicing law is not simple. In the main, practicing law means engaging in any activity that requires the exercise of judgment regarding the law or representing another person or entity in a legal capacity for compensation or otherwise. The Louisiana statute defining the practice of law is given in Figure 12-3.

FIGURE 12-3   THE PRACTICE OF LAW, AS DEFINED BY WEST'S LOUISIANA REVISED STATUTES

The practice of law is defined as follows:

(1) In a representative capacity, the appearance as an advocate, or the drawing of papers, pleadings or documents, or the performance of any act, in connection with proceedings, pending or prospective, before any court of record in this state; or

(2) For a *consideration, reward, or pecuniary benefit,* present or anticipated, direct or indirect,

   (a) the advising or counseling of another as to secular law, or,

   (b) in behalf of another, the drawing or procuring, or the assisting in the drawing or procuring of a paper, document, or instrument affecting or relating to secular rights, or

   (c) the doing of any act, in behalf of another, tending to obtain or secure for the other the prevention or redress of a wrong or the enforcement or establishment of a right. (Emphasis added)

LA. R. S. § 212

In the illustrated statute, only compensated activity is prohibited. Some states do not go along with this notion and criminalize even uncompensated activity if it impinges on the area reserved for licensed practitioners. In order to be sure of the definition and rules surrounding the practice of law in a given state, a paralegal must be familiar with the specific laws governing unauthorized practice in the jurisdiction in which he or she is employed.

Counseling and Advising Clients

We have discussed interviewing clients and witnesses at some length when we were considering trial preparation. That subject bears mention again in this section. The limits and extent of exchanges between a paralegal and a client must be considered here.

Paralegals may interview clients and work on developing a case for presentation. However, they must not mistake their role in the three-sided relationship of lawyer, client, and paralegal. A paralegal may not advise a client regarding the law. A paralegal may not offer opinions regarding the consequences of a plea or the probable outcome of a trial. Those areas are reserved for the attorney.

A client will occasionally ask a paralegal for an opinion or for counseling. At those moments, particularly if the relationship between the paralegal and the client has become close, the temptation to give in to the request may be great. The temptation, however, must be resisted. As we have seen in the standard statute cited in Figure 12-3, advising or counseling a person as to secular law is defined as practicing law.

Some paralegals worry that a client will be annoyed if a request is not answered. After all, the client is paying for the services of the paralegal as well as those of the lawyer, and he or she has a right to have questions answered. The proper approach for handling such situations is to refer the question to the supervising attorney. With a little practice, paralegals can become adept at sidestepping such requests and can do it without offending the client. One clever evasion used by some paralegals involves a self-effacing response, such as "My opinion is not very relevant to this issue; besides, the law doesn't permit me to comment. I will, however, make sure that your lawyer knows that you are concerned about this point."

Unauthorized Court Appearances

Another matter that should be well understood concerns the appearance of a paralegal in a court as a representative of a client. The rule is simple: *paralegals are not allowed to present arguments, evidence, or motions in court.*

There are no prohibitions against paralegals assisting the attorney in marshaling evidence and in organizing exhibits. We have already noted that the paralegal's duties during trial frequently include scheduling and accommodating witnesses. However, although they may be able to greatly assist in other ways, paralegals cannot make formal appearances in court on behalf of a client.

Unauthorized Practice Is a Crime

To blithely state that paralegals are not permitted to practice law may not be sufficiently emphatic to convey the significance of the matter. The fact is that the unauthorized practice of law is a *criminal offense.* A person, even a paralegal, who engages in the unauthorized practice of law may be prosecuted.

Such prosecutions are not common, but they have happened. Paralegals must be alert to the serious risks they take by stepping over the line into the domain that belongs exclusively to lawyers.

CONFLICTS OF INTEREST

The first ethical problem that we will address concerns conflicts of interest. In order to better understand the ethical predicaments involving conflicts, we will examine some situations in which conflicts could affect representation in a criminal case.

The Classic Conflict

Problems involving interest conflicts are generally thought of in the context of the same lawyer representing both sides of the same case. For example, an attorney may not represent both Smith and Jones in a case in which Smith accuses Jones of violating a contract. The problem is obvious for the lawyer who would undertake such an endeavor: he or she cannot possibly give full loyalty to either client.

Rule 1.7 of the *Model Rules of Professional Conduct* declares that an attorney may not represent one client to the adverse interest of another client. Of course, the rule allows for an exception in the case where both clients agree to joint representation and the attorney believes that such representation will not adversely affect the relationship with the other client. Usually conflict situations, such as those described here, arise only during the preliminary stages of a case. If a lawyer has an interest in both parties, he or she may make an attempt to resolve the matter short of litigation. When litigation is required, an attorney can only represent one party.

Dual Representation in a Criminal Case

In criminal law, **dual representation**, the simultaneous representation of opposing parties in a legal dispute, never happens. The same lawyer could never represent the prosecution and the defendant simultaneously. However, there are jurisdictions in which a very similar situation could develop.

In some areas, attorneys working as prosecutors are allowed to maintain a private practice. Under such circumstances, an attorney could be employed as a prosecutor in one county and attempt to represent a defendant in a criminal case in another jurisdiction. It should be clear that a lawyer may not ethically engage in such activity.

Extended to the paralegal, the situation is just as obvious. A paralegal working for the prosecution cannot simultaneously work for the defense, even in another jurisdiction.

Conflict between Interests of Codefendants

There are more subtle situations in which conflicts may arise. In the case of multiple defendants, it is quite possible to encounter a conflict even though the defenses raised by the parties do not appear to be antagonistic.

Consider the situation where **Harry** and **Barry** are charged as codefendants in the same criminal case. **Harry** is a newcomer to the criminal scene, but **Barry** is an old hand at breaking the law. The prosecutor might be inclined to go easy on **Harry** in return for his cooperation in the prosecution of **Barry**. Under these circumstances, one attorney would have a difficult time representing both defendants, even with their concurrence. In order to give maximum assistance to **Harry**, the attorney would have to turn him against the other client/defendant.

A paralegal working on a multiple-defendant case must be on guard and alert to such possibilities. If a possible conflict is detected, that information must be immediately disclosed to the supervising attorney.

Conflict at Sentencing

Even if joint representation of codefendants raises no problems and their defenses are wholly compatible, some argue that conflict at the time of sentencing is inevitable.

Sometimes the only mitigating circumstance that can be offered in a defendant's defense at sentencing is that the codefendant is even more blameworthy. In such an instance, it would be a serious breach of professional ethics for a defense attorney who represents two defendants to ask for leniency for one client because the codefendant/client is a worse scoundrel.

Former Employment

A possible area of conflict can arise when an attorney or paralegal changes employers. Today's society is very mobile. A person may change employment frequently during a career. In criminal law, employment changes become significant when they involve a move from prosecution to defense or *vice versa*.

In the case of an attorney, the general ethical standard is that a former prosecutor may not work on the defense of any person who was a defendant during the attorney's tenure as prosecutor. In some instances, a waiver may be obtained allowing the exprosecutor to represent a former defendant. A waiver will ordinarily be granted by the government if the current case is not related to the client's former prosecution and if sufficient time has passed to dispel the appearance of impropriety.

The situation is much the same for a paralegal. If a paralegal has worked for the prosecution, he or she should not participate in the defense of a former defendant without specific approval from the prosecutor.

Permission of the prosecutor for a paralegal to participate in a defense is seldom withheld without good grounds. An example of a good reason to withhold approval might be if the paralegal possesses confidential knowledge about a case gained through employment with the government.

Freelance Paralegals

A brief word is required regarding problems associated with paralegals who operate as contract employees, sometimes referred to as *freelance paralegals*. Freelancers typically provide services for several lawyers on an as-needed basis.

The chief problem to be avoided by independent or freelance paralegals concerns conflicts of interest. It is imperative that paralegals keep accurate and complete records of all clients, cases, and attorneys for whom work has been performed.

We are all aware that criminal recidivism is a problem. It seems that some people cannot stay out of trouble with the law. Recidivists always seem to be involved in a criminal case as defendants, witnesses, or victims. Their recurring presence can pose problems for paralegals who work for many different lawyers. In the event that a defendant in one case turns out to be a witness in another, a paralegal may find that he or she has information of a privileged nature that may form a conflict of interest. If that occurs, the supervising attorney must be advised immediately. If the problem is acute, the paralegal may have to withdraw from the case.

Informal Opinion of the American Bar Association

Recently the American Bar Association issued an informal opinion that touches upon the subject of paralegal mobility. (See Figure 12-4.) The opinion was not issued in connection with a criminal prosecution, but it has general applicability. The opinion recognizes the importance of allowing the paralegal great latitude in changing employers. It notes that undue restrictions could have the effect of denying qualified assistance to clients.

FIGURE 12-4   AN INFORMAL OPINION ON PARALEGAL MOBILITY

It is important that nonlawyer employees have as much mobility in employment opportunity as possible consistent with the protection of clients' interests. To so limit employment opportunities that some nonlawyers trained to work with law firms might be required to leave the careers for which they are trained would disserve clients as well as the legal profession. Accordingly, any restrictions on the nonlawyer's employment should be held to the minimum necessary to protect confidentiality of client information.

ABA Standing Comm. on Ethics and Professional Responsibility,
Informal Op. 88-1526 (1988)

American Bar Association Informal Ethics Opinion 88-1526. Copyright © 1989 by the American Bar Association. All rights reserved. Reprinted by permission of the American Bar Association.[4]

When an attorney leaves defense practice to take employment with the prosecution, the weight of authority seems to be that the attorney should not be involved with the prosecution of a former client. It must be noted that the entire prosecutor's office is not precluded from prosecuting a case because one of its attorneys defended the defendant in another case. Only the former defense attorney should be isolated from the prosecution; others on the staff will be allowed to pursue the case and prosecute the defendant.

The isolation process is sometimes referred to as a *Chinese wall*. A **Chinese wall** is a policy of isolation used within a law firm to shield an attorney or a paralegal from information or files about a client to avoid a conflict of interest. The lawyer with the potential conflict is barred from all files and records relating in any way to the former client. The exact procedures enacted to wall off the attorney may vary from office to office. Generally, denial of access is accomplished by written notice to all employees that an attorney has a conflict and that no one is to discuss the case or to disclose information regarding the defendant to that attorney. If it is possible to mechanically or electronically block the attorney's access to the files, such procedures are advised. In some offices the Chinese wall is referred to as a *screen.*

This situation is not at all clear when it comes to paralegals. It would seem that the most discreet course would be for paralegals to avoid working on any case involving a person whom they have assisted in defending. Certainly the paralegal must never assist in the prosecution of a specific case if he or she has at any time worked for the defense in the same case.

Screening for Possible Conflicts

An attorney or paralegal should perform a screening check to make certain that potential clients do not pose conflict problems. Screening procedures may vary from office to office but should be sufficiently extensive to provide reasonable assurance that the representation will not adversely affect the interest of a present or former client.

In smaller offices, the screening task is quite easy. In larger offices, the task may require extensive inquiries into the background of the prospective client. Such inquiries must be made before an attorney or a paralegal elicits confidential information from the new client.

CONFIDENTIALITY

We must also look at the ethical responsibility to maintain confidentiality. Sometimes the most significant principles are the easiest to explain. The requirement of confidentiality falls into that category.

General Rule of Confidentiality

Without the client's permission, neither a lawyer nor a paralegal may reveal what is learned in confidence from that client.

Exceptions to the General Rule of Confidentiality

Like the rule itself, the exceptions to it are straightforward:
1. Revelation may be made to prevent a crime likely to cause death or grave bodily harm.
2. Revelation may be made if a client makes a claim against a lawyer.

3. Revelation may be made if a lawyer is sued or prosecuted for conduct engaged in with a client.

Figure 12-5 reproduces the pertinent passages from the *Model Rules of Professional Conduct* that deal with issues and situations constituting exceptions to the general rule of confidentiality.

FIGURE 12-5 EXCEPTIONS TO THE GENERAL RULE OF CONFIDENTIALITY

(a) A lawyer shall not reveal information relating to representation of a client unless the client consents after consultation, except for disclosures that are impliedly authorized in order to carry out the representation, and except as stated in paragraph (b).

(b) A lawyer may reveal information to the extent the lawyer reasonably believes necessary:

(1) to prevent the client from committing a criminal act *that the lawyer believes is likely to result in imminent death or substantial bodily harm*; or

(2) to establish a claim or defense on behalf of the lawyer in a controversy between the lawyer and the client, to establish a defense to a criminal charge or civil claim against the lawyer based upon conduct in which the client was involved, or to respond to allegations in any proceeding concerning the lawyer's representation of the client.

MODEL RULES OF PROFESSIONAL CONDUCT Rule 1.6

Model Rules of Professional Conduct and Code of Judicial Conduct. Copyright © 1989 by the American Bar Association. All rights reserved. Reprinted by permission of the American Bar Association.[5]

Paralegal's Obligation

One of the highest duties of the attorney, and therefore of the paralegal, is to protect the confidences of the client. It must be understood and always remembered that *the right to confidentiality belongs to the client, not to the attorney or paralegal.*

The paralegal will encounter few problems if one simple rule is followed: *Repeat nothing disclosed in confidence by the client except to the supervising attorney.* If the paralegal believes that a public revelation should be made under one of the exceptions, the matter should be discussed with the supervising attorney who retains the responsibility and the duty to make such disclosures.

We stated that *few* problems will ensue if the paralegal restricts revelation to the supervising lawyer. Unfortunately, at least one problem can develop even under the most guarded circumstances. It involves the course of action to be taken by the paralegal if the supervising attorney fails to act in accord with the ethical conscience of the paralegal. For example, what should the paralegal do if the attorney fails to take action to prevent the commission of a crime that may result in death?

There is no clear answer to this quandary. Certainly a paralegal must act in accord with his or her conscience. At the very least, the paralegal would probably be correct in asking to be relieved of further duties involving the client.

This may be a good point at which to insert a reminder regarding the roles of the paralegal and the supervising attorney. The paralegal must not lose track of the fact that it is the attorney who represents the client. It is the attorney who must bear the consequences of a poor ethical decision. Therefore, much deference must be given to the opinion of the supervising attorney, even if it differs from the opinion of the paralegal.

Situations involving an attorney who fails to take action to prevent the commission of a crime occur so infrequently that they may have no general recognized solution. If the situation becomes critical, there is no prohibition against the paralegal seeking legal counsel from another independent attorney retained by the paralegal for counsel.

Court-Ordered Disclosure

On very rare occasions, an attorney or a paralegal might be ordered by a court to disclose information or statements made by a client. The same advice, *consult an attorney who is not involved in the case*, would apply in the event that the paralegal is ordered to make a disclosure and does not feel comfortable with the court's ruling.

Perhaps it would be better to advise the paralegal *quickly* to consult an attorney if he or she intends to disobey an order of the court. In such times, it is good to recall this old saying: "It is a foolish lawyer who would have himself as a client."

GUIDANCE FROM NATIONAL PARALEGAL ORGANIZATIONS

There are two national organizations for paralegals: the National Association of Legal Assistants and the National Federation of Paralegal Associations. In these organizations the paralegal can find guidance and direction for the ethical practice of his or her profession. Additionally, the American Bar Association's Center for Professional Responsibility is an excellent source for guidance whenever a problem arises. The American Bar Association has recently published *Model Guidelines for the Utilization of Legal Assistant Services*. It would be a good idea to become familiar with these guidelines.

As of our publication date, paralegal organizations exist in all but four states. Membership in local or national organizations is a matter of individual choice; however, it is important that paralegals be aware of the existence of groups active in the locale in which they intend to practice.

A FINAL NOTE

It bears repeating that the subject of ethics is of vast importance. What we have done is attempt to acquaint the student with the general rules of ethics that govern the paralegal profession and to point out some of the major areas of ethical concern within the criminal law specialty.

Any number of sources of information may be consulted for more detailed analysis of the subject. The student is urged to become familiar with the laws of the state and the rules of the bar in the area where he or she intends to work.

ENDNOTES

1   For an excellent treatment of legal ethics for the paralegal, see Elizabeth Richardson and Milton C. Regan, Jr., *Civil Litigation for Paralegals* (Cincinnati, Oh.: South-Western Publishing Co., 1992), 25–55.

2   Copies of this publication may be ordered from Order Fulfillment, American Bar Institute, 750 North Lake Shore Drive, Chicago, IL 60611.

3   Copies of this publication may be ordered from Order Fulfillment, American Bar Institute, 750 North Lake Shore Drive, Chicago, IL 60611.

4   Copies of this publication may be obtained from Order Fulfillment, American Bar Institute, 750 North Lake Shore Drive, Chicago, IL 60611.

5   Copies of this publication may be ordered from Order Fulfillment, American Bar Institute, 750 North Lake Shore Drive, Chicago, IL 60611.

TABLE OF CASES

GLOSSARY

Accessory after the fact   One who gives aid and support to a principal after the commission of an offense.

Accessory before the fact   One who counsels, aids, or supports another who is preparing to commit a crime. Generally, an accessory before the fact is treated as a principal to the crime.

Accomplice   One who assists another in the commission of a crime. Always treated as a principal to the crime.

Acquittal   A verdict or finding of not guilty after a trial.

Actus reus   Guilty deed. The action element of a crime. Along with *mens rea*, it forms the two essential elements of a crime.

Adjudication   In a juvenile court proceeding, the equivalent of a conviction.

Alford **plea**   A plea of guilty entered by a defendant who maintains innocence but has decided to plead guilty to avoid consequences potentially more severe. Takes its name from the case of *North Carolina v. Alford*.

Allen charge   A jury instruction by the court designed to avoid a hung jury. Usually given only if the jury is experiencing difficulty in reaching a verdict. Sometimes referred to as a dynamite charge or hammer charge. Takes its name from the case of *Allen v. United States*.

Allocution   Statement made by the defendant to the judge, at the time of sentencing, prior to sentence being imposed.

Answer   In a juvenile proceeding, the response of the minor to the petition filed by the authorities. Equivalent to the plea at arraignment made by a defendant in a criminal case.

Appellant   The title of the party who asks for a review, thus initiating an appeal.

Appellee   The title of the party who responds to an appellant's request for a review.

Argument   The fourth element of the theory of the case. A coherent presentation of the facts that supports the theory's conclusion.

Arraignment   Stage of a criminal proceeding when the defendant is officially informed of the criminal charges and is called upon to enter a formal response to the charges.

Attempt   A crime. A criminal undertaking that fails to accomplish its goal.

Beyond a reasonable doubt   The standard of proof required for each element of a criminal charge in order to support a conviction. The highest standard of proof required in any legal proceeding.

Bill of indictment   *See* indictment.

Bill of information   A document containing formal criminal charges against a defendant. May be filed by a prosecutor without action of a grand jury.

Bill of particulars   A clarification of an indictment or bill of information, detailing the specifics of the alleged offense and making the charge more easily understood by the defendant.

Bill of Rights   The first ten amendments to the U.S. Constitution.

Boykinize   Judicial interrogation of a defendant who has indicated an intention to plead guilty to a crime in order to determine that the plea is knowing and voluntary.

Brady **rule**   Rule of law growing out of the decision in *Brady v. Maryland,* calling for the prosecution to disclose information to the defendant that may be favorable in presenting a defense.

Bruton **rule**   Rule mandating separate trials for codefendants in a situation where one defendant's statement incriminates the other defendant.

Burden of proof   The duty to prove each element of the crime.

Case in chief   The first stage in the presentation of evidence at trial by the prosecution and the defense. The portion of the trial when the parties may present evidence on any and all relevant issues. Distinguished from the rebuttal or surrebuttal stage of trial when evidence may be presented only on specific issues previously addressed by an opponent.

Character witness   A witness who is allowed to testify regarding the reputation of the defendant.

Child in need of supervision (CHINS)   A classification of status in a juvenile proceeding. Less serious than a finding of delinquency.

Chinese wall   A policy of isolation within a law firm used to shield an attorney or a paralegal from information about a client or file in order to avoid a conflict of interest.

Competent evidence   Plausible evidence from a source worthy of consideration.

Conclusion   The fifth and final element of the theory of the case. The inescapable consequence of fitting relevant facts into a cogent argument.

Conditional plea   A plea of guilty entered by a defendant who reserves the right to appeal a judgment of conviction on a specific issue or issues. By written agreement, the parties consent to set aside a guilty plea if the issue is decided in favor of the defendant on appeal.

Conspiracy   A crime. An unlawful combination of two or more persons for the purpose of commission of a crime. It is a crime whether or not its criminal goal is accomplished.

Constructive intent   The element of intent "constructed," or inferred, from negligence or lack of care. Similar to criminal negligence.

Crime   A social evil, identified, proscribed, and punishable by law.

Criminal negligence   Replaces the element of intent with recklessness of the actor. Similar to constructive intent.

Deferred prosecution   An alternative to prosecution in that the defendant accepts a period of voluntary probation that, if successfully completed, will result in a dropping of criminal charges.

Delinquency   Conduct by a juvenile that is beyond parental control and is thus subject to legal action; a violation of the law committed by a juvenile. *See also* delinquent.

Delinquent   A designation given to a minor who has been adjudicated a law violator.

Demonstrative evidence   An evidence exhibit used to illustrate a factual point.

Detention hearing   A formal hearing to consider if there is probable cause to hold a person in custody.

Dismissal for cause   The rejection of a prospective juror by the court because he or she is in some manner unqualified to serve as a juror on the case.

Disposition   In a juvenile court proceeding against a minor, the action of the court equivalent to the sentence in a criminal case.

Diversion   An alternative to prosecution that moves the defendant out of the criminal justice system into an alternative program designed to correct the behavior problems exhibited by the defendant.

Documentary evidence   Physical evidence containing writings, usually in the form of papers, records, reports, or letters, relevant to the issues in the case.

Double jeopardy   Being held to answer more than once for the same criminal act. Prohibited by the Fifth Amendment.

Dual representation   The simultaneous representation of opposing parties in a legal dispute.

Due process of law   The constitutionally protected right that guarantees that a person charged with a crime must be afforded a fair chance to defend against the charge. The fundamental precept of our criminal justice system, it is first mentioned in the Fifth Amendment and was made applicable to state proceedings by the Fourteenth Amendment.

Durham test   A test for insanity at the time of commission of an offense. Excuses criminal conduct if it is the offspring or product of mental disease. Used in fewer jurisdictions than the M'Naghten test.

Elements of a crime   The *mens rea* and *actus reus* of the crime. Also, the specific component parts of an offense.

Equal dignity   Parity between the federal and state courts of comparable levels.

Evidence   Information upon which a conclusion or judgment can be based.

Exclusionary rule   The practice of not admitting illegally obtained evidence.

Excuse for cause   *See* dismissal for cause.

Expert witness   A witness qualified by training, experience, or knowledge to render an opinion on a relevant issue at trial.

Expungement   Eradication of official records pertaining to a conviction of a crime or an adjudication of delinquency in the case of a juvenile.

Fact witness   A witness giving testimony relative to the occurrence of a fact or several facts.

Federal Rules of Criminal Procedure   Official rules governing criminal procedures in U.S. district courts.

Federal Rules of Evidence   Official rules governing use and admissibility of evidence in U.S. district courts.

Felony   A transgression of the law that causes grievous social harm. A serious crime.

Formal petition   In a juvenile court proceeding, a statement of the complaint against the minor. Equivalent to an indictment or bill of information in a criminal case.

General criminal intent   The state of mind necessary to be guilty of a crime. Sometimes used synonymously with *mens rea*.

Grand jury   A body of citizens that may investigate crimes and return formal charges in the form of an indictment.

Grant of immunity   Elimination of a person's Fifth Amendment right to remain silent in return for a binding commitment from authorities not to prosecute.

Harmless error   Any error, defect, irregularity, or variance that does not affect the substantial rights of the defendant. This type of error will be overlooked by an appellate court and will not form the basis of a reversal of a conviction.

Hearsay testimony   Testimony by a witness repeating what was heard from another party.

Hot pursuit   The close, continuous pursuit of a fleeing suspect. An exception to the requirement that a warrant be obtained before conducting a search.

Hung jury   A jury unable to reach a verdict.

Hypothesis   One of the elements of case theory.

Immaturity   A defect of intent owing to the youthfulness of the offender.

Inchoate offense   A criminal act in which the perpetrator has not accomplished the criminal objective. Frequently a crime in itself.

Indictment   A formal charge of criminal conduct returned by a grand jury.

Indictment surplusage   Extraneous, unnecessary, and often inflammatory language in an indictment or bill of information.

Informal adjustment   An agreement between juvenile correctional personnel, a minor, the minor's parents or guardians, and the court, providing for voluntary behavior modification practices by the minor and some form of supervision or monitoring by authorities. Usually done in lieu of authorities filing a formal petition.

Initial appearance   First formal appearance of a defendant before a judge or magistrate to be apprised of the reason(s) for arrest, detention, or charges.

Intake   In juvenile court proceedings, the case evaluation process. Equivalent to screening in criminal cases.

Inventory search   A search of a person's belongings for the purpose of listing contents. An exception to the requirement that a warrant be obtained before conducting a search.

Involuntary intoxication   A defect of intent that can form a valid affirmative defense.

Irresistible impulse   A test for insanity at the time of commission of an offense.

Jencks Act   18 U.S.C. § 3500, requiring prosecution to disclose previous relevant statements made by a government witness. The statute mandates disclosure only after the witness has testified at trial.

Judgment notwithstanding the verdict   The entry of a judgment of acquittal by the court after the jury has returned a guilty verdict or a judgment of not guilty entered by the court when the jury is unable to reach a verdict.

Judgment n.o.v.   *See* judgment notwithstanding the verdict.

Judicial interpretation   The authority of the courts, particularly the Supreme Court, to interpret each law and make certain that it meets constitutional standards for validity and that it is applied constitutionally.

Jury instruction   A statement of the law made to the jury by the court before deliberations begin.

M'Naghten rule   The most popular test for insanity at the time of commission of the offense. The right versus wrong test.

Malum in se   An act that is a crime because it is wrong by its very nature (e.g., theft).

Malum prohibitum   An act that is a crime solely because it is prohibited by law (e.g., public drunkenness).

Mens rea   Guilty mind. The mental intent element of a crime. Together with *actus reus*, it forms the two essential elements of a crime.

Mere preparation   A defense to the crime of attempt. A criminal attempt must be more than mere preparation to violate the law.

Misdemeanor   Usually any crime not classified as a felony.

Misprison   A crime. The act of concealing knowledge of a crime committed by another.

Mistrial   A ruling during trial or jury deliberations that proceedings have been invalidated and that the trial must be abandoned. Frequently occurs because a jury is unable to reach a verdict.

Mock jury   A group of persons assembled by a party prior to trial to hear and comment on evidence and issues that may arise during trial.

Model Code of Professional Responsibility   Guidelines promulgated by the American Bar Association providing guidance for conduct of lawyers and rules to guide discipline for those lawyers whose conduct falls below the required standard. The *Model Code* is not enforced by the ABA. It is intended for adoption by appropriate state agencies.

Model Penal Code   A compilation of recommendations for criminal codes prepared by the American Law Institute. A model statute used by legislatures in drafting criminal laws.

Model Rules of Professional Conduct   Rules and comments on rules most recently promulgated by the American Bar Association intended as a guide for professional conduct of lawyers. The ABA has no authority to enforce the rules. Enforcement is left to the states and state agencies and bar associations.

Motion   An application made to a court or a judge to obtain a ruling. The title of the motion explains the relief being sought (e.g., motion to dismiss the indictment).

Motion for judgment of acquittal   A procedural device, authorized by Rule 29 of the Federal Rules of Criminal Procedure, requesting that the court enter a judgment of not guilty after the government has concluded its case or after all evidence has been presented by the prosecution and the defense but prior to the rendition of a verdict by the jury.

Motion for a new trial   A procedural device available only to defendants that enables them to request that a case be retried after a guilty verdict has been issued by a judge or a jury or after a finding of guilty has been made by the court.

Motion practice   The maneuvering of parties by use of formal pleadings, usually before trial.

Motion to suppress evidence   A formal request of a party to prevent (suppress) the use of certain evidence by another party.

Nolle prosequi   Dismissal by the prosecutor of an indictment or a bill of information.

Nolo contendere   Plea of a defendant amounting to ''no contest'' to criminal charges contained in a bill of information or an indictment.

Notice   A requirement of a valid criminal law necessitating the specific identity of the deed that the law forbids. ''The first essential of due process of law.''

Peremptory challenge   The dismissal of a prospective juror by a party. There need be no cause stated by the dismissing party.

Personal recognizance   A form of bail by which defendants are allowed to remain free pending trial by merely giving a written assurance that they will appear when required. It eliminates the necessity of posting cash or surety bond.

Petit jury   A group of citizens that acts as the trier of fact during a trial.

Plain view   An exception to the requirement that a warrant must be obtained before conducting a search that states that police officers do not have to close their eyes to evidence of a crime that inadvertently comes into their view.

Poisonous tree doctrine   Rule that holds that evidence derived from an illegal search or arrest or confession is itself inadmissible. Comes from the case of *Silverthorne v. United States.*

Poll of the jury   The examination of each juror to determine if the verdict announced is the one actually reached during deliberations.

Predisposition report   In juvenile court proceedings, a report on the background of a minor containing recommendations to the judge relevant to disposition alternatives.

Preliminary examination   A hearing held before a judicial officer to determine if there is probable cause to retain a charge against a defendant.

Pretrial intervention   *See* diversion.

Presentence investigation (P.S.I.)   An investigation into the personal background and criminal history of a defendant awaiting sentencing, the results of which are usually formulated into a presentence report, which includes sentencing recommendations and an analysis of sentencing guidelines.

Primacy The first position in an argument or statement.

Principal A person who actually commits the crime, as contrasted with an accessory. There can be more than one principal to an offense.

Probable cause Evidence that constitutes more than suspicion but less than the amount of proof needed to convict.

Pro bono Legal representation without financial remuneration.

Re-arraignment A pretrial procedural device usually employed to allow a defendant to change a plea of not guilty to a plea of guilty.

Reception statute Statute receiving common law crimes into a state's body of law.

Record on appeal The transcript, or such portions thereof as may be designated by the parties as pertinent to the issues to be raised before the appellate court, along with the original papers (pleadings, motions, orders, judgments, and exhibits) and copies of all docket entries.

Relevant evidence Evidence that pertains to a fact or occurrence at issue.

Requested special charge An instruction of law for the jury requested by one of the parties. Usually involves an issue specific to the case not found in all cases. The court has the discretion to accept or reject the request.

Res ipsa loquitur Literally, "The thing speaks for itself." Sometimes used as a test to determine if preparation to commit a crime has become an attempt to commit a crime.

Responsive verdict A permissible verdict by a jury.

Screening cases for prosecution The evaluation process used to select cases for prosecution.

Search incident to a lawful arrest An exception to the requirement that a warrant be obtained before conducting a search.

Sentencing guidelines A schedule employed by the courts to ensure uniformity of sentence among persons convicted of similar offenses.

Severance Separation of codefendants or counts of a formal charge for separate trials.

Shadow jury A group of persons, with no official status, who resembles the actual jury demographically. It is allowed to sit through trial and hear only the evidence heard by the actual jury. It is used and paid for by a party who wishes to test the effectiveness of evidence and presentation.

Specific intent A higher form of *mens rea* than general criminal intent. A necessary element for some crimes, such as murder.

Speedy trial   The requirement that all criminal cases be resolved expeditiously.

Status offender   In juvenile court proceedings, a finding that a minor is not yet a delinquent but is in need of behavior modification. *See also* child in need of supervision (CHINS).

Stop and frisk   Refers to a search conducted without a warrant by police who are exercising a right to momentarily detain suspicious persons. An exception to the requirement that a warrant be obtained before conducting a search.

Subpoena   An order commanding the person named in it to appear at court.

Subpoena duces tecum   An order to a witness to appear and produce specified documents.

Substantial act   A test employed in some jurisdictions to determine if preparation to commit a crime has become an attempt to commit a crime.

Substantial assistance   A term used in the U.S. Sentencing Guidelines. It is not defined in the guidelines, but it is a means of allowing a sentencing judge to depart downward from guideline sentence ranges in consideration for meaningful cooperation by the defendant with law enforcement officials.

Supporting facts   The second element of the theory of the case. Those facts that can be established through competent evidence to substantiate the hypothesis.

Surrebuttal   The portion of the trial, coming after the prosecution's rebuttal, when the court may allow the defense to present additional evidence, usually on very narrowly defined issue(s).

Tacit agreement   An unwritten nonspecified understanding between prosecutor and defendant.

Testimonial evidence   Spoken and sworn testimony of a witness at trial.

Theory of the case   Method of demonstrating the truth of a position taken by either party.

Transferred intent   A fictionalized intent supplying the element of *mens rea* when the actual result of an action was unintended by the actor.

Trier of fact   The entity, either a judge or a jury, that weighs evidence and determines the verdict.

Truth   The first element of the theory of the case. The proposition that explains a party's position on an issue.

Two-phase trial   A trial in which the jury is required to reach a second verdict regarding the sentence. The second phase of the trial is conducted only if there is a verdict of guilty in the primary phase.

Unauthorized practice of law   Generally, counseling, advising on legal matters, offering legal opinions, or representing a client before a court or other official forum with or without compensation by any person who is not licensed to practice law. Specific definition varies from state to state.

Uncodified   Unwritten.

Unreasonable search   A warrantless search that is not covered by a recognized exception to the requirement that a warrant be obtained before a search is conducted.

Venire   The general array of prospective jurors from which a jury pool is selected.

Venue   The place (location) where a criminal charge is lodged.

Voir dire   The selection process used to test the qualifications of prospective jurors.

Voluntary intoxication   A defect of intent that usually does not form a valid affirmative defense.

Waiver   A determination that a minor who has committed an offense should be subjected to an adult criminal prosecution.

Writ of *certiorari*   In the context of criminal law, an order from the Supreme Court to a lower court to transmit a case to it for review. Review *via certiorari* is the usual method for bringing criminasl cases to the Supreme Court. The decision of the Supreme Court to grant *certiorari* is strictly discretionary. Petitions for writs of *certiorari* are usually denied.

Writ of *habeas corpus*   A procedural device, distinct from an appeal or a writ of *certiorari*, designed to prevent injustice that may have resulted in the illegal imprisonment of a person by securing postconfinement relief.

INDEX